AGRICULTURAL TRANSFORMATION, FOOD AND ENVIRONMENT

KW-241-876

WITHDRAWN
FROM
UNIVERSITY OF PLYMOUTH
LIBRARY SERVICES

Agricultural Transformation, Food and Environment

Perspectives on European rural policy
and planning - Volume 1

Edited by
HENRY BULLER
KEITH HOGGART

Ashgate

Aldershot • Burlington USA • Singapore • Sydney

© Henry Buller and Keith Hoggart 2001

All rights reserved. No part of this publication may be reproduced, stored in a retrieval system, or transmitted in any form or by any means, electronic, mechanical, photocopying, recording or otherwise without the prior permission of the publisher.

Published by
Ashgate Publishing Ltd
Gower House
Croft Road
Aldershot
Hants GU11 3HR
England

Ashgate Publishing Company
131 Main Street
Burlington, VT 05401-5600 USA

UNIVERSITY OF PLYMOUTH

Item No. 9004709535

Date 2 6 JUL 2001 S

Class No. 338.184 AGR
Cont. No. ✓

PLYMOUTH LIBRARY

Ashgate website: http://www.ashgate.com

British Library Cataloguing in Publication Data
Agricultural transformation, food and environment
 Vol. 1: Perspectives on European rural policy and planning
 edited by Henry Buller and Keith Hoggart. - (Perspectives
 on rural policy and planning)
 1.Agriculture and state - Europe
 I.Buller, Henry, 1956- II.Hoggart, Keith
 630.9'4

Library of Congress Control Number: 00-110695

ISBN 0 7546 1736 X ✓

Printed and bound by Athenaeum Press, Ltd.,
Gateshead, Tyne & Wear.

Contents

Figures

Tables

Contributors

Henry Buller
Professor of Rural Studies, Cheltenham and Gloucester College, and Maître de Conférences in Geography at the University of Paris 7

Jean-Paul Charvet
Professor of Geography, University of Paris 10

Keith Hoggart
Professor of Geography, King's College London

Pierre Lenormand
Maître de Conférences in Geography, University of Paris 7

Mara Miele
Lecturer, Department of Agricultural Economics, University of Pisa

Larisa Mokrushina
Senior Research Fellow, Institute of Geography, Russian Academy of Sciences-Moscow

Angel Paniagua
Senior Researcher, Instituto de Economía y Geografía, Consejo Superior de Investigaciones Cientificas-Madrid

Hilary Tovey
Senior Lecturer in Sociology, Trinity College Dublin

1 Is this the European model?

Henry Buller

Introduction

This book is the first in a series of edited volumes concerned with the evolution, implementation and analysis of European rural policy during recent years. Two parallel series of volumes are also being produced, the first on British rural policy (Gilg, 1999) the second on North America (Furuseth and Lapping, 1999). Together, the three series follow from a previous annual edition, published by GeoBooks, Belhaven and Wiley during the 1980s and early 1990s (see for example, Gilg, 1993). Within the new European series, the current volume will be followed by a second on rural economic development and the new service economy (planned for 2003), with a third on European rural social change (planned for 2006).

This first book is about the shifting relationship of agricultural, environmental and food policy within Europe. It has been over two years in the making; two years that have seen a number of critical changes both in agricultural, environmental and food politics and in the way these domains have been investigated by European social scientists. The chapters in this book do not seek to provide a global overview of these changes. Rather, they focus upon specific areas of change, most notably agricultural restructuring (in the face of globalization, Europeanization and the collapse of the former Soviet model of agricultural organization, (Chapter Two, Chapter Four, Chapter Five), agriculture-environment relations (Chapters Six, Chapter Seven) and consumer preferences (Chapter Three). A final chapter (Chapter Eight) seeks to close the book with a review of recent literature in the field of European agricultural change, in a context of environmental and food policy initiatives.

From all of the chapters included here, a fundamental interrogation emerges, whether explicitly or implicitly. This is that of the relative autonomy both of the current European (in the largest possible definition) agricultural experience and of future European trajectories with respect to wider forces of economic globalization, as well as environmental normalization and standardization. To what degree does Europe offer a 'unique' and identifiable

1

rural experience? Is the *'exception européenne'*, whether it be defined in terms of 'blue' or 'green' box agricultural aids, a particular sensitivity to rural (and agricultural) landscapes, a unique socio-economic composition yielding a distinctive pluri-functionality, or simply a prior historical evolution, both real and sustainable? Is a European rurality different from that of the 'colonies of settlement' (Bolton, 1973), such as the United States, Canada, Australia and South America. How far does the European imperative differ from these nations, as they strive to define the world economic agenda within which regional and national policies relating to agricultural activity, landscape protection and human migration are ordained to comply? In short, is there (still) a European model?

A European model?

The idea of a European model of agriculture has achieved a certain prominence in recent years, largely as a result of the eminently political need. On the one hand this has resulted from the need to defend existing policies of European agricultural support under the Common Agricultural Policy (CAP) in the face of growing international demands to reduce, and ultimately do away with, farm subsidies. On the other hand, it emerges from the need to achieve a coherent and harmonious domestic agenda for agricultural policy development, particularly in the face of increasingly divergent Member State views with respect to CAP spending and future EU enlargement. Both as a leitmotif for European exceptionalism and as a reaffirmation of European rural identity and, crucially, the legitimacy of agriculture within that identity, the notion of a European model is seductive and fundamentally political.

The diversity of European ruralities and rural traditions (Hoggart *et al.*, 1995; Jollivet, 1996), the variety of national cultural and institutional differences within Europe (Lowe, *et al.*, 2000), and the different trajectories of agricultural modernization (Buller *et al.*, 2000b), all suggest that any single, all-embracing 'model' can only be a contrivance of limited empirical or analytical value. Indeed, as recently defined by the EU's Agricultural Commissioner (Fischler, 1998), the 'European model' is essentially a series of broad policy objectives, most of which are still far from being achieved. These objectives include the intention that:

- European farming must perform its market function, providing consumers and the processing industry with healthy, high-quality food and renewable raw materials;
- European farming must carry out its environmental functions, ensuring the sustainable use of natural resources, safeguarding the wide variety of ecosystems and protecting the diversity of Europe's farmlands;

- European agriculture must provide a wide range of services, performing new functions for which there is increasing public demand, such as tourism or in the social sector; and,
- European farming has a major role to play in providing employment in rural areas.

The European model is founded upon a set of relationships that are held to be distinctly 'European' (as opposed to, for example, North American). These exist: between nature (essentially domesticated, altered and portrayed through a long history of agricultural endeavour) and society (ancient and settled, whose 'civilization' has largely been defined in terms of its relationship to nature); between town (as the current demographic and economic focus and a as the birthplace of modern socio-economic stratification and industrial capitalism) and country (as an 'alternative' to the town); between farming (as a spatially dominant but economically and demographically shrinking sector) and the wider rural economy (whose overall well-being has long been considered dependant upon agriculture); and, between units of agricultural production (the farm) and the organization of agricultural labour (the family). These components are deeply embedded in the European tradition (Jollivet, 1996) and, perhaps more significantly, in the process of European construction and modernization. Hence, an early Franco-German concern for the well-being of the family farm, both as the basic unit of agricultural enterprise and as the emblematic expression of rural social organization, largely underscored the establishment of the Common Agricultural Policy. Leading on from this, and finding resonance with the UK's 1942 Scott Report on rural land use, was the principle that agricultural policy should *de facto* be a rural policy in that the rural economy is best served by a healthy farming sector. The emergence of an environmental agenda in agricultural policy in the 1980s (Whitby, 1996; also Chapter Six and Chapter Seven in this book) extended the belief that farming has a critical role to play in supplying and managing public goods. This had already been made visible in some national expressions of Less Favoured Area and Mountain Area policy. From this history, the European model emerges as a pluralistic conceptualization of farming's vocation, even though the reality, as we are only too aware today, is very different. Under the CAP agricultural modernization has often pursued a diametrically opposite trajectory to this model. This has led to regional specialization and mono-production, to environmental degradation on a wide scale, to a shrinkage of farm diversification, to conflict between town to country, to a lack of traceability in the production of foodstuffs and so on.

If we come back to the two fundamental needs that drive adherence to the notion of a 'European model' (first, an internal need to encourage, promote and finance farming in an increasingly plural rural policy agenda, and, second, an external the need to legitimize new and alternative forms of agricultural support in the face of increasing agricultural trade liberalization), then both find expression in the operationalization of recent Agenda 2000 reforms. The first is seen through the support of agricultural multifunctionality. The second is evident in the policy of degressivity.

Multifunctionality

The European model, as a political construct, has yielded the more pragmatic notion of agricultural 'multifunctionality'. As defined by the EU Agricultural Commissioner, multifunctionality is the fundamental link "... between sustainable agriculture, food safety, territorial balance, maintaining the landscape and the environment and what is particularly important for developing countries, food security" (Fischler, 2000). Multifunctionality is a word that enshrines the essence of the European model. This ideal has become the lynchpin of Agenda 2000 agricultural reforms (Lowe and Brouwer, 2000). The Rural Development Regulation (Regulation 1257/99), which is the central component of the so-called 'second pillar' of the reformed CAP (Lowe, 1998), combines rural development objectives, agri-environmental schemes and other largely pre-existing agricultural structural mechanisms into a package of measures that in many member states will place farming once again at the centre of a broader rural development agenda. Although the financial support of this 'second pillar' remains slight compared with that reserved from the traditional domain of CAP spending, market and commodity support (though it will be derived essentially from the EAGGF Guarantee), 'cross-over' measures such as 'modulation' will permit certain member states, notably Britain and France, to derive additional funding for rural development and agri-environmental schemes from direct payments (Buller *et al.*, 2000a; Falconer and Ward, 2000).

To a large degree, the idea of agricultural multifunctionality is based on an assumption of the greater and wider integration of environmental management into production systems. For sure, debate over multifunctionality cannot be disassociated from the emergence of an agri-environmental agenda over the last 20 years. As a component of multifunctionality, improved management of the environmental impact of farming (both positive and negative) can be seen as an attempt to shift agricultural policy objectives that until comparatively recently were markedly monofunctional in mechanisms and outcomes. However, the measures proposed by the Rural Development Regulation go further than agri-environmental schemes have done in the past to include the maintenance and reinforcement of a viable social fabric in rural areas, the promotion of non-food production, farm diversification, the creation of rural employment, plus a series of additional measures targeted at farmers and non-farmers within rural areas (known as the Article 33 Measures). Hence, within the definition of multifunctionality advocated by the Rural Development

4

Regulation, as well as by domestic legislation such as the French *Loi d'Orientation Agricole* of 1999 (Laurent, 1999), European agriculture is called upon to play a productive and market function, a territorial management function, an environmental management and protection function, as well as a rural development function.

Whether a clever marketing ploy or a genuine attempt to identify a real European distinctiveness, the European model of agricultural multifunctionality is a potent icon in the global debate over agricultural subsidies and their seemingly ineluctable reduction, even though it remains more a set of aspirations than a plausible *'etat des lieux'* of European farming. For some, the 'model' is a step backwards, towards renewed public support at a time when agricultural trade is being increasingly liberalized. Sir Leon Britton (quoted in Grant, 1999, p.3) maintained in 1999 that: "Some people still advocate a type of 'European agricultural model' which would involve a retreat behind high tariff walls, closing our farm industry off from growing world markets and leaving only our internal market. This is not the 'European model' that I would want to defend or create". Others (for example, Grant, 1999) might argue for a clearer separation of the social and environmental components of European agricultural support, thereby escaping the wrath of the US and the Cairns Group. Yet, the very term multifunctionality seems to imply, indeed necessitate in certain regions/countries, particularly where there are few economic alternatives, some form of limited recoupling of agricultural support, albeit within the context of a broader rural agenda. Different strategies for recoupling suggest themselves. 'Green coupling' is when farmers receive public money for the provision of environmental goods to help compensate for the loss of production related payments (as has been the case for certain agri-environmental schemes). Cross compliance is when commodity supports become conditional upon the provision of certain base-level environmental standards (as has been advocated by Agenda 2000 but as yet not implemented by Member States). Then there is the more holistic approach to farm support, under which the productive, environmental and rural development contribution of farming activities are recognized and supported (the model the French have adopted in the *Contrats Territoriaux d'Exploitation* following the 1999 Agriculture Act).

The degressivity debate

The second set of concerns that underlie the concept of a 'European model' relate to the need to maintain public support for an agricultural policy that is frequently perceived as excessively expensive, anti-liberalist, environmentally damaging and unfairly distributed; all in all a rather damning assessment in the light of the CAP's original aims. In addition, the existence and uniqueness of the European model is held up as justification for certain financial supports that might otherwise be denounced by the World Trade Organization. Between the two, a subtle equation has to be met. Inevitably, as European agriculture aligns itself further with world markets and the rules that govern international commerce, prices will fall and existing support mechanisms (such as export aids) will eventually be dismantled. To maintain Europe's agriculture and with it Europe's rural tissue, new sources of finance will have to be sought and new justifications for these will have to be advanced. As Potter (1998, p.152) has pointed out: "The challenge here will be to balance the need to meet international obligations under the WTO to decouple CAP support, with the desire to retain a broad base of support in order to preserve the social and environmental fabric of a managed countryside much more vulnerable to the restructuring effects of world market forces". Demonstrating farming's contribution to rural sustainability, through measures that encourage agricultural multifunctionality, and thereby gaining public support for the continued financial underwriting of European agriculture, is a key objective of current policy. However, remunerating farmers for environmental and other rural development actions has so far proved to be small beer compared with the compensation payments currently made to offset price falls and decreasing commodity support. One of the key issues to emerge from the Agenda 2000 proposals, and one of the central areas of discord amongst member states, has been the increasingly necessary reduction of the CAP budget and, more particularly, the part given over to direct payments. Some states, notably Britain and France, have favoured reducing direct payments chiefly to cereal farmers. Partly as a means of addressing public concern over the uneven distribution of monetary aids (see Charvet, Chapter Two), and partly as a means of transferring money from the 'first' to the 'second' pillar of the modified CAP, these states modulate direct aids, albeit in radically different ways. France has adopted a redistributive principle, removing some subsidies from larger and more successful arable farms. By contrast, the UK has chosen an across-the-board application of degressivity (Buller *et al.*, 2000a). Other states, notably Germany, have so far resisted degressivity and modulation. Yet the uneven distribution of compensatory payments, the continuing high cost of the CAP and the incompatibilities of applying existing support schemes to potential new East European members (see Lenormand, Chapter Four), mean these issues will remain high on the agenda for some time to come.

The contribution of this book to the debate

Through the analysis of current debates on contemporary European agriculture and agricultural policy, the chapters in this book address the multiple and shifting ruralities that comprise the wider Europe (which we take to stretch to the Ural Mountains). Many of the chapters approach these debates in terms of choices for the future. Charvet (Chapter Two), in analysing the relationship of post-1992 reforms CAP to world agricultural trade, begins by asking whether the EU should seek greater liberalization and consequently greater degressivity or should seek to address essentially internal agricultural, food and social priorities. Similarly, Lenormand (Chapter Four), in examining the future trajectory of Central and East European farming systems asks what sort of 'integration', either at a global or a greater European level, the current Central and East European states should ultimately seek. Mokrushina (Chapter Five), like Lenormand, considers the 'benefits' and 'disbenefits' of shifting from a state-regulated agricultural economy under the former Soviet model, to a free-trade environment, for which the principal beneficiaries are far from traditional rural and agricultural communities. Both Tovey (Chapter Six) and Paniagua (Chapter Seven) explore the notion of 'post-productivist' agriculture and its relation to agri-environmental policy and future rural development. They do this from substantially different viewpoints, with Paniagua identifying a critical implementation failure in achieving genuine environmental policy integration in Spain, and Tovey raising a more fundamental critique of the basic assumptions of so-called 'post-modern', post-productive agriculture. Throughout the chapters of the book, there is a concern with linkages between agricultural and food economies. In Chapter Three, Miele focuses explicitly on the food dimension, by considering how food consumption has changed over time within Europe. The theme presented here is that in the midst of food abundance and homogenization trends, a 'remoralization' of food is occurring today. As a review of contemporary issues in European agricultural policy, the chapters in this book demonstrate the societal, economic and environmental roles of contemporary farming.

What emerges most strongly from these different chapters is the extent to which conceptions of rurality are intrinsically linked to processes of social modernization (Mormont, 1997); processes that are no longer restricted to rural concerns but extend into national, international, even global socio-economic configurations. The transformation of farming into a multifunctional activity is not only a response to an increasingly differentiated rurality, nor to a shifting political agenda, but also to an evolving set of societal relationships that define quality of life and access to it. Does this make the 'European model' a referential for future society-nature relations?

References

Bolton, G.C. (1973) *Britain's Legacy Overseas*, Oxford University Press, Oxford.

Buller, H., Lowe, P.D. and Ward, N. (2000a) *Setting the Next Agenda? British and French Approaches to Common Agricultural Policy Reform*, University of Newcastle-upon-Tyne Centre for Rural Economy CRE Working Paper 45.

Buller, H., Wilson, G.A. and Höll, A. (2000b, eds.) *Agri-Environmental Policy in Europe*, Ashgate, Aldershot.

Falconer, K. and Ward, N. (2000) *Modulation and the Implementation of CAP Reform in the UK*, University of Newcastle-upon-Tyne Centre for Rural Economy CRE Working Paper 44.

Fischler, F. (1998) 'A Strong Agriculture in a Strong Europe: The European Model', Speech to the European Agriculture Congress, Ljubljana.

Fischler, F. (2000) 'Framework for World Agri-Food Trade', Speech to the Dublin Castle Centenary Conference, Dublin.

Furuseth, O.J. and Lapping, M.B (1999, eds.) *Contested Countryside*, Ashgate, Aldershot.

Gilg, A.W. (1993, ed.) *Progress in Rural Policy and Planning: Volume Three*, Belhaven, London.

Gilg, A.W. (1999) *Perspectives on British Rural Planning Policy, 1994-1997*, Ashgate, Aldershot.

Grant, W. (1999) Wyn Grant's Common Agriculture Policy page, 02/03/1999, at http// members.tripod.com/WynGrant/WynGrantCAPpage.html

Hoggart, K., Buller, H. and Black, R. (1995) *Rural Europe*, Arnold, London.

Jollivet, M. (1996, ed.) *Vers un Rural Post-Industriel*, L'Harmattan, Paris.

Laurent, C. (1999) Activité agricole, multifunctionalité et pluriactivité, *Pour*, 164, pp.41-46.

Lowe, P.D. (1998) *A 'Second Pillar' for the CAP?*, University of Newcastle-upon-Tyne Centre for Rural Economy CRE Working Paper 36.

Lowe, P.D. and Brouwer, F. (2000) Agenda 2000: a wasted opportunity?, in F. Brouwer and P.D. Lowe (eds.) *CAP Regimes and the European Countryside*, CAB International, Wallingford, pp.321-334.

Lowe, P.D., Flynn, B., Just, F., de Lima, A., Patricio, T. and Povelatto, A. (2000) National cultural and institutional factors in CAP and the environment, in F. Brouwer and P.D. Lowe (eds.) *CAP Regimes and the European Countryside*, CAB International, Wallingford, pp.257-280.

Mormont, M. (1997) Belgique: à la recherche des spécificités rurales, in M. Jollivet (ed.) *Vers un Rural Postindustriel*, L'Harmattan, Paris, pp.17-44.

Potter, C. (1998) *Against the Grain*, CAB International, Wallingford.

Whitby, M. (1996, ed.) *The European Environment and CAP Reform: Policies and Prospects for Conservation*, CAB International, Wallingford.

2 European farming and world markets

Jean-Paul Charvet

During the current series of debates over the reform and financial management of the Common Agricultural Policy (CAP), two essentially opposing viewpoints have emerged. For some, and this is widely shared view in France, even if it is not unanimously held, the European Union (EU) should be a major presence within world markets for agricultural commodities. As such, the Union must be able to export large amounts of agricultural produce on a regular basis and, in doing so, enter into commercial competition with the current world leader in agricultural exports, the USA. For others, the EU should first and foremost assure the provision of sufficient quantities of agricultural produce for its own domestic consumption. Europe must produce primarily for itself. In such a scenario, the Common Agricultural Policy would need to be re-focused towards the internal European market - a market composed of some 375 million consumers with a relatively high standard of living - while at the same time anticipating the future enlargement of the Union towards the east. Exports beyond Europe's frontiers towards 'third' countries would consequently become largely marginal and occasional, resulting chiefly from temporary production surpluses during exceptional productive seasons.

The economic, social and environmental implications behind these alternatives are considerable. In particular, any reduction in agricultural production from levels reached under a generalized productivist model could lead to improvements in agriculture-environment relations and maintain a slightly larger agricultural population than is currently the case. Such a reduction could also facilitate the reorientation of certain production sectors toward commodities of higher quality and greater added value. At the same time it could induce better management of landscapes, themselves the product of generations of European rural history. Inversely, the choice of maintaining the EU's presence as a major competitive exporter on world markets might increase environmental degradation and further reduce the European farm population.

With the 1992 reforms of the CAP, European agriculture found itself at a critical turning point with respect to its position vis-à-vis world markets; all the more so as the 15 EU Member States were far from being in agreement over which ultimate direction to take. The first part of this paper considers the foundations upon which the relationship between European agriculture and world markets has been established in the context of the pre-1992 CAP. The second section examines world markets themselves and their recent evolution. The debate between the two options for European agriculture identified above turns critically around the question of whether or not international exchanges in agricultural commodities will grow in the medium-term. Finally, in the last part of this chapter, new relations between European farming and world markets following 1992 CAP reforms will be explored. This final section will provide a close look at the problems raised and new questions posed by change since the 1992 reforms.

World markets and the CAP of the 1960s

The original objectives of the CAP, as laid out in the early 1960s, need to be understood in terms of the political and economic context of the period. Europeans, particularly the increasingly important urban population, had been confronted by real food shortages during the Second World War and in the years that immediately followed its end. The memory of these shortages was very prominent in the collective European memory long after the War ended. With the exception of the UK, which joined the Common Market in 1973, farmers were still numerous in the European countryside, especially in some regions. While it is possible to argue that the European farm population suffered less from food shortages during the War than town dwellers, their economic and social situation remained very difficult. Low levels of productivity, both per hectare and per labour unit, characterized much European farming in the early post-war years, with low incomes an associated characteristic.

Reflecting these underlying concerns, the dominant concerns of the post-war period were specified in the four objectives of the first CAP, as laid down by Article 39 of the 1957 Treaty of Rome:
1. To guarantee the security of food provision, with the notion of food security having a different emphasis to that of today, as it was defined essentially by quantitative rather than qualitative criteria.
2. To raise agricultural productivity through technical progress, both by raising yield per hectare and by raising the productivity of labour units.
3. To stabilize markets, with the dual aims of protecting the interior European market from large-scale fluctuations in world prices and making allowance

for such price fluctuations within the European Community by establishing a relatively narrow set of price bands.
4. To assure an equitable standard of living for European farmers, with this objective being largely dependent upon a policy of establishing and maintaining relatively high agricultural prices.

Principles and mechanisms of the CAP

In order to achieve the objectives fixed by Article 39, European legislators focused upon five basic principles. Each of these was to be operationalized by a specific intervention mechanism. These principles and mechanisms are still in place. They continue to regulate relationships between European agriculture and world markets, despite recent adjustments that shall be discussed below.

The first principle is the free circulation of agricultural commodities within the EU (at the time of the Treaty of Rome, the European Economic Community or EEC). In reality, for a long time the operation of this single market was disrupted by fluctuations in the relative value of national currencies within the EEC (e.g. CEC, 1989). This situation has only been corrected by the introduction in 1999 of the Single European Currency within a majority of EU States.

The establishment of the free market area was greatly aided by the setting up, at EEC frontiers, of a uniform system of import levies, which enshrined the (second) principle of 'Community Preference'. Import levies were placed upon agricultural commodities coming from outside the CAP zone, thereby making the cost of imported products slightly higher than those produced within the EEC. Before their more recent 'tarification' (see below), these levies proved extremely efficient in limiting imports from outside the EEC. All the more so as these levies were not fixed import taxes, as (say) a proportion of the value of the commodities concerned, but rather were variable entry payments. As such, they were periodically altered to take account of both fluctuations in world prices and variability of the dollar exchange rate with respect to the ecu. France and the Netherlands, as the major agricultural exporters in the EU at this time, were undoubtedly the principal beneficiaries of 'Community Preference'. This system opened up for them what was, in effect, a captive market. However, beyond Europe, criticisms soon began to mount, particularly from the USA and from members of the Cairns Group[1] of 'Fair Trader' nations with Australia at their head.

A guarantee of single minimum prices within the EU was the third principle. This was assured by the mechanism of market intervention. The intervention price that is set by the EU is a 'floor' price. However, this does not necessarily guarantee prices to producers. In the case of cereals, for example, the price might be received by a cooperative or a private dealer.

This is an important point when we examine international comparisons. In nations such as the USA guarantee prices usually go directly to producers.

Where European agricultural commodities are sold on world markets, significant differences can exist between European and world market prices. In order to compensate European exporters for losses resulting from these differences, a series of export subsidies (or *restitution* payments) were incorporated into the CAP. The level of these payments depends, as in the case of levies, on the difference between the world price and the European price (Figure 2.1). As a result, the value of financial aid varies significantly across time, in line with both price movements and dollar exchange rate fluctuations.

The fifth and final principle of the CAP is financial solidarity amongst Member States. This is maintained by the EAGGF (FEOGA), a financial agency the EEC set up in 1962. The EAGGF assures the financial management of market intervention, as well as levies and *restitution* mechanisms. At the beginning of the CAP system, the European Community had an overall deficit in agricultural production (relative to demand), so levies on imported agricultural commodities were able to finance, through *restitution* payments, relatively small volumes of European farm exports. However, as the modernization of European agricultural continued under the aegis of the CAP, particularly since the 1970s, exports increased significantly. Restitution payments similarly grew dramatically, as European produce came increasingly to be exported, while import levies declined. A new source of finance was required. The solution was to seek CAP funding via VAT payments. These were paid by consumers and taxpayers throughout Europe.

Types of production and world markets

Although commodity regimes have been set up within the CAP for all major types of European agricultural production since the 1960s, not all sectors benefit equally from the five principles (and associated mechanisms). Most of the major production sectors of the northern Member States (cereals, milk, sugar and beef and sheep meat) benefit wholly from intervention prices, *restitution* payments and so on. However, for other farming sectors (notably pork production, fruit and vegetables, and table wine), although intervention is possible under the CAP, it has been used rarely. Alternative subsidy mechanisms, such as direct aids, have been more common. For around a quarter of European agricultural output (poultry, eggs, flowers and certain fruits and vegetables), there is no system of intervention, only protection from imports from outside the Community. Furthermore, for the most part, for these latter sectors exports are unaided.

Another important difference exists between oil-seed and protein crops (rape, sunflowers, soya) and cereal substitutes. The latter are extensively used

12

Figure 2.1
Relationship between world and European cereal prices

a)   When world price is lower than European price

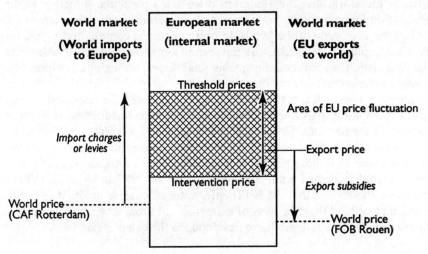

b)   When world price is higher than European price

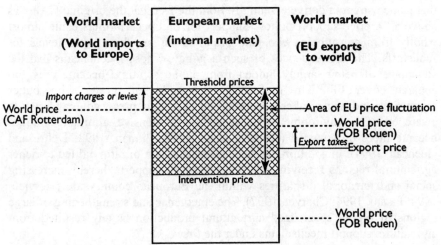

NB CAF Rotterdam is the indicator for the price paid for cereals imported to the EU from outside
    FOB Rouen is the indicator for the export price paid for EU exports (Rouen being the most
    important cereal export port within the EU)

in industrial husbandry units, particularly those involving pigs and poultry. The most common cereal substitutes are corn gluten feed, manioc and sweet potatoes. These products, derived essentially from non-EU states, are unique in that they have successfully penetrated the European market without having to pay levies or customs duties. For these products, there is no difference between the world and the European price. This particular situation is the result of diplomatic negotiations immediately preceding the setting up of the CAP at the beginning of the 1960s. In order to get the commodity regime for cereals accepted by the USA, the European Community agreed to allow the free circulation of oil-bearing plants and cereal substitutes within the European market area. At the time, imports of both were negligible. However, as intensive livestock units multiplied, so did the need for imported animal feed, explaining in part by the development of intensive units around major ports in the Netherlands, Brittany, northern Germany and Cataluña. European imports of soya thereby rose from 2.5 million tonnes in the middle of the 1960s to some 15 million tonnes in the middle of the 1990s. Imports of cereal feed substitutes[2] passed from 5 million tonnes in 1975 to over 20 million tonnes by the end of the 1980s (Toepfer International, annual). It is worth noting that without these imports of animal feed, Europe's capacity as a major exporter of cereals would not have developed to the extent it has.

Criticisms of the former CAP

Internal criticisms Particularly during the 1980s, the criticisms of the CAP that gained strength derive essentially from the fact that the original CAP was above all a price support policy. Support for European farmers came almost wholly from consumers, who paid prices far higher than world levels for foodstuffs. The consequences of such a policy, whose mechanisms had the advantage of being largely hidden from public scrutiny, became only too apparent over time. In particular, over-production grew, with butter mountains and wine lakes receiving considerable press coverage, while awareness of the environmental consequences of intensive farming techniques became more pronounced (Arnould *et al.*, 1992; Pitman, 1992; Deltre and Gueneau, 1994). In addition, the unequal distribution of farm aid led to richer agricultural regions receiving the lion's share of support; thereby increasing social and territorial disparities within the European countryside (Hervieu, 1994; Pisani, 1994; Charvet, 1997). The emergence and strengthening of large regions of highly specialized agricultural production largely resulted from agricultural support mechanisms under the first CAP.

External criticisms In addition to the perceived failures and injustices of the CAP within Europe, the policy drew considerable criticism from outside the EU. These critiques became particularly evident with the political negotiations accompanying the Uruguay Round of the GATT from 1986 to

1993 (e.g. Miller, 1986; Hathaway, 1987; Ingersent *et al.*, 1994). The approach adopted by negotiators during these lengthy negotiations consisted of classifying different forms of farm aid from which European farmers benefited into three (and later) four categories, according to actual or potential impacts upon world markets. Each category was termed a 'box' and each 'box' was given a colour. The colours of the first three categories were those of traffic lights. What were placed in the red box were farm aids and subsidies that should be removed as fast as possible because they had major distorting effects upon world markets. Most notable in this regard were CAP *restitution* payments (viz. export subsidies). The aids and subsidies placed in the 'yellow' box were those that should be removed progressively; for example price supports under the original CAP. These measures were felt to affect markets indirectly by influencing production costs. Finally, 'green box' entries were aids that were not considered to have a major impact on the strength and direction of market exchanges. This green box was comprised of aids that have subsequently been 'decoupled' from production. Farm training aid, agri-environmental aid and pre-retirement aid are examples.

Significantly, dispute over trade in agricultural commodities was such that Uruguay Round negotiators were only able to reach a final agreement once a fourth box (a 'blue' box) was established. This contained so-called 'tolerated' payments. These included the direct aid that US farmers had been receiving for decades (viz. US deficiency payments, which were renamed transition payments), which European farmers received after the 1992 CAP reforms as compensatory payments.[3] Similar aids in other countries were excluded from the 'blue box'. These direct payments, also know as deficiency payments, were to be paid to cereal growers according to the size of their cultivated area and on the basis of an established threshold of existing yields. They were justified on the basis that farmers had to be compensated from falling world prices. However, the originality of 'blue box' aids was that they were conditional. To obtain them, farmers had to set aside part of their cultivated area in order to reduce farm production.

Compensatory payments have become an important element in European farm revenues during the 1990s. Indirectly, they play a decisive role in the competitiveness of European agriculture on world markets, as demonstrated below.

Retrospective and prospective change in major agricultural markets

Given the substantive differences that exist in world markets for primary agricultural commodities, with these differences impacting on relationships with European agricultural sectors, this section examines the three key trading commodities of cereals, oil-seed plants and meat in turn.

Cereals are at the heart of the world food system as well as being the most traded of all agricultural commodities. Shifts in world cereal markets are therefore of critical importance for trade relations in agriculture. Having progressed at a slow rate throughout the 1950s and 1960s, international cereals commerce underwent a veritable explosion in the 1970s, passing from 100 million tonnes exchanged in 1970 to 200 million in 1980. This was an expansion of some 10 million tonnes per year. The ex-USSR, which prior to the 1970s was outside the world cereals market, rapidly became the world's leading importer. Thus, its imports rose from zero to 40 million tonnes from the beginning to the end of the 1970s. Amongst the other factors that contributed to the growing price of cereals, rising petrol costs were one of the most important. The oil crisis of the early 1970s opened the door to potentially high foodstuffs demands from a number of developing countries, particularly those in northern Africa and the Middle East. An additional factor was the growing industrialization of the Pacific Rim states and Latin America, which led to improved living standards and thereby increases in food consumption.

From the early 1980s onwards, however, the world price of cereals gradually stagnated. The volume of cereals moving through world markets reached a ceiling during the 1980s and 1990s at around 200 million tonnes per year. With this loss of dynamism, the trade battle between the principal exporting nations (the USA, Australia, Argentina, Canada and the EU) became increasingly aggressive. After many difficulties, the commercial negotiations of the Uruguay Round ultimately ended in agreement, with a number of concessions made to the EU. Yet these eventually became the source of an increasingly difficult relationship between the EU and other world trading nations. This tension has led to growing demands for further reform of the CAP and its mechanisms. As a result, up to 1999, a ceiling of 23.5 million tonnes per year was placed on European cereal exports that benefited from *restitution* payments (CEC 1995, 1996; Charvet, 1997; Loyat and Petit, 1999). In addition, a new system of tariffs was applied to levies imposed by the EU on imported agricultural products. In this way, the levies, whose exact amounts fluctuated according to world price variations and the dollar exchange rate, were transformed into 'tariff equivalents' or fixed duties that were to be reduced progressively by 36% over six years. Finally, the EU agreed to open up its internal market at reduced import duty rates, for quantities of agricultural produce representing 5% of total European consumption (Le Roy, 1994; CEC, 1995, 1996).

In this new context, the question of whether the EU should participate even further in international trade, both as an importer and as an exporter of agricultural products, or should concentrate more on its own food needs without exporting, becomes crucial. The current stagnation of world cereal exchanges would suggest the second option. If international markets are not operating to the EU's advantage, is it reasonable to reinforce an agricultural policy that favours exportation? This question is particularly pointed given that the stagnation of world cereal prices is likely to last for some time as a result of the current Russian crisis, the economic downturn in the Far East and the difficulties currently experienced by a number of Latin American countries, especially, Brazil. However, other factors, such as strong demographic growth and urbanization within developing countries, as well as economic recovery in some Far Eastern states, suggest that cereal prices could start rising again in the medium term. A significant number of prospective studies, undertaken by the FAO, the World Bank, the International Cereals Council and the US Department of Agriculture, appear to share the same view (Conseil International des Céréales, 1994 and 1995 editions; Alexandros, 1995; USDA, 1996 edition). But will the EU be willing to participate in what seems to be an inevitable growth in world cereal trade, and on what basis?

Oil-seed plants

While cereal exchanges have remained practically stagnant since the early 1980s, the demand for oil-seed and protein crops has been far more dynamic. World exports of soya grains passed from 16 million tonnes in 1972/74 to 30 million during 1992/94, to reach 80 million tonnes at the end of the 1990s. A similar path has been followed by exports of soya oil-cake, which rose above 36 million tonnes in 1998/99 from a base of only 8 million in 1972/73. The production of oil-seed and protein crops is one of the deficit areas of European agriculture. In fact, the European deficit has grown with the expansion of industrial pork and poultry husbandry over the last 10 years. This is despite the fact that European production of oil-seed and protein crops has been strongly encouraged since the 1970s (Charvet, 1997; Loyat and Petit, 1999). For both climatic and agronomic reasons, initiatives for these products have centred more on colza and sunflowers than on soya. To compensate for the difference in remuneration between what is considered 'normal' for a European producer and the much lower world price for these commodities, European farmers received 'deficiency payments'. However, under the terms of the Uruguay Round agreements, the EU had to make a significant concession to the United States in limiting the land area given over to oil-bearing plants. This imposed a ceiling of 5,482,000 hectares. Under such a constraint, the only viable way to reduce the EU's high level of dependency on imports has been to intensify production within the existing area.

Turning finally to world meat markets, it is useful to distinguish between red meat (beef and sheep) and white meat (poultry and pork). With consumers in the industrialized countries eating less and less red meat, both for dietary and for financial reasons, coupled with traditionally low consumer demand in developing countries, the international beef market is currently depressed; total trade amounts to under three million metric tonnes per year. From the middle of the 1980s to the middle of the 1990s, the consumption of beef and veal in the USA fell from an average of 50 kg per person to 45 kg. During the same period, average consumption declined within the EU from 24 to 17 kg per person, a fall of over 25% (FAPRI, 1996). In 1996 the EU produced 75 million tonnes of beef and veal while consuming only 6.5 million, thereby raising the issue of surplus disposal (FAPRI, 1996).

While demand for red meat in developing countries has traditionally been low, consumers in industrialized countries are increasingly shifting to poultry and other less fatty meats. Countless cookery books and magazines bear witness to this shift in consumer preference. In terms of production costs, beef, which requires longer to produce and demands higher per unit vegetable feed inputs, is much more expensive than poultry and other 'white' meats. It is widely known that 7 calories of vegetable input are required to produce every calorie of beef. For a single calorie of chicken meat, only 2.0-2.5 vegetable calories are required. The price variation between beef and poultry is of the same level of difference. The recent BSE crisis has reduced consumption levels even further, with hygiene and health issues becoming increasingly important to consumers and, as a result, to the beef trade and world prices.

While world average red meat consumption per person has fallen during the 1990s to the level of the early 1960s (around 11.5 kg/person/year), that of white meat has strongly increased in both rich and poor countries, going from 11 kg/person/year in 1960 to 24 in 1997/98. Over the last five years, poultry meat in particular has become the dominant meat product in world exchanges. While the price of red meat within Europe is approximately twice that found on the open world market, over half of EU poultry meat exports take place without recourse to *restitution* payments, for internal EU prices are much closer to world levels. As a result, the EU is currently the second largest exporter of poultry meat in the world (after the USA). This owes much to the highly effective intensification of the Dutch and French poultry sectors in response to the shifting consumer demands.

The post-1992 CAP and its relations to world markets

The rules of the reformed CAP were applied during 1992/93. For a number of farm commodities, relations with world markets were largely unaltered from their pre-reform state. Thus, for wine, fruit and vegetables, oil-seed plants, milk and white meat, no immediate changes were apparent. For the cereal and beef sectors, however, major shifts in the relationship between the EU and world markets followed CAP reform.

Given relative surpluses in EU agricultural production at the beginning of the 1990s, alongside the environmental consequences of intensification in the more specialized agricultural regions of the EU, the transformation of productivist models of farming to more extensive forms was actively encouraged by 1992 CAP reforms. From that point on, EU policy was that gains in productivity should come from better farm management. In addition, within the framework of constraints resulting from the GATT agreement, agricultural product prices within the EU were to be realigned closer to those of world markets. However, the partial abandonment of the classic mechanism of farm income support through the maintenance of high prices created a need for other forms of income support. Hence, following 1992 reforms, temporary deficiency or compensatory payments were permitted under the Uruguay Round of the GATT, so long as they were phased out by 2002 (Figure 2.2). One of the more important consequences of such shifts in payment systems was to make the nature and level of agricultural support within the EU more visible to the European public. The passage from an aid system financed essentially by higher consumer prices to one financed essentially by taxpayers had the effect of raising the whole issue of agricultural subsidies onto the wider public agenda. The upside was that prices were to fall, bringing internal European prices closer to those of world markets and opening, at least cost, European markets to world markets.

Although less that at the beginning of the 1990s, the agricultural trade balance deficit between the EU and the rest of the world in 1997 stood at around five billion euros. Imports to the EU in 1997 amounted to around 131 billion euros, against exports to the value of 126 billion. The largest deficits occur in trade between the EU and the two Mercosur[4] nations of Brazil and Argentina, from whom the EU imports large amounts of soya and soya oil cake. The EU also has a net trade deficit with the USA, which is the largest market for EU agricultural produce and its largest supplier (GraphAgri Europe, 1999).

At a world trade level, the EU is a net importer of fruit and vegetables, tropical foodstuffs and oil-seed plants. While the deficit for the first of these has remained relatively constant since 1990, at around 6.5 billion euros, it has doubled for tropical foodstuffs, as well as for oil-seed plants and their derivatives, the latter going from 3.5 billion euros in 1990 to 5 billion euros in

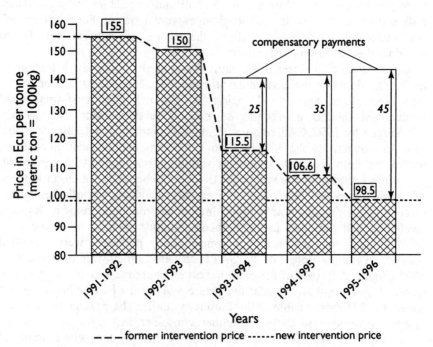

Figure 2.2
Impact of the 1992 CAP reform on cereal prices

Source: Author, adapted from data from the
Féderation Nationale des Syndicates des Exploitants Agricoles

1997. Alongside massive imports of oil-seed plants, those of cereal substitutes have been maintained at a high level (3.3 billion euros in 1997), despite the recent expansion of the European animal-feed cereal market following 1992 CAP reforms (see below).

Though post-1992 meat and live animal trade between the EU and the rest of the world remains relatively balanced, in some sectors, notably alcohol and drinks, EU exports have expanded dramatically. Here, the trade balance is increasingly favourable, going from 5 billion euros in 1990 to over 8 billion in 1997. It is notable that these products benefit from no export aids. Cereals are a second group of products for which the EU has a favourable trade balance. Increasingly, as Agenda 2000 reforms take effect, cereal exports will be made without export aid. A final group of products with a favourable trade balance come from the dairy sector, particularly for cheese (with a positive trade balance to the order of some 3.8 billion euros in 1997).

Beyond general trends, we should examine in detail how CAP reforms have affected the EU's position with respect to international agricultural markets and trade. As before, we propose to examine each of the principal product sectors in turn, beginning with those that have undergone few major changes and ending with those where market shifts have been particularly marked.

Milk

The EU milk regime was substantially altered following the imposition of milk quotas in 1984. As a result of these and other mechanisms, milk prices during the early 1990s were on average double the world price level (although these were low as international milk trading is relatively slight). Only cheese sells relatively well on the world stage, as there is strong demand amongst the richer nations and few subsidies exist to perturb world trade. But milk producers are affected by beef markets, for at least half of European beef production comes from dairy herds. To a far greater degree than for the USA or Australia, the European beef sector is in co-production with the milk sector. Changes in one sector are likely to have major implications for the other.

Oil-seed and protein crops

The reorganization of the oil-seed and protein crop regime dates from 1991, just before the final Uruguay Round negotiations. Changes made at this time were the result of considerable tension developing between the EU and the USA. When the CAP was originally set up in the 1960s, the US accepted a high degree of protection for European cereal producers with respect to world markets. But this initial concession was only made on the basis of EU acceptance of the unrestricted importation of US oil-seed and protein crops (chiefly soya) and their derivatives. In short, the US accepted the loss of the European cereal market (particularly at the height of the Cold War, when European support was considered essential) as long as it could maintain its dominance of the oil-seed plant market. The USA correctly calculated that, with the development of industrial animal farming, trade in animal foodstuffs had a solid future. Understandably, therefore, every time the Europeans sought to promote their own oil-seed plant production, they came up against strong US resistance, with the imposition of limits on EU action justified under previous GATT agreements.

In the years immediately following CAP reform, few significant changes were recorded in absolute EU price levels or in their relation to world prices. To all intents and purposes the European price was the same as the world price. One reason is that the EU does not tax oil-seed and protein crop imports from non-EU states. The only substantial modification that has occurred for these commodities since 1992 has been in the nature of the support mechanism for oil-seed and protein crop producers. Prior to reform, subsidies within the EU were paid to the agri-industrial sector, which then redistributed them, where appropriate, to producers. Under the post-1992 system, compensatory payments have been paid directly to producers. However, these payments, which are as much as £350 per hectare in France, are considerably higher than those paid to cereal farmers (on average, around £250 in France). If aid for oil-seed and protein crops is ultimately to be brought into line with those for cereals, there is likely to be a rapid and extensive reduction in the area given over to these crops within Europe. This scenario is increasingly likely as, under the recent Agenda 2000 agreement, compensatory payments will be the same for oil-seed and protein cops as for cereals. Without doubt, the most important change regarding the oil-seed and protein crop regime following 1992 reforms has been acceptance by the EU (under strong US pressure) to limit the total European area given over to oil-seed crops to 5,482,000 hectares. As this ceiling is laid down in area and not in tonnage, it leaves the door open to intensification. It nevertheless keeps EU Member States highly dependent upon oil-seed imports (Charvet, 1997; Loyat and Petit, 1999).

Poultry and pork

As these regimes operated largely independently of price support and export subsidies, the reforms of the 1990s have not had a major impact upon their relationship with world markets. However, the 1992 CAP reforms did have an indirect effect upon these sectors which effectively rendered them more competitive on international markets. Pig and poultry breeders, as large consumers, have benefited more than other sectors from a lowering of cereal prices in the 1990s, following the 1992 reforms. It takes approximately two kilograms of cereal to produce one kilogram of poultry meat, and four kilograms of cereal to produce one kilogram of pork. The lower feed costs engendered by dropping cereal prices allowed poultry and pig breeders to gain a competitive advantage over beef producers. This situation prevailed until the final years of the decade, when a dramatic fall occurred in pig meat prices, largely due to over-production in the sector (GraphAgri Europe, 1999).

Beef

For red meat, as for milk, the internal European market price is about double that of traded prices on the world market. Despite an enforced price reduction of 15% between 1992 and 1995, the situation remains largely unchanged today. European beef producers benefit from a number of different aid

22

schemes, including the suckler cow premium and the male calf premium. In a situation where supply is structurally greater than demand, these premiums are subject to a series of ceilings and quotas. Thus, individual farm quotas exist for the suckler cow premium and a ceiling of 90 animals exists for the male calf premium. In addition, the extensification of beef production has been actively encouraged through the use of supplementary subsidies that come into operation when stocking levels fall below 1.4 units per hectare. These link up with accompanying agri-environmental measures, which were also introduced by 1992 CAP reforms, under which a number of Member States seek to encourage upland pasture protection through the maintenance and encouragement of extensive forms of animal husbandry (Charvet, 1997; Loyat and Petit, 1999). Finally, Less Favoured Area and Mountain Area subsidies are employed in many EU Member States, notably France and the UK, for the support of beef, mutton and lamb-meat producers. Both these nations possess vast areas of mountain pasture of high and medium grazing quality. Landscape management in these areas, where population (and farmer) densities are low, is largely achieved through extensive or semi-extensive grazing practices, which are consequently encouraged and supported. The issue in these regions is not to increase per hectare production but to manage the land for environmental, social and landscape reasons.

Cereals

It is for cereals that we find the greatest shifts in relations between EU and world prices. A 1992-1995 drop of over a third in the EU intervention price for cereals was programmed by 1992 reforms. In real terms, this meant moving from a floor price of 155 ecu/tonne in 1992 to one slightly under 100 ecu/tonne in 1995.The 1992 reforms also brought all cereals under the same intervention price. Although price divergence between different cereals was never that great before, this convergence was partly in recognition of the increasing diversity of end uses, for example their use as animal feedstuffs. For producers, the price fall was to be tempered by offering compensatory payments. Since 1995 these have been calculated on the basis of 45 ecu per tonne, multiplied by a variable regional coefficient. The initial aim of the regional coefficient was to encourage producers who obtained yields above the regional average to reduce their inputs (pesticides, fertilizers and so on). However, the passage from price supports to income supports via compensatory payments still favours major farm producers and principal producer regions. Even if subsidy levels are only partially proportional to quantities produced, they remain largely dependent upon another unevenly distributed factor in agricultural production, namely the amount of land given over to cereals. Hence the major cash grain farming areas of Europe, such as the Paris Basin, East Anglia and Lincolnshire, the Borden region in Germany or the Po Valley in Italy, remain as the principal beneficiaries of European cereals support.

In addition to the reorganization of support mechanisms, the introduction of 'set-aside' in the 1990s facilitated improved management of European cereal production, for the amount of land to be 'set aside' each year is determined by the volume of cereals on the market and in storage. Thus, 'set-aside' levels have shifted through the decade, from 15% of the arable area (including oil-based and protein plants) in 1993, when there was enforced rotation of set-aside land, to 10% in 1995 and 1996, which were years characterized by a buoyant world cereals market and by relatively elevated European and world prices (see Figure 2.3), and eventually to 5%, with rotation being no longer mandatory, in 1997.

Figure 2.3
Changes in world and EU wheat prices from 1992/93 to 1998/99

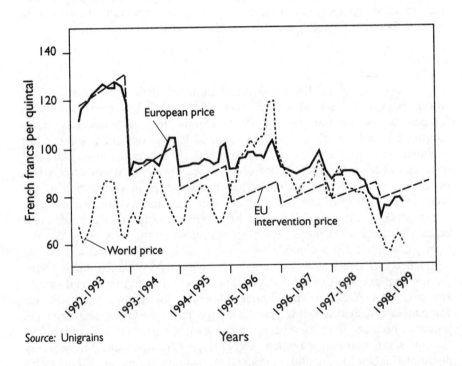

Source: Unigrains

With the fall in world and European prices from the end of 1997, set-aside levels have once again been revised. For farmers wishing to benefit from compensatory payments introduced by 1992 reforms, the setting aside of arable land is obligatory. However, the obligation only applies to those producers who annually harvest over 92 tonnes of grain, which corresponds to the European yield on an average 20 hectares of arable land. This equates to around 10 hectares of land in the richer cereal regions of the UK and northern France.

During the course of commercial negotiations under the GATT Uruguay Round, the United States succeeded in obtaining from the EU an agreement that European import levies would be transformed into fixed tariff equivalent levels. These would then be dismantled gradually over the period 1995 to 2000. Under this process of 'tarification', the entry price for foreign cereals was set in 1995 at 155% of the internal EU intervention price. This level was considered sufficiently high to protect the European grain market from the world market. The agreed gradual lowering of the tariff level over six years, coupled with a parallel lowering of the intervention price under the Agenda 2000 agreement, will ultimately have the intended effect of greater price alignment. Increasingly, therefore, cereals available on the world market will be able to penetrate the internal European market, even though a temporary glitch in the operation of world cereal markets caused world cereal prices to rise for a few months in 1996 to a higher level than the internal EU price. The European Commission, in a substantial about-turn, was forced to call a temporary halt to export aids as well as being obliged, for the first time, to tax European wheat exports for a short time.

As before, it has been pig, poultry and other intensive animal breeders who have been the primary beneficiaries from these changes. The general fall in European cereal prices, and their gradual alignment with world levels, have lowered breeders' input costs. Indeed, since European cereal prices have fallen considerably over the 1990s, foreign cereals are increasingly dominating the internal animal feed market. From 1994 to 1997, Europe's intensive husbandry units consumed an additional 7-8 million tonnes of cereals. By contrast, imports of cereal substitutes have fallen over the same period by around seven million tonnes. Moreover, with cereal-based animal feed becoming cheaper, pork and poultry is becoming more competitive against red meat. This situation is largely at odds with EU policy, which, largely for social and environmental reasons, has sought to encourage the maintenance and development of extensive pasture-based beef and sheep farming, particularly in upland and mountain areas. The European urban population, for whom cow and sheep grazing on rural and mountain pastures is integral to conceptions of the European countryside, is nevertheless eating less and less red meat.

Conclusion

The Common Agricultural Policy is at a critical stage in its history, with new reforms on the table and a new round of global trade negotiations forthcoming. The current situation for different production sectors of European farming, as well as their relationship to world exchanges, is highly variable, as too are methods of farm support. The effectiveness of the mechanisms set up to protect internal European production from risks associated with world market fluctuations are also highly variable, with all the economic, social and environmental consequences that such variability implies. While these mechanisms are generally effective in achieving their broad objectives with respect to beef production, they are markedly less so in the case of cereals, whose EU prices, like those of fruit and vegetables, are increasingly dependent upon world prices.

While one of the objectives of 1992 CAP reform was to maintain as many farmers as was possible within the European countryside, the rate of their decline at the close of the century has never been so rapid. In France, the decline in farm numbers during the 1990s reached a level of over 4% per year against around 2% during the preceding decade. For the 15 EU Member States, the number of farms has dropped from 8,497,000 in 1990 to 7,342,000 in 1995, a fall of 13.5% in five years (Eurostat, 1998). Food production chains and farmers alike frequently react to imposed reforms by expanding units of production. They thereby contribute to an ever-increasing decline in the number of European farmers.

At a moment when the enlargement of the EU towards the east is high on the political agenda, even if the dates of accession for the first East European states is continuously pushed back, and at a time when the World Trade Organization is having a growing impact upon European agricultural markets, with respect to world markets the CAP is in an intermediate position between being a price support policy, which has only been partly abandoned during the 1990s, and a direct income support policy, which remains partial and fragmented. The equivocal position makes it more and more difficult for the CAP to address another, increasingly central contemporary debate, which is that of the role of modern European farming in environmental, landscape and countryside management.

Notes

1 The Cairns Group is an informal group of agricultural-exporting countries from the 'North' and the 'South' that has sought to mediate between the USA, Japan and the European Community. Australia, Canada and New Zealand are leading members. These countries are in favour of greater

trade liberalization and the removal of agricultural subsidies, whether direct or indirect.

2 Imported cereal substitutes are made up principally of corn gluten feed, manioc, citrus pellets and molasses. Oil meals have not been included in these figures.

3 The appearance of compensatory payments during the course of the 1992 CAP reform process represented a substantial shift in the nature of EU farm aid away from production-related subsidies toward direct to-the-farmer payments. Henceforth, European farmers were to be compensated for the potential loss of income resulting from the lowering of EU market prices through payments that are calculated on the basis of the farmed area (for cereal and oil seed plants), as well as being dependent upon farmers agreeing set aside from production an agreed proportion of their arable land. In moving from production-related payments to area-related payments, it was hoped to halt the productivist drive towards greater production volumes and, thereby, to reduce the cost of storing and disposing of output that could not be sold on the open market.

4 Mercosur is the South American Free Trade Area.

References

Alexandratos, N. (1995) *Agriculture Mondiale: Horizon 2010*, Food and Agricultural Organization, Rome.

Arnould, P., Veyret, Y. and Wicherek, S. (1992) *Agriculture et Environnement*, Bulletin de l'Association de Géographies Français, Paris.

CEC (1989) *A Common Agricultural Policy for the 1990s*, Office for Official Publications of the European Communities, Luxembourg.

CEC (1995) *Rapport Annuel sur la Situation de L'Agriculture dans L'Union Européenne*, Office for Official Publications of the European Communities, Luxembourg.

CEC (1996) *Rapport Annuel sur la Situation de L'Agriculture dans L'Union Européenne*, Office for Official Publications of the European Communities, Luxembourg.

Conseil International des Céreales (annual) *Rapports Annuels*, London.

Charvet, J-P. (1997) *La France Agricole dans son Environnement Européen et Mondial*, 2nd edition, Liris, Paris.

Deltre, G. and Gueneau, M. (1994, eds.) *Agriculture et Environnement: Etat des Lieux*, L'Harmattan, Paris.

Eurostat (1998) *Agricultural Statistical Yearbook*, Office for Official Publications of the European Communities, Luxembourg.

FAPRI (1996) *Prospective 2005*, Food and Agricultural Policy Research Institute, Washington DC.

GraphAgri Europe (1999) *L'Agriculture dans l'Europe des 15*, GraphAgri, Paris.

Hathaway, D. (1987) *Agriculture and the GATT: Rewriting the Rules*, Institute for International Economics, Washington DC.

Hervieu, B. (1994) *Les Champs du Futur*, F. Bourin, Paris.

Ingersent, K.A., Rayner, A.J. and Hine, R.C. (1994, eds.) *Agriculture in the Uruguay Round*, Macmillan, Basingstoke.

Le Roy, P. (1994) *La Politique Agricole Commune*, Economica, Paris.

Loyat, J. and Petit, Y. (1999) *La Politique Agricole Commune*, La Documentation Française, Paris.

Miller, G. (1986) *The Political Economy of International Agricultural Policy reform*, Australian Government Publishing Service, Canberra.

Pisani, E. (1994) *Pour une Agriculture Marchande et Ménagère*, Editions de l'Aube, Paris.

Pitman, J.I. (1992) Changes in crop productivity and water quality in the United Kingdom, in K. Hoggart (ed.) *Agricultural Change, Environment and Economy*, Mansell, London, pp.89-121.

Toepfer International (annual) *Statistische Informationen zum Getreide und Futterlittelmarkt*, Toepfer International, Berlin.

USDA (annual) *Grain*, Washington DC.

3 Changing passions for food in Europe

Mara Miele

Despite a seemingly rapid pace of change in the food sector there are well-established traditional cuisines in Europe. These have evolved over the centuries, but even with the present-day 'questioning of traditions', such cuisines have maintained a strong national specificity (Beck *et al.*, 1994, pp.65-110). As Geertz (1986, p. 105) put it: "We may be faced with a world in which there simply are not any more head-hunters, matrilinearists, or people who predict the weather from the entrails of a pig... [but]... the French will never eat salted butter". This comment underlines the fact there are enduring differences in cultures of food. Yet some common traits and a common 'nutritional language' is shared by the majority of Europeans, so there are bridges across the sharpest divides. These common facets are deeply rooted, originating in the fifth or sixth centuries AD, when the Western Roman Empire was dissolved. According to the Italian historian Massimo Montanari (1996, pp.5-37):

> The Romans - like the Greeks - did not show great appreciation of nature in its wild state and the uncultivated had little or no place in the value system of Greek and Roman intellectuals. It was in fact the antithesis of *civilitas* - itself a concept linked etymologically and otherwise to that of *civitas*, the city - an artificial order created by man [sic] in order to distinguish and separate him [sic] from nature.

For Graeco-Roman culture, the ideal productive space consisted of rural areas organized around cities. The Romans called this space *ager*, the sum of cultivated lands, and distinguished it from *saltus* (virgin or unproductive nature). Agricultural cultivation was the basis of the Graeco-Roman economy and culture. Wheat, grapes and olives were the most important crops. In addition to the harvesting of field, vine and tree, horticulture played an important albeit secondary role, as to a lesser extent did the pasturing of sheep, the only use of natural resources for which Greek and Latin writers showed serious attention. Out of this productive system developed a diet, which we may call 'Mediterranean'. This was characterized by a dominant vegetable component - grain preparations and bread, wine, oil and greens - complemented by a little meat and cheese. Goats and sheep were raised principally for the production of milk and wool.

Montanari (1996) contrasts this Mediterranean cuisine with the modes of production and cultural values of the 'barbarians', as the Greeks and Romans called them. Celtic and Germanic populations had for centuries criss-crossed the great forests of central and northern Europe and had developed a strong preference for the products of uncultivated spaces. Hunting and fishing, the gathering of wild fruits, and the free pasturing of livestock in woods (especially swine, but also horses and cows) were central to their way of life. Meat, rather than bread, was the most important element of the diet. Instead of wine (known only in areas bordering the Empire), Celts and Germans drank mare's milk and its acid liquid derivatives, or cider (made by fermenting wild fruits), or beer in areas where grains were grown in small plots carved out of the forest. Instead of oil, butter and lard was used for greasing or cooking.

As Montanari shows, a key trait in cultural differences was the role of specific foods in nutritional regimes, for their status within societies was organized in very different ways. Differences in food hierarchies served to establish cultural identity and distinguish one group from another. Hence, before the fifth of sixth centuries, while the Romans consumed some meat, this foodstuff was not central to the basic diet and did not have a high cultural status. On the contrary, a near vegetarian diet constituted the ideal food culture of the ruling class and intellectuals.

Both Romans, with their celebratory vision of humans as 'bread eaters', and Germans and Celts, with their preference for meat, were proud of their respective food cultures and consequent cultural identity. Even though these two worlds were profoundly separated by differences in values and systems of production, a process of value blending started during the fifth and sixth centuries which developed further in the following centuries. The political and social predominance of the Germanic tribes, who became the ruling classes of the new Europe during the so-called 'Dark Ages', spread the Germanic outlook, along with its nutritional values, especially into those areas that were most directly dominated (England, Germany, France and northern Italy). In this process uncultivated land lost the marginal role attributed to it by Roman culture and become a space 'to be used' for rearing animals (mainly swine). Meanwhile meat became the most valued element of human nutrition. Even though the Roman physician, Cornelius Celsus,[1] maintained that bread was unquestionably the most nourishing kind of food, the nutritional handbooks that appeared after the fifth century gave clear priority to meat (Montanari, 1996, p.13).

The history of food consumption in Europe, such as that provided by Montanari, shows that even though the scarcity of meat kept consumption low until the end of the Second World War, especially for the lower classes, the food culture hierarchy established in earlier centuries arrived almost untouched into the present century, with meat as the most valued food (Harris, 1989, Lyman and Merzer, 1998).

In the 1990s, however, the hegemony of meat has started to be questioned, especially among the middle and wealthier classes. As Fiddes (1992, p.29) has noted:

> ... probably for the first time in history abstinence from meat eating is now more a question of choice than necessity, and is prevalent among those in better economic circumstances and better informed.

This quotation shows that the vegetarian antecedents of Mediterranean cuisine tend to be neglected in northern European perspectives on food culture. The contrasting histories of vegetarianism and meat eating are consequently often downplayed. Yet these contrasting histories run through European food cultures and yield a set of distinctive characteristics for the European food sector.

The interaction between these distinctive characteristics and contemporary cultural change in Europe will be described in the following sections. In the first section a brief overview of the shift from scarcity to over-production is provided. In the second section changes that have taken place in the 1990s are described, as these indicate key trends in food culture, including fragmentation at the micro-level, in the context of growing homogenization at the macro-level. The processes underpinning fragmentation and homogenization are then discussed, including time-saving, alongside shifting health and safety concerns, plus a growing interest in food quality. In the final section vegetarianism is discussed as an example of a new sensibility towards food. The reason for selecting this case is that it not only illustrates contemporary change, but also shows how ancient food values can be rediscovered by (post)modern consumers.

From food scarcity to overproduction since 1945

Food consumption in Europe has changed rapidly over the last 50 years. During the 1950s and 1960s, in tandem with rapid economic growth, there was an exponential increase in consumption, which made marked impressions on human nutrition. The new social pattern that emerged was generally referred to as *mass society* (Fabris, 1995), whose characteristic features were defined as a growing uniformity of culture and values. In a nutshell, people were believed to share the same basic values (and above all to want the same things), to share the same objectives in life and to crave for the same consumption goods and corresponding services. Differences in consumption were essentially concerned with the *quantity* of goods consumed rather than the *quality* of such goods.

During the 1960s, economic growth promoted social mobility (in the form of an expanded middle class) and, while the increase in consumption impacted upon the nutritional regime mainly in terms of quantity and calorie intake, the issue of quality started to be discussed. During the 1970s growing importance was attached to food quality and quality differentiation processes started to multiply. The quantity of food that was produced continued to rise and, in a context of over-abundance, more affluent consumers began to become more discerning. This trend became very clear in the 1980s, which has been commonly defined as the years of *hedonistic consumers*. By this time, the agro-food market had become segmented into different market *niches*. Much importance was now attached to food brands that shaped consumer preferences. During this period the quantity of consumption (most especially of food) increased more slowly than in the previous 20 years. Indeed, the share of food expenditure in household income started to decline rapidly. In Italy, for example, food expenditure accounted for 24% of household spending in 1984, which was a huge drop from the 1950s figure of 50%. Such trends prevailed across Europe and North America, with the typical 1980s share of household income spent on food being around 20% (15% in the USA). In lower income nations of the EU (Portugal, Greece, Spain and Ireland), the tendency was the same, but food accounted for a higher share of the household budget.

In the 1990s attention turned to quality issues with even more vigour, as market segmentation increased and the share of food in household income continued to fall. By 1997, food accounted for just 17% of the average Italian household budget, and this fell to 14% in 1998. Subsequently a growing number of consumption studies pointed out that traditional economic variables, such as food price or household income, no longer explain household purchasing strategies at the micro-level (Rosa, 1998, p.400). In support of this view, market analysts such as Malassis and Gersi (1995, pp.71-75) pointed to the fact that in most industrialized countries the energy limit has been achieved (viz. calorie intake per head per year has not changed over the last 10 years). This has led to the 'saturation' of the market for several food items (i.e. a number of products are coming close to their consumption limit). Connected to such saturation, as well as to the trends previously explained, a further key reason for the poor explanatory power of 'traditional' economic variables is that, when overall food expenses draw a minimal amount from available income, food price and personal income no longer determine consumer choice. This is because most products are effectively costed within the same 'price bracket'.[2] Conversely, increasing relevance is now given to socio-economic variables, such as formal education, lifestyle and rural-urban residence, in explaining differences in food consumption (Fabris, 1995; Malassis and Gersì, 1995).

The main effect on the food sector can be described as a growing complexity in food supply processes. This is represented most starkly by the activities of retail companies in moulding food choices. Such developments have resulted in two contrasting tendencies. At macro-level, there has been a growing homogenization within EU countries in food consumption (Rosa, 1998). At the micro-level, there has been growing fragmentation in food demand. These coexisting and contrasting trends have characterized food consumption trends over the last decade.

Consumption in the 1990s: micro-*fragmentation* and macro-*convergence*

Alan Gordon in the OECD report on the *Future of Food* (1998) argues that within Western Europe, there are two different approaches to food. These he terms the *'fuel'* and the *'pleasure'* approaches. The United Kingdom, the Netherlands and to some extent Germany, have traditionally been linked to the 'fuel' approach. France, Spain, Italy and Belgium are in the 'pleasure' camp. The former is characterized by standardization and homogenization, while the latter is marked by strong regional influences and culinary traditions.

The same author argues that, apart from the above-mentioned differences in food consumption, there are several factors that promote similarities:

> Until the first half of the nineteenth century, what people ate was mainly influenced by the natural endowment of their country: Mediterranean climate versus Northern Europe, types of fruit, vegetables and oils cultivated, pasture availability for cattle (beef meat, milk), appropriate conditions for wine, cider, beer or spirits, and so on. These influences remain in varying degrees, but have been attenuated by such factors as industrialization (urban living); the development of the food processing industry to meet the needs of the city-dwellers; organized food retailing; and the intermingling of food cultures (immigration, travel and media). (Gordon, 1998 p.93)

Gordon maintains (it would be better to say that he *laments*) that the countries that first industrialized lost their traditional foods and have developed a modern, more international food system. For instance:

> ... the United Kingdom was the first European country to receive (or suffer) the impact of the Industrial Revolution, and 'cheap food for the labour classes' became a necessity from the mid-nineteenth century onwards. The peasant farmer had already been eliminated by the

enclosures of the sixteenth, seventeenth and eighteenth centuries. The result: very little attachment to the soil, destruction of food culture, low value attachment to bread, regional cheeses and fresh fruit and vegetables. (Gordon, 1998 p.93)

Comparing consumption trends with food price and income, Rosa (1998, p.396) highlights converging processes amongst EU countries. In his conclusion, notwithstanding differences in food price and household income in each country, EU food consumption tends to be homogeneous at the macro-economic level. After comparing current trends in the West and East European countries, other commentators agree with this view (see Rosa 1998). In order to explain this finding, Rosa outlines the evolution of food expenditure in total family spending from 1970 to 1995 (Table 3.1). He shows how, in all European countries, food expenditure has decreased in comparison with total family expenditure This process is particularly strong in the decade 1980-1990, when expenditure on cereals, fats, meat, fruit, vegetables, coffee and sugar was stable, while that for fish and milk was growing. Demand for proteins also increased, and vegetable proteins began to be substituted for animal proteins. As for cereals, consumption of corn flakes, bakery products and crackers grew, because these products began to be valued for their high fibre content. Consumption of animal fats fell and in recent years has been replaced by organic fats. These trends indicate a growing consumer awareness of the effects of food on health, as well as a deeper understanding of medical information.

Table 3.1
Percentage of total consumption spent on food in European countries

Country	1970-1975	1975-1980	1980-1985	1985-1990	1990-1995
Belgium	24.8	22.7	21.9	20.8	19.1
Denmark	25.5	23.9	25.1	23.2	22.7
Germany	20.1	18.5	18.7	17.5	16.4
Spain	25.4	24.5	25.3	23.4	20.1
Greece	43.2	40.3	40.5	39.4	37.2
France	23.4	21.6	28.8	20.0	18.8
Ireland	44.4	42.7	42.5	36.4	33.5
Italy	31.4	28.2	25.7	23.4	22.4
Luxembourg	26.0	23.8	23.9	21.4	18.2
Netherlands	21.0	19.7	19.8	19.3	18.7
Portugal	n.a.	38.8	37.8	36.1	33.1
UK	30.6	29.4	27.1	23.1	20.9
Mean average	29.7	29.9	28.1	25.4	23.4
Standard deviation	8.5	8.3	7.9	7.5	7.0

Source: Rosa (1998)

34

The same author underlines the growing relevance of supermarket chains on the homologation process (Rosa, 1998, p.403). Distribution chains have helped change consumer habits (with decreases in the number of shopping trips, in changed shopping time, and new shopping hours), and have influenced the typology of purchased food, with a strong dominance of branded items over unbranded. Choice in buying a product is now inclined to come from a comparison between different brands and prices, rather than from perusal of a limited number of locally produced, traditional agricultural products, that are available in corner shops. With the emergence of supermarket chains, consumption has tended to become more similar in both the northern European and Mediterranean countries, even though in these latter areas anthropic and cultural factors still maintain a degree of specific influence.

Owing to its minimal food 'price elasticity', its pronounced development of retailing chains, and the widespread habit of eating out, the United Kingdom is considered the country in Europe with the most modern food system (McMichael, 2000; Rosa, 1998); which places the UK closest to patterns in the USA. There is speculation that the UK-USA model will be reproduced in other European countries (as promoted by some of the largest transnational companies, such as McDonald's).

Another significant contributor to changes in food consumption is the general shift in shopping habits that has emerged in the 1990s. One element of this is increased purchases of durable goods, and an especially significant trend in additional expenditure on health and leisure. This latter trend is one that experts forecast will continue to rise. Expenditure growth in these sectors is seemingly a common occurrence across Western Europe and North America and is a sign of a shift in values toward health and leisure. Health has become a prerequisite for a high quality of life and, for the first time in history, leisure time has become a scarce resource for the wealthier classes (Fabris, 1995; Warde, 1999). This cultural change has had a marked impact on perceptions of food quality.

Quality in food is a complex concept. We might distinguish the following qualities in the food chain: productive quality (e.g. efficiency and cost), ecological quality (e.g. sustainable production), brand quality (trademarks, labelling) and consumer-perceived quality (taste, nutrition, lifestyle) (Murdoch and Miele, 1999; Murdoch et al., 2000). There is a growing literature showing that consumer-perceived quality affects consumer purchasing choice the most (Becker at al., 1998). In this context, Peri (1990, p.189) provides a classification of consumer requirements for food quality in terms of the perceivable and not-perceivable (Figure 3.1). Perceivable attributes refer to the contents of service and sensorial quality (convenience and organoleptic charactistics), whereas non-perceivable quality features

Figure 3.1
Perceivable and non-perceivable requirements of quality of food

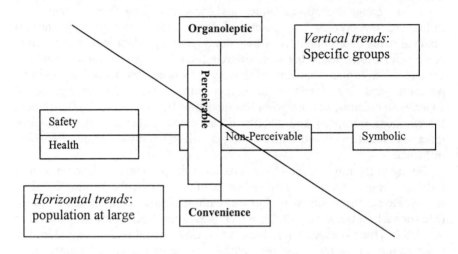

pertain to health, safety and symbolic values, such as 'organically produced' or 'animal friendly', 'fair trade', 'country of origin', and so on.

Amongst multifarious demands for improved agro-food quality characteristics (Figure 3.1), the most pressing are demands for healthy food and for higher food safety. These create conditions for the development of dietetic or *light* product lines, as well as for the decline/substitution of meat. The demand for services (simplification of preparation, higher conservation, saving time, etc.) lead to an increase in the market for 'convenience' products. Both 'convenience' and 'health/safety' are food characteristics that have gained enormous relevance in the last decade (even though convenience foods have been evident in Europe since the end of the 1950s). Concerns about simplifying food preparation (or conservation) and about health are common to a wide range of consumers. Such concerns are not strongly segmented by socio-demographic characteristics or lifestyle (Gordon, 1998), so they can be defined as *horizontal* trends. They represent key elements in homogenization - the common lines of evolution in food consumption in Europe. The new relevance attributed to symbolic aspects of food, alongside the sophistication of consumer taste, represent elements driving the segmentation and fragmentation of food demand.

Saving and shifting time, safety and health concerns: horizontal trends

Convenience

Convenience foods are a growing segment of the food market. They meet a relatively new social demand for simplification of meal preparation. A large number of items (packaged, canned, frozen, pre-cooked, ready meals) are commonly referred to as 'convenience foods'. Warde and associates (1998, p.2; also Warde, 1999, p.6) say the term convenience has been used in English since the 15th century and identify three meanings for the term. The first refers to something that is suitable or well adapted to the performance or attainment of some satisfaction (fit-for-purpose). A second meaning concerns avoidance of personal trouble in particular practices, and also the material advantage and personal comfort so derived (saving trouble, saving toil). A third sense refers to furnishing an opportunity or advantage. Basically, 'modern' conveniences are those oriented towards comfort and labour saving. The instruments of modern convenience reduce the amount of work required in the accomplishment of routine domestic tasks.

It was only during the 1960s that another usage was imported from the USA. The term 'convenience store' suggested that the organization of shopping or goods might be 'designed for convenience' or used when needed. At that time the term convenience became linked with the re-ordering of time. Warde and associates connect the evolution of the meaning of 'convenience' with a new relevance attributed to 'time management' in everyday life: "... the concept has changed recently, perhaps because shortage of time has been identified as a contemporary 'trouble' which requires 'saving', or more properly re-ordering" (Warde *et al.*, 1998, p.3).

Interestingly, many studies have tried to test whether or not the 'availability of time' was the main explanatory variable in people purchasing convenience foods, but results showed that 'household income' rather than 'free time' is the main factor affecting the purchasing of convenience foods (Bonke, 1992). These findings are consistent with recent market analyses pointing to increased demand for organic or animal-friendly foods (even though such foods are more expensive than conventional products). This fact suggests that convenience foods have gained legitimacy. Previous opposition to the use of convenience products because of a reduced 'care' or 'authenticity' in food preparation is not felt so strongly today (although issues of acceptability or appropriateness do survive for baby foods; Miele and Neri, 2000).

With regard to the role of time (availability) in affecting attitudes towards convenience foods, Warde (1999, p.6) suggests:

> The alternative explanation that I wish to canvass is that the appeal to convenience increasing involves appeal to a new way of conceptualizing the manipulation and use of time. It speaks to the problem (sic) of living in a

social world where people in response to the feeling that they have insufficient time, set about trying to include more activities into the same amount of time, by arranging or rearranging their sequence. *This is about timing rather than about time.* Peas in the freezer reduce the number of shopping expeditions and provide vegetables to hand at whatever time it might be desirable to eat .... What certainly is *eliminated is any need to include shopping into the schedule every day* of the week. (emphasis added)

One can conclude from Warde that the desirability and increased popularity of convenience foods rely on them acting as both time-saving and time-shifting devices. They help free leisure time, that today is perceived as a scarce resource, especially in terms of quality-time (e.g. enjoying the company of one's co-residents, which for middle class dual-earner households appears to be a real concern; Gregson and Lowe, 1994, cited in Warde, 1999, p.9).

Health and Safety

In the 1990s, health and safety concerns have become pivotal in purchasing food products. For a large number of consumers these concerns manifest themselves in the selection of products, as seen in increased purchases of diet and low-fat foods. For example, by 1987 diet products covered 37% of all processed foods in Germany, while 'light' foods account for half the supermarket supplies in the USA (Malassis and Ghersì, 1995, p.79).

Health and safety are two different concepts, since safety involves production, processing and sales, which can be achieved without food being particularly healthy; as seen in many 'junk foods'. Safety issues relate to questions of codes and standards, whilst health issues focus on the impact of food consumption. That said, in reality it is extremely difficult to define the contribution of food to consumer health.

In the 1950s and 1960s consumers were barely aware of health and food safety issues. There were groups seeking to protect the environment who warned about risks to health from food based on refined, processed methods, which were associated with the widespread application of chemical pesticides (Milenkovich, 1978; Tovey 1997). But these were minority groups, involving a small number of consumers. They were very marginal in political terms. The large majority of consumers tended to be concerned merely with seeking quantitative increases in food consumption. It was not until the 1980s that the agro-food sector really witnessed an increase in healthy food lines. Principally this was as a result of growing concern that diets should be healthy and nutritional. In Italy and other southern European countries, the ideal of a healthy diet has imposed itself even more recently, for in the previous decade this ideal was the focus of attention in northern Europe and North America.

Healthiness is not an inherent characteristic of a single product, nor is it solely dependent on food consumption. Moreover, owing to the multitude of elements of lifestyles and living conditions that impact on health, insofar as consumers conceptualize a role for food in health promotion, this is dependent on personal perception. For individual products this will be influenced by the general pattern of food consumption into which a single item is inserted, which can hardly be codified or standardized.[3]

Fabris (1995, p.55), who is one of the most attentive experts on consumption trends in Italy, has noted that there has been an evolution in people's understanding of the concept of health: "... the attention to health issues, which was typical of the most aged or hypochondriac segments of the population, has nowadays changed and is fuelling a large phenomenon whose starting point is redefinition of health to a previously inconceivable extent and size". This new orientation (see Figure 3.2) affects large population segments, irrespective of age and economic status. It is moulding consumer behaviour across a wide range of choices, from food to holiday locations, from items of clothing to use of leisure time, from avoiding certain products (like cigarettes and alcohol), to the rise of new market sectors (e.g. the low-fat sector and organically-produced products; see, for example, Schifferstein and Oude Ophius, 1998). What lies behind these new concerns is an evolution in citizen understanding of the concept of health. Until the 1960s and 1970s, the concept of health was used either as the opposite to traumatic events, including illness, or else indicated treatment and recovery. During the 1980s the concept became something more. Certainly it no longer became a factor to be considered when traumas occurred. Rather it was a prerequisite in order to reach specific aims (viz. the improvement of one's body, physical beauty, etc.). In the 1990s a *holistic* concept of health has become a dominating element in fields from which health concerns had previously been excluded (Fabris, 1995). For example, health is seen as a prerequisite for energy and fitness, for efficiency and well-being, for balance and harmony, for longevity, and as a key element in quality of life in a broad sense.

This understanding of health has become especially relevant in the food sector, and has gained enormous potency so far as consumer choice is concerned. Lying behind this, Levenstein (cited in Gronow, 1997) identifies progress in scientific knowledge about nutrition as the most influential determinant of our perception of food and eating. This progress has created a situation in which we assume:

> ... that taste is not a true guide to what should be eaten; that one should not simply eat what one enjoys; that the important components of food cannot be seen or tasted, but are discernible only in scientific laboratories; and that experimental science has produced rules of nutrition which will prevent illness and encourage longevity. (cited in Gronow, 1997, p.113)

Figure 3.2
Dimensions of health

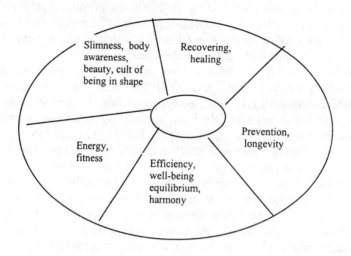

Slimness, body awareness, beauty, cult of being in shape

Recovering, healing

Prevention, longevity

Energy, fitness

Efficiency, well-being equilibrium, harmony

Source: Elaboration from Fabris (1995, p.58)

Often, health and nature are now seen to be closely connected. This vision is more and more a key distinguishing element in consumer choice, which is fostering the development of new markets. Most evident in this regard is decline/substitution in the consumption of red meat (beef) with white meats (poultry and pig meat) or meat substitutes (tofu and seitan), alongside the rise in consumption of *light* or dietetic products, foods enriched with fibres, minerals and vitamins or less processed foods.

Several studies hold that Europe has reached saturation level in meat consumption, so the European market is not anticipated to see further increases in meat consumption (Becker, 2000). On the contrary, substitution among different types of meat can be forecast, such as white meat replacing red, or exotic meats like oyster or kangaroo becoming more popular.

That said, we need to recognize differences across Europe. For example, pig meat is consumed in greater quantities in northern European countries and in Spain. Italy and France are characterized by high beef consumption, although recently poultry-meat has become more popular. Qualitative substitution across meats began to be noticed in the 1980s, as the humblest cuts (offal, fore quarters) were neglected in favour of choice cuts, and as white meats were substituted for red. In the Italian meat sector, consumption trends followed this general path, with exponential growth in meat consumption recorded around the 1960s and 1970s. From that time on there has been an increase in annual consumption from 10 kilos per capita to the current 86 kilos. Noticeably, in the early 1990s, meat consumption did not increase, which suggests that a consumption limit was reached. In the UK, decline in meat consumption started even earlier and, after the 1996 'mad cow disease' scandal, meat sales collapsed. Although this situation has now reversed, and current consumption is at the same level as that preceding the BSE scare, total meat consumption is stationary (and is falling for red meat; see Miele and Parisi, 2000).

But health and safety concerns are not the only reasons for decline in meat consumption. Thus Franklin (1999, p.51) ascribes the *'demise of meat'* to a general loss of 'image':

> First, the quantities of meat eaten have declined in response to health scares and raised thresholds of repugnance. Meat is no longer required to centrepiece meals or as a symbol of social progress; high consumption can indicate vulgarity. Meat is increasingly sold in marinades, stir fries or sauces as a pre-prepared meal with exotic origins, thus further disguising its animal beginnings; ... Fordist mass-production, factory meat systems have attracted substantial criticism and [a] section of the service class avoid their products. A substantial minority has become semi-vegetarian.

Franklin points to the rise of a new sensibility towards animals in postmodern culture, one that leads to a growing legitimacy or attractiveness of lifestyles once perceived as extravagant and radical, such as vegetarianism. The diffusion of these values among some consumer elites, such as the service classes, the young, and highly educated segments of the population (Kafka and Alvensleben, 1998), has promoted the advance of new consumption styles and new niches in the food markets. These are defined here as vertical trends.

Vertical trends: the rise of new food consumption styles

New orientations in food consumption are also affected by what David Chaney (1996, p.123), in his book on lifestyles, calls a "... moral and aesthetic concern in contemporary culture". Chaney points to three areas of change in discourses about food. The first refers to a shift from seeing food as a matter of practicality to food as an aesthetic concern that is a display of social competence or even sophisticated taste. The second is the vast increase in the "... disciplinary focus upon regulating the amount and types of food eaten, with a consequent industry of advice on the need for, and most effective modes of, dieting". This latter point links to the third area, which refers to an enormous increase in moral discourse around the symbolic meaning of food (also Mennel *et al.*, 1992). Moral concerns are perhaps most evident in the ideas and values associated with terms like 'organic', 'natural', 'traditional' and 'animal-friendly':

> Common to these values are beliefs that the mass marketing of food has led to bland, tasteless merchandise that not only exploits the raw material of animal products but also the producers of vegetable products, has contributed to the chemical destruction of the soil and other natural resources, and is harmful to consumer's health through over-use of pesticides, chemical ingredients and ingredients such as salt and fats. In addition to those who value more traditional style of production and preparation of food items, there are consumers who seek assurance that their food has been produced in ways that are not exploitative of their environment. In these moral concerns over food it is unsurprising that vegetarianism, in a variety of guises, should be a growing aspect of lifestyle practice. (Chaney, 1996, p.124)

Investing food with moral significance is not peculiar to the current era. However, a genuine innovation is what Chaney refers to as 'lifestyle politics', by which he means the politicization of many lifestyle choices. This process of politicization has generated a large number of new social movements, some of which have come to concern themselves with the production and consumption of food. Examples include those who promote animal welfare through to concern about animal rights and environmental concerns (see Tester, 1991 quoted in Chaney 1996; Miele and Parisi, 1997; Alvensleben, 1998), those who oppose the diffusion of so-called 'Frankenstein Foods' (i.e. genetically modified organisms), and opponents of the McDonaldization of world food, who act to protect traditional cuisines and local production (e.g. the Slow-Food movement; Miele and Murdoch, 2000). It is in this context that we can assess the emergence and diffusion of new niche-markets, like 'animal-friendly produce', 'suitable for vegetarians', 'organic products' or 'typical products' (Arvola, 1998; Miele, 1998; Alvensleben and Schrader, 1999; Marsden *et al.*, 1999).[4] This new interest in local foods is also reflected in the number of local, regional, national and transnational policies aimed at organic and 'typical' production. Such policies have been evident for some time in the European context, as seen for instance in the European Council Regulation 2092/91, which defined the rules for certifying organic production, in European Council Regulation 2081/92, which allowed food producers to register products with geographical names if they could show that region of origin gave special characteristics (e.g. Ilbery and Kneafsey, 1998), and in European Council Regulation 2082/92, which was concerned with specific product types (traditionally processed foods; Sylvander, 1996). 'Animal-friendly produce' and 'suitable for vegetarians' foods have been developed mostly by private retail companies (with the exception of Sweden, where animal welfare has represented a focus of attention in public policy towards animal products). These 'cruelty free', 'traditional', 'authentic' foodstuffs have become highly valued in the 'moralized' culture of contemporary food consumption. The growth of the market for vegetarian foods and the increased popularity of vegetarianism represent a good example of this trend.

Vegetarianism

Many people think vegetarianism is a trendy new fashion, but, as indicated in the introduction, it has a long history (Simons, 1994).[5] Nevertheless, it is only during the last decade that there has been a remarkable growth in the total number of vegetarians in Europe, as well as in social movements concerned with animal welfare and animal rights, who criticise the way in which animals are treated in the production process. Indeed, some commentators believe that vegetarianism in Europe is now becoming part of the mainstream:

> Vegetarianism is an acceptable religion in Britain today. No one asks any longer why you hold this particular belief. Even though followers of the vegetarian faith are still technically in a minority, they are nowadays treated to equal rights wherever they go. What really matters in an acceptable religion is that no one asks or cares whether its members are true believers. Only a few modern-day vegetarians presume they have the moral high ground, giving them the right to make themselves a social nuisance. In their case there is a faint tension about the land, in otherwise carnivorous restaurants and at similar dinner parties. (Chamberlain, 1998, p.72)

During the last 10 years the general perception of vegetarianism has also changed. A mere decade ago, anyone who declared themselves to be vegetarian was likely to be considered weird or cranky, and was expected to be adopting this nutritional stance as part of a radical lifestyle. Nowadays, vegetarians in Europe tend to be well educated and belong to the higher socio-economic classes, so they have disposable income to spend on animal welfare and green issues (Harper and Henson, 1998). Yet they are less likely to be seen as self-denying, compared to the rest of the population. Indeed, they are frequently viewed as people to be emulated.

In Europe, the UK is the country with the highest number of vegetarians. It is estimated that vegetarians numbered around 100,000 in 1945. Today 7% of the population declares itself to be vegetarian, and the number of young people adopting this style of consumption is increasing steadily: 12% amongst 15-24 year olds, who are the consumers and parents of the future.

It was not until the 19th century, however, that any attempt was made to organize a vegetarian movement in the UK (the first in West Europe). In the 1950 and 1960s, the British public became increasingly aware of the poor living conditions of animals in factory farming, which had been introduced following the Second World War. Vegetarianism increased steadily throughout the 1970s and 1980s, with The Vegetarian Society taking a prominent lead in campaigning and education. By 1983, demand was so great that the Food and Cookery Section of The Vegetarian Society was replaced by The Cordon Vert Cookery School, which today runs courses almost every week of the year, for all levels of expertise from beginners to professional chefs. During the 1980s and 1990s, vegetarianism has been given a major growth impetus as part of the process of change and conservation of resources. More recently, food scares, such as 'Mad Cow Disease', Lysteria and Salmonella, have broadened concerns about meat consumption and have echoed to the public issues of animal welfare in modern animal farming systems (Miele and Parisi, 1997). Thus, in a report published in 1998, Mintel estimated that 25% of consumers in the UK were potential purchasers of vegetarian food. Almost one-quarter of women aged 16 to 34 no longer ate red meat. Moreover, between 1992 and 1997 the market had grown by 70%. According to Mintel, this trend is evident in the rest of Europe (see http//www.The Vegetarian Society UK/).

In Stockholm 'Meaning Green', the world's first vegetarian and organic fast food chain was opened in November 1998. The owner's intention is to open 100 restaurants in West Europe and the USA over the next five years, starting with London. The vision of a growing market for vegetarian food is supported by various research findings. Thus, a survey sponsored by Dalepack in 1998 showed that 82% of those asked felt there would be more vegetarians in the future, and, according to the UK Vegetarian Society, if the actual rate of change towards vegetarianism continues, everyone in the UK will be vegetarian by 2035 (a similar forecast has been made by the US Vegan Society, which puts the year at 2075 for the USA).

In the final years of the millennium, more people in Europe have begun to change their attitudes towards animals and have started to share the view that the meat industry is intrinsically cruel and responsible for environmental destruction. Such people have begun to look for animal-friendly products or meat substitutes. Perhaps one of the most surprising changes, at least in the Western world, has been the growth and availability of vegetarian targeted products. Until the 1970s vegetarian foods were not available in supermarkets. One could find them only in specialized, expensive health stores filled with unfamiliar or exotic ingredients. During the last decade, restaurants, caterers, supermarkets and manufacturers have broadened the food stocks that are 'suitable for vegetarians'. Today, the main supermarket chains sell an abundance of tasty, ready-made meals, a huge variety of vegetarian burgers, sausages, bacon, pates, sandwich fillings, and colourful vegetarian foods, garnered from all over the world.

According to *The Grocer* (March 1998), which is the bible of the UK food trade, "the meat free market has changed dramatically", with a "growing moral awareness" playing a part in driving consumer demand to make the vegetarian market one of the most dynamic growth areas in modern times. The continued development of vegetarian convenience foods has played a key role in market expansion for a wider number of consumers, and not only for those that are strictly vegetarian. The availability of convenience foods opens this moral choice to a large group of people without compromising practical aspects of their life. *The Grocer* estimated that the 1997 commercial value of prepared vegetarian food in the UK was £388 million and forecast a rise to £600 million in 1999. The largest UK supermarket chain, Tesco, has claim that of the 8 million customers it serves each week, 50% are meat reducing. Nearly half of this supermarket chain's pasta range is vegetarian and around a third of their ready-made meals are vegetarian. The market for 'suitable for vegetarian' foods seems to be expanding much faster than the number of self-declared vegetarians.

In a recent article, Chamberlain presents a small story that gives insight on the fashion for vegetarianism, and its consequences:

> The television cameras recently went behind the scenes at one of Britain's largest hotels, the Adelphi in Liverpool, and it was amusing to watch the traditional-minded chef dealing with the vegetarian 'problem'. He was in the kitchen, preparing a banquet for 640 people, and the number of vegetarian reservations kept rising by the hour. The BBC bleeped out the besieged cook's comments as unsuitable for family viewing. His brief was originally 47 vegetarians, 8 vegans, and two people who don't eat food touched by other people. By the evening there seemed to be 'a few hundred' who 'had decided overnight or this afternoon' that they weren't going to eat meat. Had the chef been the owner of the restaurant, and able to afford a loss of business, he might have turned them away. In any case he suspected them of being somehow fake. Well, vegans aren't fake. They don't eat meat, or fish, or any dairy produce, not even eggs, and if they're not careful they can leave their children malnourished. There have been some published cases. But some vegetarians eat fish, some not, and some even eat the occasional bacon sandwich. Plenty more people, less conceptually confused, describe themselves as 'mostly vegetarian'. The poor chef was right to feel there was something elusive about the opposition to his menu that night, but what he hadn't grasped was that purity of belief doesn't matter much to vegetarianism any more. Most people just want the option, without putting in a special advance order. And they expect

to be able to do it in restaurants, if not at dinner parties. (Chamberlain, 1998, pp.72-75)

As the same author has noted, if the rich and beautiful give up meat, many will copy them, but they will not necessarily share any commitment to a full vegetarian lifestyle.

Conclusion

During the 1990s a new culture of food seems to have emerged. It is associated with a discerning attitude towards many aspects of food. What is striking about this new culture is that it is being asserted in a context of *abundance*: European societies, in many respects, have too much food. Abundance allows the expression of this new sensibility. Once consumers stop worrying about getting enough to eat they begin to concern themselves with the quality of that which they have. In the case of food, quality comes to be linked to health and taste. This new culture follows from a growing homogenization of food consumption across food cultures. This homogenization has been based on a distinctive hierarchy of values and traits, in which meat consumption has been central. More recently, new commonalties in consumption have emerged from a decline in meat consumption and from new concerns about health and convenience (viz. time availability).

However, abundance also leads to fragmentation in food markets as greater choice enables consumers to express a variety of ideas and desires. One set of ideas currently being expressed is associated with a new morality of food. This new morality stems, in part, from a changing perception of animals. It marks a shift from a utilitarian view (in which animals are seen as machines whose only value is derived from the way they meet human demands) to a more compassionate and altruistic view (wherein animals are seen to have intrinsic value). This shift is taking place across Europe. It appears to be associated with a context of abundance, for consumers now have access to various sources of protein (vegetable sources of protein are now widely available); thus, animals are potentially freed from the role of protein source. As a result, growing numbers of consumers have come to see vegetarianism as a dietary option. In exercising this option these consumers promote a healthy (more animal-friendly) food culture. We can conclude, therefore, that the increased homogenization (and abundance) of food products within the European economic and cultural space has not prevented a remoralization of food consumption. This remoralization perhaps points towards a food future in which various European cuisines rediscover the virtues of vegetarianism.

Notes

1 Cornelius Celsus, *De Medicina*, II, 18, translated by W.G. Spencer, London, 1948, pp.191-193.
2 This is a technical term in marketing. It means all the possible final prices for a category of products. Especially when the product costs little money (let us say eggs or milk), prices vary within a limited range that does not influence consumer choice.
3 As 'health' is an inexpressible and elusive concept, that can hardly be measured, there are direct consequences for rules governing food advertising. Within the European Union any reference to the healthiness of a food product is forbidden, or at least open to regular challenge, as 'the facts' cannot be verified. By contrast, in the USA so-called 'health claims' are allowed, with many producers making extensive use of this freedom, as seen in promotions of meat originating from maize-fed or free-range livestock.
4 In Regulation 2081/92, the EU sought the protection of typical products PDO/ IGP by 'country of origin designation'.
5 See http//www.The Vegetarian Society UK - The History of Vegetarianism in the UK/htm.

References

Alvensleben, V.R. (1998) Ecological aspects of food demand: the case of organic food in Germany, in *Health, Ecological and Safety Aspects in Food Choice*, EU Project AIR-CAT-Measurement of Consumer Attitudes and their Influence on Food Choice and Acceptability Reports Volume 4, Number 1, Matforsk/Norvegian Food Research Institute, pp.68-80.
Alvensleben, V.R. and Schrader, S.K. (1999) Consumer attitudes towards regional foods products: a case study for northern Germany, in *Consumer Attitudes Towards Typical Foods, The European Food ConsumerI*, EU Project AIR-CAT-Measurement of Consumer Attitudes and their Influence on Food Choice and Acceptability Reports Volume 5, Number 1, Matforsk/Norwegian Food Research Institute, pp.10-20.
Arvola, A. (1998) Beliefs and purchase intentions concerning organic pork in UK, Denmark and Finland, in *Health, Ecological and Safety Aspects in Food Choice*, EU Project AIR-CAT -Measurements of Consumer Attitudes and their Influence on Food Choice and Acceptability Reports Volume 4, Number 1, Matforsk/Norwegian Food Research Institute, pp.80-83.
Beck, U., Giddens, A. and Lash, S. (1994) *Reflexive Modernization*, Routledge, London.
Becker, T. (2000, ed.) *Quality Policy and Consumer Behaviour in the European Union*, Wissenschaftsverlag Vauk, Kiel.

Becker, T., Benner, E. and Glitsch, K. (1998) *Summary Report on Consumer Behaviour Towards meat in Germany, Ireland, Italy, Spain, Sweden and The United Kingdom*, Final Report for Fair Project CT-95-0046 Quality Policy and Consumer Behaviour, available at: *www.unihohenheim.de/~apo420b/eu-research/eu.htm.*

Bocock, R. (1993) *Consumption*, Routledge, London.

Bonke, J. (1992) 'Choice of Foods: Allocation of Time and Money, Household Production and Market Services', MAPP Working Paper 3, Copenhagen.

Buttel, F.H. (2000) The recombinant BGH controversy in the United States: towards a new consumption politics of food?, *Agriculture and Human Values*, 17, pp.5-20.

Chamberlain, L. (1998) A new religion, *Slow*, 9, pp.72-75.

Chaney, D. (1996) *Lifestyles*, Routledge, London.

Fabris, G.P. (1995) *Consumatore & Mercato, le nuove regole*, Sperling & Kupfer Editori, Milano.

Fiddes, N. (1992) *Meat a Natural Symbol*, Routledge, London.

Franklin, A. (1999) *Animals and Modern Cultures: A Sociology of Human-Animal Relation in Modernity*, Sage, London.

Geertz, C. (1986) The uses of diversity, *Michigan Quarterly Review*, 25, pp.105-123.

Gordon, A. (1998) Changes in food and drink consumption, and the implications for food marketing, in OECD *The Future of Food: Long-Term Prospects for the Agro-Food Sector*, Organization for Economic Cooperation and Development, Paris, pp.91-110.

Gronow, J. (1997) *The Sociology of Taste*, Routledge, London.

Harris, M. (1989) *Cows, Pigs, Wars and Witches: The Riddles of Culture*, Vintage, New York.

Harper, G.C. and Henson, S.J. (1998) *Consumer Concerns About Animal Welfare and the Impact on Food Choice: The Comparative Report*, University of Reading EU Project CT98-3678, Reading.

Ilbery, B.W. and Kneafsey, M. (1998) Product and place: promoting quality products and services in lagging rural regions of the European Union, *European Urban and Regional Studies*, 5, pp.329-341.

Kafka, C. and Alvensleben, V.R. (1998) Consumer perceptions of food-related hazards and the problem of risk communication, in *Health, Ecological and Safety Aspects in Food Choice*, EU Project AIR-CAT-Measurement of Consumer Attitudes and their Influence on Food Choice and Acceptability Reports Volume 4, Number 1, Matforsk, Norway, 21-41.

Lyman, H.F. and Merzer, G. (1998) *Mad Cowboy: Plain Truth from the Cattle Rancher Who Won't Eat Meat*, Scribner, New York.

Malassis, L. and Ghersi, G. (1995, eds.) *Introduzione All'Economia Agroalimentare*, Il Mulino, Bologna.

Marsden, T.K., Murdoch, J. and Morgan, K. (1999) Sustainable agriculture, food supply chains and regional development, *International Planning Studies*, 4, pp.295-303.

McMichael, P. (2000) The power of food, *Agriculture and Human Values*, 17, pp.21-33.

Mennel, S., Murcott, A. and van Otterloo, A. (1992) The sociology of food: eating, diet and culture, *Current Sociology* 40, pp.32-41.

Miele, M. (1998) *La Commercializzazione dei Prodotti Biologici in Europa*, Effemmelito, Firenze.

Miele, M. (1999) Short circuits: new trends in the consumption of food and the changing status of meat, *International Planning Studies*, 4, pp.373-387.

Miele, M. and Neri, C. (2000) La carne da allevamenti biologici in Toscana, in M. Miele and V. Parisi (eds.) *Atteggiamento dei Consumatori e Politiche di Qualità*, Franco Angeli, Torino.

Miele, M. and Parisi, V. (1997) *National Report on Consumer Concerns about Animal Welfare and the Impact on Food Choice*, Report for EU FAIR-CT- 98-3678, Università di Pisa, Pisa.

Miele, M. and Murdoch, J. (2000) 'Fast Food/Slow Food: Standardization and Differentiation in Culinary Networks', paper prepared for Workshop 21, World Congress of Rural Sociology, Rio de Janeiro, July-August 2000.

Miele, M. and Parisi, V. (2000, eds.) *Atteggiamento dei Consumatori e Politiche di Qualità*, Franco Angeli, Torino.

Milenkovich, L. (1978) *Agricoltura Biologica in Europa*, Clesav, Torino.

Montanari, M. (1996) *The Culture of Food*, Blackwell, Oxford.

Murdoch, J. and Miele, M. (1999) Back to nature?: changing worlds of production in the food sector, *Sociologia Ruralis*, 39, pp.465-483.

Murdoch, J., Marsden, T.K. and Banks, J. (2000) Quality, nature and embeddedness: some theoretical considerations in the context of the food sector, *Economic Geography*, 25, pp.58-78.

OECD (1998) *Future of Food*, Organization for Economic Cooperation and Development, Paris.

Peri, C. (1990) Qualità e certificazione dei prodotti agro-alimentari, *Bollettino dell'Agricoltura*, 3/1990, pp.185-198.

Rifkin, J. (1992) *Beyond Beef: The Rise and Fall of the Cattle Culture*, Dutton, New York.

Rosa, F. (1998) Consumi alimentari nell'UE: modellizzazione e convergenze, *Rivista di Economia Agraria* Anno L III (3), pp.395-423.

Schifferstein, H. and Oude Ophius, P. (1998) Health-related determinants of organic food consumption in The Netherlands, in *Health, Ecological and Safety Aspects in Food Choice*, EU Project AIR-CAT -Measurements of Consumer Attitudes and their Influence on Food Choice and Acceptability Reports Volume 4, Number 1, Matforsk, Norway, pp.63-68.

Simons, F.J. (1994) *Eat Not This Flash: Food Avoidances from Prehistory to the Present*, University of Wisconsin Press, Madison.

Sylvander, B. (1996) Normalisation et concurrence internationale: la politique de qualité alimentaire en Europe, *Economie Rurale*, 231(Jan-Feb).

Tovey, H. (1997) Food, environmentalism and rural sociology: on the organic farming movement in Ireland, *Sociologia Ruralis*, 37, pp.21-38.

Warde, A., Shove, E. and Southerton, D. (1998) 'Convenience, Schedules and Sustainability', University of Lancaster Department of Sociology paper at: http://www.comp.lancaster.ac.uk/sociology/soc006aw.html.

Warde, A. (1999) 'Convenience Food: Space and Timing', University of Lancaster Department of Sociology paper at: http://www.comp.lancaster.ac.uk/sociology/soc006aw.html.

4 Political mutation and agricultural change in Eastern Europe

Pierre Lenormand

The major changes that have hit East European farmers since the beginning of the 1990s derive from political shifts linked to the weakening of a model of society which, confronted by a planet-wide liberalist offensive and enfeebled by its own failure to move forward, finally collapsed. This collapse precipitated a subsequent fall of the Soviet system, which was the lynchpin of the 'global' socialist model. Even accepting that this model contained diversity, it nonetheless had certain number of distinctive characteristics (e.g. Dawson, 1986). Once freed from these essential features, the former socialist countries sought integration into the capitalist world economy, the decollectivization of agriculture in favour of family farming and a rapid accession to the European Union (EU). These three major objectives were adopted virtually unanimously by governments succeeding the former socialist authorities after the Autumn of 1989 in what became the 15 Central or East European (CEE) states. These 15 countries[1] exactly match the current number of EU Member States.

This chapter shows how the post-socialist agricultural reconstruction has taken a number of often very different forms across these 15 countries. It has, in fact, led to social and territorial changes that in many cases are far removed from those originally intended (for example, Conté and Giordano, 1997). The result has been the emergence of a wholly new and never-before-seen agricultural situation whose diversity relates, at least partially, to varied national trajectories dating to before and during the period of 'real socialism'. The impact of these national trajectories has been sufficiently strong to leave a permanent mark.

The agricultural heritage of the socialist era

With some 10 years of hindsight, it is useful to recall, albeit briefly, the major features of agriculture in countries that, following the Soviet Union, and under governing communist and workers' parties, defined themselves as socialist. First and foremost, their agricultural systems were characterized by a dualism based upon the co-existence of large socialist agricultural enterprises and very small individual farms. The first of these, the production cooperatives and state farms, closely resembled the Soviet *Kolhoz* and *Sovkhoz*. They were comprised of several thousand hectares, indeed in some cases tens of thousands of hectares. They covered the major part of the national agricultural land surface and made up the major part of national production. Huge land parcels were characteristic, with complex crop rotations involving industrial crops, cereals and feed crops (though rarely grass), interspersed with giant stables and husbandry units, workshops and hangers. Administrative buildings were often several storeys high. Such 'farms' produced the characteristic landscapes of socialist agriculture, with these landholdings themselves often based upon the large feudal estates that dominated northern Europe for many centuries to the East of the line joining Trieste to the Elbe. This generalized system of mixed husbandry and arable farming reinforced the broad homogeneity of regional agricultural systems from the Baltic to the Black Sea. It allowed for little regional distinction, except in a few cases where local climatic and national variation yielded distinct regional production systems, such as the southern wine and fruit regions.

The second agrarian form that was characteristic of socialist agriculture was the very small domestic farm. These often occupied well under a single hectare, and were generally found on the outskirts of towns and villages (see Chapter Five; Morgan, 1987). Four types of small plots can be distinguished: private plots or 'lopins' belonging to cooperative farm workers; garden plots farmed by industrial workers; weekend or second home retreats; and, small kitchen gardens attached to the individual houses that make up so much of the East European countryside.

With varying degrees of competition and complementarity, these two classic agricultural forms co-existed throughout the East European rural landscape, save on mountain slopes, which were almost exclusively given over to state-owned forests. Plains and plateaus were dominated by state and cooperative farms. They employed a large workforce, and often utilized an impressive level of mechanization. The hills and peri-urban areas were the domain of small holdings. These were intensively farmed by family members, almost always manually.

Variations in these archetypal East European agrarian landscapes reveal the impact of distinct national histories. These were seen in highly diverse patterns of land-use control by state forces following post-war agrarian

Figure 4.1
Diversity of farming systems under socialism at the end of the 1980s

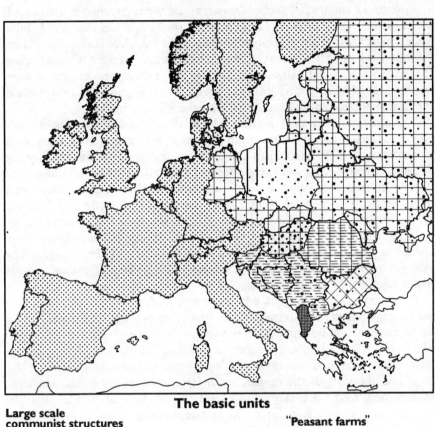

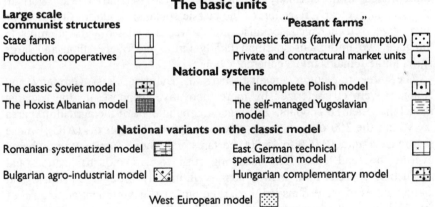

The basic units

Large scale communist structures

State farms

Production cooperatives

"Peasant farms"

Domestic farms (family consumption)

Private and contractural market units

National systems

The classic Soviet model

The Hoxist Albanian model

The incomplete Polish model

The self-managed Yugoslavian model

National variants on the classic model

Romanian systematized model

Bulgarian agro-industrial model

East German technical specialization model

Hungarian complementary model

West European model

Source: Author

reforms, differences in the form and intensity of agricultural collectivization and departures, more or less pronounced, from the basic Soviet model (Figure 4.1).

Prior to the collapse of the Soviet system and the emergence of the 15 CEE states, some of the original East European socialist states (the three Baltic States, Czechoslovakia, Byelorussia, Ukraine and Moldavia, the latter three falling outside the CEE states), offered classic forms that were relatively close to the Soviet model. Unequal technologies, differences in the relative importance of state farms and the presence of large areas of grassland distinguish these countries somewhat from the Russian archetype.

The others offered more diverse models of agricultural organization, that were all somewhat different from the Soviet system. Two were long characterized by an isolationism and dogmatic purism. This was the case for Albania, where recent emergence from a particularly frugal, isolated and heavily policed socialism has led to a general climate of ubiquitous social delinquency. It also fits Romania, where the hardening of the regime came later. This latter state, however, is one of the few in which rural and agrarian contestations, notably against the policy of emptying and liquidating town centres in the name of modernization under Ceausecu's 'Systemization' policy (forcibly relocating residents into collective housing centres), played a major part in toppling the socialist regime.

Poland and Yugoslavia took a far more non-conformist line with respect to Soviet agricultural organization. In the former, the resistance of a demographically important peasantry was largely successful in preventing the setting up of vast cooperative farms at the onset of the socialist era and in maintaining over two million small family farms. These co-existed, in the north and the west of the country, with large state-owned farms that were expropriated from Germany at the end of the Second World War. In Yugoslavia, the early rejection of the classic socialist model in favour of an alternative, self-managed socialist model, was associated with attempts to integrate two million or so small family farms and over a thousand large agricultural domains into a coherent whole.

The three remaining socialist states of Bulgaria, East Germany and Hungary were characterized by more innovative responses to the socialist model than their neighbours. In Bulgaria, around 85% of the agricultural area lay within the 300 or so enormous Agri-Industrial Complexes (AIC), whose size ranged from 10,000 to 15,000 hectares and whose employees numbered over a thousand each. The headlong rush toward industrialization and production concentration in this country ultimately brought gigantism and diseconomies of scale. This led the last communist[2] government getting rid of the AIC in 1988 and replacing them with village cooperatives (McIntyre, 1988; Lenormand, 1996). The model favoured by the German Democratic

Republic was one founded upon product specialization and the technical separation of animal (*Tierproduktion*) and crop farming (*Pflanzenproduktion*). As specialist production cooperatives and state farms were linked by highly regulated contractual relations (Lacquement, 1993), the result was that huge areas were given over exclusively either to arable farming or to husbandry. The final socialist state to be considered here is Hungary. Despite the short-lived challenge to collectivization in 1956, this nation displayed a classic model of socialist agrarian organization, tempered by the encouragement of internal competition between complementary but diverse forms of socialist agriculture, each fulfilling the niche for which it was best adapted. Here, state domains were characterized by high levels of investment and technological innovation. Cooperatives proved to be particularly effective in mass production, while individual farms provided the framework for specialized animal and crop production (such as vines, vegetables and fruit). Technological and scientific innovation, illustrated best by 'technological production chains', an early concern for market relations and diverse forms of cooperative membership, in many ways combined to make Hungarian farming the showpiece of European socialist agriculture.

From this considerable variety of organizational models, one can draw a single all-embracing concern; namely, to produce at low prices and on a national basis, the food necessary for the domestic population. Yet the insistence on national supply often led to emphasis on basic food supplies alone (such as cabbage, potatoes and pork in the north and corn, fruits and mutton in the south). Initially at least, trade and exchange between members of the socialist bloc were seen only as temporary correctives of domestic supply shortfalls (Lavigne, 1979). Adherence to this principle partly explains the fact that states in the Council for Mutual Economic Aid (CMAE, which is also known as COMECON) traditionally insisted both upon the rule of unanimity and upon essentially bilateral exchanges. A Charter, established in 1959, and subsequently revised in 1962, 1971 and 1974, set out the principle of socialist economic integration. This led to cooperation programmes and a certain degree of economic harmonization. Sectoral commissions were set up, including one for agriculture and the food industry, based at Sofia. Several international management organizations were constituted, such as Agromach for agricultural machinery. Potentially, these appeared to open the door to greater cohesion, to the creation of 'socialist multinational corporations', and ultimately to the establishment of a single market area, reflecting the construction of a similar space in the West (exchanges between CMAE states represented around 60% of total CMAE exports in 1983; Lavigne, 1985, p.247). However, these cooperative innovations fell foul of jealously guarded national prerogatives, of a multiplicity of different national currencies and of the heterogeneity of internal price systems within nations (Lavigne, 1985). As a result of the state monopolies over foreign exchanges, the very idea of a common agricultural policy was in good measure alien to the principles of the CMAE. Yet so too was the notion of protectionism.

More sparing but also more wasteful in their use of entrants than Western agriculture, these different forms of socialist farming give the overall impression of having been less efficient, particularly with respect to labour productivity, which was low in all sectors. In following its established objectives, farming appeared expensive for the state, both in production investments and in consumer subventions. The contradictions of the system, which could lead Polish pig farms to feed their animals with bread rather than forage crops produced on the farm, are well known. By the end, and in order to respond to unmet food needs, the USSR and other states decided to operate within the world market. Although their participation in world exchanges was limited by their lack of exchangeable currencies, benefits did accrue from the low prices of world markets, particularly for forage crops and the cereal substitutes used to feed animal stocks.

At the heart of socialist agricultural models, the mode of regulation was typically state-led. This was frequently through a State Plan, which laid down with greater or lesser success production targets per farm sector. Initially defined in terms of volume, these targets came to be set increasingly in terms of value, production gain or even export receipts. Mechanisms of state planning gradually incorporated greater degrees of incentive into pricing systems that rewarded producers for growing more than set targets (which encouraged local officials in state and cooperative farms to set targets low). This was achieved through subventions and through the granting fiscal advantages. With little room for negotiation over the overall objectives of an economic planning system that was oriented essentially around grand socialist enterprises, the agricultural sector was dominated by the state (with the exception of Poland), through a virtual monopoly over the purchase, conditioning and distribution of food products. At the same time, a small-scale production sector, oriented toward a 'free' market and domestic production, continued to thrive. Though substantially different from its equivalent in Western Europe, this production sector represented between a quarter and a third of total output for fruit and vegetable products.

Although priority under state planning was heavy industry, at least until the 1970s, the food industry, which was of equal importance strategically, was organized vertically by branch or sub-branch. Apart from the Soviet AGROPROM, which Gorbachov created when he was Minister of Agriculture, Bulgaria was the most advanced country in developing a unified agro-industrial complex. The Bulgarian Agro-Industrial National Council (AINC) replaced the Ministry of Agriculture at the beginning of the 1980s, although this was dismantled in 1986 when Bulgaria began it process of *perestroika* (known as *preustroistvo*). Although there were differences in form, all East European states (including Poland and, to a lesser extent,

Yugoslavia), were characterized by a large public agro-food sector, for which the state, as representative of the interests of 'all the people', had overall control.

The shift away from socialist agriculture

From the 1970s onwards, researchers finally moved on from the ideological 'for' and 'against' positions that had so characterized commentaries of Eastern Europe up to this point, and began to analyze the largely unknown real world of Eastern Europe. Stressing both the convergences and divergences of East European farming systems, both with respect to themselves and with respect to Western models, geographical and other social science research during the 1980s focused on a comparative approach that revealed the juxtaposition of two parallel 'crises'. On the one hand, there was the commercial 'crisis' of the productivist model in the West. On the other hand, there was an efficiency crisis of the extensive model that prevailed in the East. The developing ecological crisis revealed itself to be common to both models.

In an ideological climate increasingly dominated by neo-liberalism, a new analysis emerged towards the end of the 1980s. This has proved so accessible that little has emerged to contradict it. According to this reading, commentators set a Western model, which is portrayed as largely the victim of its own success, against the socialist model, which is characterized as being distinguished by three fundamental failures. The first of these was economic failure, which was underlined by slow growth rates and by an increasing recourse to major grain imports. The second was an ecological failure, which was symbolized by the Chernobyl disaster, the desertification of the Aral Sea and extensive soil pollution. The third failure was a socio-political one, in which collectivization irredeemably separated 'people from the land' (for example, Streih, 1997). It is on the basis of the supposed original sin of the socialization of private property that much of the discourse of the contemporary political leaders in the East is constructed. This applies no matter what their particular neo-liberal variant is. This diagnosis, and the political advantages to be won from advocacy of land redistribution, has meant that against all expectations about agrarian issues are once again placed upon the political stage. Indeed, they have dominated political debate in the new pluralist assemblies since 1990.

The countryside of Central and East Europe is currently undergoing a far-reaching process of restructuring that has largely been imposed from above (Blaas, 1993; Dontchev and Lenormand, 1993; Lacquement, 1993). Over a period of a few years, complex edifices and structures of the socialist era have been torn down. This dismantling of the socialist agrarian heritage has two key aspects, which have been described as a short 'functional transition' and a longer 'structural transition' (Maurel, 1992; Blanchet and Revel, 1997).

Functional transition

From 1990 onwards, new political leaders have resolutely sought to establish a market economy by adopting macro-economic measures designed to break with the principles of socialist reproduction. Underlying these policies has been a desire to impose on economic actors, almost all of whom were largely unprepared for this systematic bifurcation, the rules of market competition, both internally and externally (Lavigne, 1979). Different forms of 'shock therapy' have been implemented, with policies of structural adjustment, which were already tested in Third World countries, constituting the central strategy of this functional transition.

The first 'therapy' has been monetary. Destabilized by a ubiquitous black market, to varying degrees national currencies have been massively devalued to the detriment of people's savings and spending power. The deregulation of prices has brought sharp rises in product costs, accompanied by a concomitant fall in consumption. An increasingly differentiated pattern of demand has led to a new structuration of the market. This has led to a polarization of consumption, with reduced demand for basic consumer items, which are still largely supplied by domestic outlets, and the satisfaction of new demands for largely imported food (and other products), which is particularly notable amongst the developing middle and upper classes.

The absence of command and control mechanisms after the end of the Soviet system has led to market chaos, with speculative market trading dominant. Thus, Romania has been condemned to import cereals after speculators and traders exported the bulk of domestic production. Such negative outcomes have provoked virulent criticism, not so much on the part of consumers, who are largely deprived of a collective voice, but from farmers. This is particularly the case in Poland, where farmers have experimented with a large range of measures designed to challenge state agro-food policy, such as speculative food stocking, the development of parallel markets and, somewhat paradoxically, state aid (Halamska, 1992, 1995).

In the name of de-monopolization, a process of state disengagement has been initiated. With respect to agriculture, former collection and distribution centres have either been closed down or have been decentralized to much weaker regional structures (whose names often belie their public status), which have largely inherited the installations and sometimes the food stocks of former state enterprises. Yet these are still public segments of former agro-food complexes. They are dependent either upon a de-legitimized central state or upon impoverished and weak local or regional authorities. These public segments are incapable of providing the guarantee and orientation roles they formerly held under the socialist period (Lenormand, 1997). The short and, for many states, sharp 'functional transition' of the CEE states is thus characterized by the process of state de-monopolization and the subsequent weakening of public sector roles in the agro-food sector. This has been followed by a much longer period of structural transition, the essential component of which has been a growing privatization.

Structural transition

Within the new macro-economic framework, the substitution of private for formerly public operators, privatization in other words, is at the centre of a process of structural transition that touches diverse sectors of the economy. The Hungarian experience serves as a good example. Hungary, where recent history, including the period of 'entrepreneurial socialism', lent itself to a relatively easy conversion. Perhaps not surprisingly, early privatization took place through the widespread establishment of private firms. This involved one person in 10 (or one active person in five), with private firm formation being most notable in the commercial and service sectors, which were comparatively undeveloped under the preceding political regime (Lenormand, 1997). In the Hungarian agro-food sector, privatization was highly selective (as in other sectors). Many socialist agricultural production structures were simply dismantled and liquidated, with their equipment and installations sold or abandoned. A t least partially, a second group of structures has remained in production, essentially due to being taken over by local and regional governments or by private investors. Today, a lack of available capital, the difficulty of raising bank loans, and exorbitant interest rates, all hinder the modernization of the nascent Hungarian private sector and limit the durability of enterprises. Any further major restructuring risks provoking profound change, which could engender severe difficulties, even in sectors of the agro-food economy, whose strategic position and contribution to employment would otherwise justify public support. From this sombre political landscape, more often than not, the only really emerging enterprises are those that are supported by foreign capital. Around a quarter of the Hungarian agro-food sector depends today upon foreign investment. Yet this investment is limited to the highest performing firms, in the most viable sectors, such as brewing and sugar. Outlets in these sectors are increasingly controlled by major European and world agro-food companies, like Nestlé, Danone, Unilever and Feruzzi. Even the celebrated vignoble of the Tokai region has recently been subject to an influx of foreign capital, which is largely French but also embodies Japanese and British concerns.

As with the agro-food sector, for agricultural production, 'structural transition' has taken the form of a widespread but highly variable process of de-socialization. Yet privatization processes in agriculture initially appear to

59

be more complex than for the agro-food sector. This is because they centre around the two distinct processes of reforming land ownership and restructuring of farm holdings.

Land reform

A policy of re-establishing full private property rights has been actively engaged in by East European political leaders. At a fundamental level, this policy has been ideologically and politically motivated, with new political elites seeing private property as the means of re-establishing the 'lost' link between society and the land. As such, agricultural land represents a relatively easy and uncontentious starting point, given that the farming population is numerous and the political advantages to be drawn from giving land to farm workers are expected to be significant. 'Give the land back to its owners' comes across as a straightforward objective, particularly as much of the land that has been farmed under cooperatives that remained in private ownership. In this, East European states differed substantially from the ex-USSR, in that land reforms after the Second World War tended to expropriate only larger estates or foreign-owned agricultural land. The remainder of the land that was in private hands either stayed in private ownership or was distributed amongst farm workers. In addition, the family farm appeared as a recognizable and relevant base for the reconstruction of a post-socialist farming organization, as well as being seen as a significant departure from inefficient state enterprises.

However, if the principle seems simple at the outset, its implementation has raised serious problems. Land could be redistributed according to the principle of 'redistributive justice' ('the land belongs to those who work it') or according to the principle of 'reparatory justice', to former owners and their inheritors who had been disadvantaged by collectivization (Maurel, 1994a). In the bulk of the Central and East European countries, the majority of elected leaders, who were keen to eradicate all traces of one of the key building blocks of former socialist regimes, voted between 1990 and 1992 to re-establish the fundamental law of private property and thus 'return' land to prior owners and their descendants.

For societies marked for almost half a century by an 'egalitarian paradigm' (Maurel, 1994b), such a return to the prior *status quo* raised two political limitations. First, there was the spectre of foreign capital having a key economic role. Second, there was the possibility of (former) large landed estates being re-constituted. For these reasons, the reference date for property restitution was generally set at a date subsequent to the redistributive land reforms of the immediate post-war period, although in practice a number of exceptions to this broad rule were allowed. One such exception was the 1995 Hungarian Amendment, which allowed foreign ownership of farmland but only by individuals. Meanwhile, in the Länder of what is now eastern

Germany, the policy of giving indemnification for expropriations that took place before 1946, coupled with the sale of former state farms, allowed a number of large landowners to take repossession of part or all of their former estates (Gerbaut, 1997).

The restitution of land to its former owners also revealed two technical limitations. The first of these was juridical. With the passage of time, especially given that the lands concerned had experienced warfare, it has often proved extremely difficult to ascertain ownership. This has led to innumerable court cases and, as a result, to lengthy periods of uncertainty for all involved. The second difficulty, which is of a more practical nature, arose following the collapse of Bulgarian communist government, at which point it was decided to return land to its 1945 pattern of ownership, despite the considerable changes that the landscape and land-use had undergone over the last half century. With popular opinion strongly opposed to this policy, it was later abandoned as being impossible to implement. At the end of the day, and contrary to the declared policy at the time, many land parcels were maintained in the socialist form (Billaut, 1996).

Despite their generally common goals, these land reforms reveal a variety of solutions, ranging from full restitution of 1945 boundaries, in the case of Bulgaria, to a more tempered land reform, cushioned by compensation, as undertaken in Hungary (Figure 4.2). Albania is the only East European state to have adopted a policy of egalitarian redistribution between former and existing landowners and occupiers, that includes the partial indemnification of former property owners. By 1993, only a handful of large privately owned farms existed (often jointly held). Most of the 600,000 hectares that were formerly held by 492 cooperatives had been broken up into 467,000 farm units of around one hectare each (Civici and Lerin, 1997). Finally, with the exception of Russia, the Commonwealth of Independent States[3] (CIS, where the totality of the agricultural land surface was state-owned) and Bulgaria (where state farms grew out of the original cooperatives), state-owned land was usually treated differently. Generally, a small proportion was sold off, with the rest remaining in different forms of public ownership, which was subsequently either let to private concerns or farmed by state enterprises (as in the former East German Länder, in Poland and by the new 'commercial societies' in Romania; Hirschausen, 1996).

Farm organization

The restructuring of farm holdings themselves has been guided by a single principle. This has been adhered to by international experts and the new governments, as well as by policy-makers within the European Union. It has been reinforced by assessments of the various land reform processes outlined above. This is that the family farms represent the most adaptable and effective

Figure 4.2
Diversity of land reforms in the post-socialist period, 1990-1995

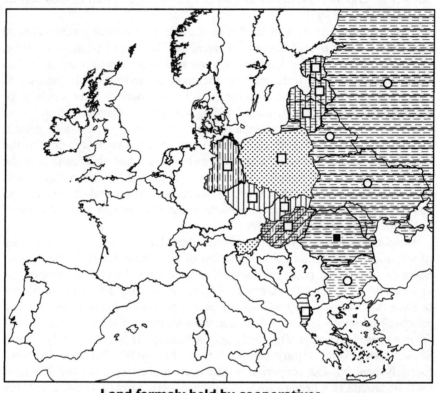

Land formaly held by cooperatives

Returned to former owners	Shared out amongst those having use rights
1 2	1 2
I Partial or very partial levels of return	I Little information
2 Complete or nearly complete return	2 Not applicable

Indemnisation or compensation

Land formerly owned by State farms

Maintaining the status quo ■ Leasing and sale □ No distinct reform ○

Source: Author

units for reorganizing agricultural production. To this end, and in parallel with land reform legislation, a series of measures were introduced throughout post-socialist Central and East Europe that forced former cooperatives to respect newly established private property rights and adopt new forms of agricultural organization. From this legislation and its application, four very different forms of agricultural holding emerged.

The initial intention to create numerous small family farms soon encountered a number of obstacles. Despite the establishment of a series of aid schemes, and irrespective of official encouragement, the family farm sector today is very minor, both in terms of the number of farms and the surface area covered. Poor and ill-adapted agricultural machinery, the cost of becoming an entrant into the sector, including the prohibitive cost of credit, the contraction of the market and the absence of appropriate commercial networks, have all hindered the establishment of everything but larger farms (Duval, 1997). Commentators have underlined the importance here of the enduring presence of a socialist work culture, that was "heterogeneous, segmented and de-territorialized" (Maurel, 1994a, p.20). Certainly, this has not been conducive to stimulating a new enterprise or even an artisan culture. Agricultural investment has also had to compete with more rapidly expanding economic sectors (commerce, banking and private services). Finally, an additional structural factor has had a generally negative effect. The passage of the ubiquitous and recently restored small landholdings to viable farm units supposes a far-reaching process of land concentration. While this certainly occurred, it only really concerned a relatively small proportion of middle-sized farms. At the bottom end of the scale, small holders are reluctant to give up their land, while, at the top end, larger scale farm operations have already captured much of the appropriate land market (see below).

By far the most common production unit, amongst contemporary farming types, is the self-help micro-farms that derive from the former socialist tradition of the cooperative micro-plot. Extended almost universally to urban and rural households by land reform, these very smallholdings have become indispensable for the survival of a large and impoverished sector of the population (Chapter Five). They are relied upon for basic, if minimal, food needs. As a result of their continuing importance for so many households, alongside the difficulty of accumulating them into a larger landholding so as to constitute a viable farm production unit, these structures are marked by strong inertia (Duval, 1997). Yet the number that will ultimately survive is dependent upon the rhythm and modes of property concentration within the land market as a whole, as well as to the dynamics of the agricultural land concentration.

A third form of landholding, which some link, erroneously in my mind, to the Anglo-Saxon or even American model, are large private or entrepreneurial farms with salaried workers. These are generally holdings of several hundred hectares, the majority of the land being rented. This capitalist model owes its relative strength to a number of factors. The emergence of a small entrepreneurial class, derived chiefly from those who are well-qualified, as well as being well-connected, embodying techno-structure personnel of former cooperatives and state farms, has enabled some to grab opportunities that have accompanied privatization (Simon, 1994). These operatives have had the capacity to create large-scale agricultural enterprises and other agricultural services. Foreign investors have also emerged within these larger farm structures. In the former East German Länder in particular, West German investors have acquired farms far larger than those available in the West (Lacquement, 1993; Gerbaud, 1996, 1997). These entrepreneurs have proved adept at using the necessary material and the qualified agricultural workforce to their advantage; thereby renewing the tradition of large private estates that was present in Central Europe before the post-war land reforms. As such, they are an increasing source of concern for a growing number of Western agricultural leaders, who see in them a strong competitive challenge to the West European family farm model. Yet the viability of these enterprises, which is without real parallel within the EU, lies chiefly on an inherited competitive advantage that is derived from low labour costs.

The fourth and final model, which is entirely specific to Central and East Europe, brings together various forms of neo-collective farming that have emerged from former grand socialist agricultural enterprises. These bear witness to the capacity of resistance and adaptation to structures, that too often is relegated to history as purely artificial and ineffective, despite their complexity and relative longevity (Maurel, 1992). Current structures associate numerous worker groups with extensive arable farms or husbandry units and, in doing so, offer a high degree of labour division. Several new structures of this type, that specialize in particular forms of agricultural production, have taken up the relay, albeit generally over smaller surfaces, of former production cooperatives and state farms. Within this fourth model, we find variety in the dimensions and status of individual farms. These range from the Romanian 'commercial societies', which are often presented as simple clones of former state farms, although in reality the economic and legislative environment of their operations have completely changed, to new 'hybrid' forms, which present traits that are at one and the same time old and new. The 'registered cooperatives', or *Eingetragene Genossenschaft*, of the former East Germany, the Hungarian Agricultural Limited Companies (or KFT) and the 'landowners cooperatives' of Bulgaria or the former Czechoslovakia, exemplify this latter combination. These forms reflect the diversity of social relations of production within new structures. They bring together landowners, stakeholders and salaried workers, in a way that has no recent precedent, despite the contradictions that are becoming ever more apparent over time. Behind the facade of their new juridical status, the question of the real and durable functioning of these agricultural enterprises is raised, particularly in the face of increased hoarding, either by individuals or by small groups, with or without devious intent. The future for these hybrid forms is controversial. Many observers see them simply as a transitional form, not really viable outside the micro-climate of the socialist economy (Maurel, 1995) and therefore condemned in an open economy where competition is free. Yet one can also interpret them as a response to the incapacity of small landowners to create viable production units. They are potentially a more economically effective and politically acceptable alternative, that conforms to the ineluctable processes of land concentration without the dispossession that usually accompanies the process (Lenormand, 1996).

If economic restructuring, in agriculture as in other sectors, has introduced a profound and far-reaching process of social differentiation, the new rules of the game have also instigated an equally important process of spatial differentiation. This is leading to a major territorial recomposition, at virtually all geographical scales. At the intra-state regional level, numerous authors have showed how, contrary to the stated political objectives of attaining regional balance, the concentration of trade flows and commercial relations has widened the pre-existing distance between the metropolitan and the peripheral regions (Maurel, 1995; Lenormand, 1996; Rey, 1996a). In the latter, unemployment is consistently higher and firm creation rates markedly lower than in metropolitan centres. From an agricultural point of view, the periphery has been less affected by change and retains a closer resemblance to its socialist past. Inversely, in Hungary or the Czech Republic, the influence of the capital cities has been to concentrate investment and economic change in metropolitan areas (Rey, 1996b). This has led to a rapid growth in production, alongside decline in the agricultural and rural population.

At the international scale, Maurel (1995) and Rey (1996b) also demonstrate how frontier effects have operated in favour of the more western regions positioned along the former Iron Curtain. Once marginalized and under-populated, these frontier zones have become the focus of significant migration and investment since the early 1990s. This investment often originates in the West, both in the agricultural and food sectors. The new German Länder, western Poland, Hungary and the Czech Republic all provide examples of this phenomenon, thereby underscoring the geopolitical importance of the Austrian-German axis in the future economic development of Europe. Towards the eastern edge, however, the situation is very different. Although open to western imports and seeing a developing manufacturing sector that is specializing in low cost discount products, the eastern-most regions have suffered far more from the dissolution of COMECON. For them, the former Iron Curtain has simply been moved eastwards. A second frontier has also developed between the north east states (the so-called Visegrad triangle or quadrant) and those of the south east. This is obviously revealed in the size and the economic contribution of the agricultural workforce since 1989 (Table 4.1).

Table 4.1
Contribution of agriculture to the economies of eight CEE states

Country	Agricultural employment as % of total employment		Agriculture as % of total Gross Domestic Product	
	1989	1995	1989	1995
Albania	49.0	53.0	33.0	59.0
Bulgaria	18.0	22.0	11.0	10.8
Czeck Republic	9.4	4.7	6.3	3.1
Hungary	17.9	8.5	15.6	6.4
Poland	26.4	25.0	11.8	6.1
Romania	13.7	21.6	28.2	35.7
Slovakia	12.2	7.1	9.4	6.1
Slovenia	11.8	10.0	4.4	4.4

Source: from Lhomel (1996) and Pouliquen (1996)

With the exception of Slovenia and Poland, where modest structural changes have led to the maintenance of a relatively large agricultural workforce, one can distinguish two distinct trends in agricultural employment. In the ex-Czechoslovakia and in Hungary, the drop in agricultural jobs has led to a similar fall in the economic contribution of agriculture to the national GDP. By contrast, in all the southern states, falls in the state agricultural sector have been largely compensated (and indeed exceeded in the case of Albania) by the emerging private agricultural sector and the multiplication of small farms.

Finally, and at an altogether different spatial scale, that of the locality, geographers have observed a detailed and generalized process of re-territorialization. In a trend that is increasingly bringing Eastern and Western Europe closer together, the local level is emerging as the most pertinent scale for agricultural production and land management. This has been clearly revealed in the new German Länder (Lacquement, 1993), where a considerable and ancient diversity of configurations and local power structures exist, even if they were long hidden by the socialist regime. It is also seen in the new distribution of farm structures in Romania (Rey, 1996a, 1996b; Hirschausen, 1996). Some see in this return to localism evidence of a return to territorial democracy. Others, more sceptically, see the re-emergence of longstanding and traditional struggles between different components of the local oligarchy.

Table 4.2
Average percentage of household income spent on food

	1989	1995
Albania	56.5	72.0
Bulgaria	29.5	40.0
Czech Republic	32.9	32.0
Estonia	28.2	30.0
Hungary	25.4	22.3
Latvia	30.3	41.5
Lithuania	34.9	57.5
Poland	36.9	28.0
Roumania	48.0	66.0
Slovakia	35.4	37.4
Slovenia	25.7	25.0

Source: Pouliquen (1996, from OECD statistics)

What future for the 'second Europe'?

Taking care to distinguish, as far as one can, what one knows or observes from what one might imagine or suppose, the position of agriculture in the Central and East European states raises four central questions relating to the integration of these nations into an enlarged Europe.

The place of farming

The first question centres the place of farming in these nations and the need to re-evaluate the issue of agricultural production. Following a period of massive farming retreat, at present the agricultural sector in these Central and East European nations is marked by a regaining of strength, albeit unequally distributed across states and the agricultural sectors concerned. With the exception of Hungary, arable production as a whole has returned to a level similar to the beginning of the 1980s. Animal production remains well below former levels, however, as a result of wide-scale decapitalization of large livestock units. In the southern states, the resurgence of the Bulgarian agricultural sector in the mid-1990s remains fragile, while Albania and

Figure 4.3
Changes in agricultural production in northern and southern East European states, 1983-1995

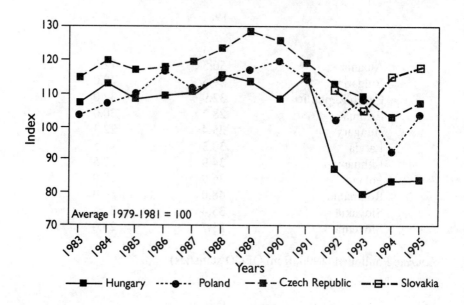

Average 1979-1981 = 100

Years

—■— Hungary ····●··· Poland —■— Czech Republic —□— Slovakia

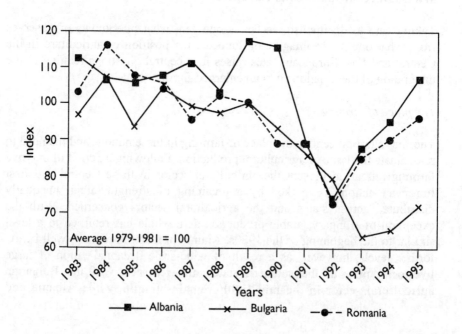

Average 1979-1981 = 100

Years

—■— Albania —✕— Bulgaria —●— Romania

Romania have returned to production levels of the early 1980s (largely as a result of the development of small private livestock farms). Yet general decline in the early years of the 1990s permanently aggravated the structural backwardness of Central and East European farming.

Throughout Central and East Europe, but particularly in the Baltic and southern countries, the agricultural production crisis has been fuelled by the fall in the overall value of household foodstuffs. At the same time, as incomes have fallen, and increased proportion of individual household budgets are being spent on food. Only in Hungary and Poland has there been a significant fall in household food spending. Everywhere else, this has either risen dramatically or has been maintained at a high level (Table 4.2). Yet average figures should not hide considerable social differentiation within food markets. The most plausible hypothesis, that future research needs to verify, is that of the coexistence of the middle or upper classes, who have achieved an improved lifestyle and degree of consumption, and an often numerically superior segment of the population living in hard and durable poverty. This contrast appears to be particularly potent in the south and in the Baltic states (with the possible exception of Estonia).

Change in popular dietary habits, new demands from the middle and upper classes, and largely foreign investment in the food sector, have promoted growth in food imports. In part this has been compensated by local food processing industries operating at Western standards (e.g. ice cream and deserts, dairy products and pre-cooked meals). This shifting situation corresponds to discernible changes in food industry markets (Figure 4.3).

To these shifts in the domestic food markets of the Central and East European states, can be added other changes in their performance in world agro-food markets. For the reference period, the trade balance for the six ex-socialist states portrayed in Figure 4.4 appears less uneven that is generally thought. Most countries recorded a positive trade balance in 1989, so the total surplus was more than three million US dollars. In terms of their world trade position (rather than that with the EU), export levels remain relatively constant. The single major shift is rapid growth in imports; most of which come from the West (Pouliquen, 1996), particularly the EU.

However, these exchanges reflect an evolving situation. In the early 1990s, under a process of de-capitalization in East European agriculture, when large and unproductive units sought to sell their assets, even though they were relatively limited in volume, exports of meat products from the CEE states (particularly Hungary and Poland) to the EU were sufficient to provoke a temporary fall in EU meat prices. This immediately provoked the ire of West European farmers towards what they were quick to label 'dumping' by states with a high agricultural potential and the possibility of becoming competitors in agricultural trade. Later, however, it became widely accepted that the ex-socialist states, including Russia, would constitute a net importing bloc for

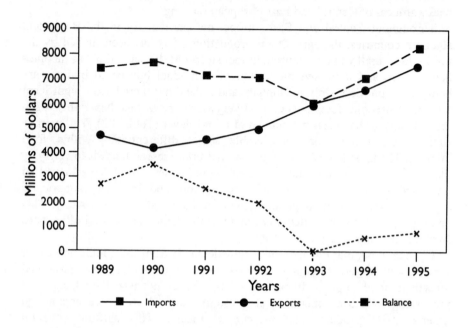

Figure 4.4
Agro-food trade in six CEE states, 1989-1995

many years (Pouliquen, 1996). Eastern Europe was thereby seen to represent a significant market (for as long as countries were solvent) for OECD farmers, and for US and EU farmers in particular. Observers noted that agricultural production continued to be held back in these states as a result of the lack of technological investment and agricultural productivity levels that were from two to eight times lower than in the EU (Pouliquen, 1996). The only factors in favour of their participation in world markets were their low labour unit costs, which low agricultural prices reinforced. Yet an arsenal of import restrictions, alongside export aids, were set up by supposedly liberal governments. Often, as in the case of Romania, these measures were introduced following protests from local farmers, who argued that they were increasingly denied access to foreign markets. Yet the true export or import capacity of these 'second Europe' states has divided experts for over a decade. As a provisional conclusion to the debate, I offer a hypothesis. If, in the medium term, agricultural development can satisfy effectively both internal consumer demand, that will hopefully rise, and produce substantial surpluses, then the short-term scenario appears to be one of straightforward maintenance of export levels and continued growth in imports. However, the current EU objective of limiting or even reducing its own agricultural production can only be a source of concern for the states in the East. In no way can reduced output become a policy objective in these countries, as basic food security is still not assured. Moreover, agricultural productivity is still seen as a means of gaining access to world markets, so importation of the foodstuffs they increasingly require can be paid for.

What relations to world markets?

The second series of questions is more general and political, in that it concerns trajectories for inserting these states into world markets. Two distinct and alternative strategies might be identified here. Full integration into the capitalist global market is the first. Hungary, when still a socialist country, chose this path by joining the Cairns Group (within which it became a leading European state) and adopting the free-market ideology of the Group.[4] Since then, and rather ironically, Hungary has been accused by other Cairns Group members of distorting competition through protectionism and export subsidies. In the name of market freedom, and in opposition to over-regulation, several opponents of European integration, such as the Polish lawyer Szlamacha, offer similar arguments in the East. Though their views stand little chance of getting wide media coverage, they can be usefully employed by national governments in forthcoming negotiations.

An alternative approach might be national autonomy. For economies with feeble buying power on international markets, agricultural self-sufficiency and the legitimation of the 'right of peoples to feed themselves' (as Hervieu's 1996 book is entitled) can be attractive goal. Similar concerns, operating at the fringe of the world capitalist order, have been expressed in the Czech Republic, where the liberalism of Vaclav Klaus has been tempered by pragmatism to promote, in the absence of any ambition to be a major exporter, a national agricultural policy based upon supply to domestic markets. More generally, this vision of 'an alternative way' (as a national or multi-national strategy) finds sympathy with nationalist and populist groups that are omnipresent on either side of the Oder River. It also finds support amongst farmers' groups that are still linked together by the inherited techno-structures of the former socialist period and by agrarian and neo-communist political affiliations. Here, calls for guaranteed prices, import restrictions or taxes on imports, export subsidies and so on, all receive a warm welcome. The general mistrust of the market economy is very strong. For example, in Poland, three-quarters of the peasantry believe that market forces should be 'controlled by government' (Gorlach, 1993). Significantly, only 11% of the Polish peasantry believes that 'market forces should work in agriculture as in any part of the economy', which is equal to the 11% who believe that 'market forces should not work in any economy at all'. Handicapped from the outset by the extreme heterogeneity of political forces who are likely to define it, and lacking genuine cooperation between countries and peoples, a national autonomy strategy has not yet proved a credible way forward (Lhomel, 1996). Changes in the electorate, shifts in the global situation and the position of the EU in forthcoming negotiations, all seem likely to support such a conclusion.

For the moment, therefore, the way forward would appear to be the European model of integration into world markets. Support for this view is particularly strong amongst the political elite and the emerging middle classes, who have made this a key objective, along with the permanent establishment of parliamentary democracy. As such, they wait, in the name of enlarged European solidarity, for the subsidies and aids that will bring about the economic and social improvement to which everyone aspires. The new elites also see this as a way of consolidating their power and confirming their still fragile social status. Yet on adhesion to the EU, large sections of the population are sceptical. According to a recent survey, 57% of Poles hold that the adaptation of Polish farming to the EU's Common Agricultural Policy will be either difficult or very difficult. Only 5% think it will be easy (Jaruga-Nowacka, 1998). Initial illusions have disappeared. While the political will to join 'Europe' as soon as possible remains strong, the difficulties multiply. The first setbacks emerged from the Association Accords, that were signed between the EU and the Central European countries in 1991, when the restrictive nature of imports into the EU became apparent, as well as the incapacity of certain countries to honour them (e.g. Hungary with respect to poultry products). The announcement of further agricultural price falls can only be a source of concern to producers already exposed to price cuts (Simon, 1994; Pouliquen, 1996; Rey, 1996a). Ultimately, preserving the gains of EU Member States runs against the aspirations of others to improve their standard of living. Hence a partial, progressive and conflictual Europeanization is likely to result. Whatever the final configuration, in agricultural terms, Eastern Europe represents a major issue for the EU.

Ten Central and East European states have so far begun negotiations for EU entry. These represent over 100 million people and over one million square kilometres of territory. In other words, they constitute 28.3% and 32.8% of the current population and surface area of the EU (see Table 4.3). In these countries, around 39 million people live in rural areas (which is about half the number of rural residents in the current EU). More than eight and a half million people are employed in farming; which is equivalent to the current EU total. In total, six million hectares of Utilized Agricultural Area would be added to the 4.7 million that exist in the EU today. Before further EU expansion to incorporate this 'third circle', and even more so before the potential long-term goal of bringing in a 'fourth circle' [5] (which together would give potentially 18 Central and East European states equivalent or even greater representation on the Council of Ministers as the 15 current EU Member States), it should be grasped that the accession of these 10 nations represents a significant shift in the EU centre of gravity towards more agricultural and rural states. This is in direct opposition to the oft-stated wishes of the European Commission and the European Parliament to reduce the importance of agricultural spending in the EU budget.

Table 4.3
The four circles of European Union enlargement

Group of countries	Total area	Total population	Total rural population	Millions employed in agriculture	Agricultural area
	1000 km²	millions	millions		1000 ha
1st circle states [1]	540	62.7	24.0	5.1	3,132
2nd circle states [2] requesting EU membership	519	42.8	15.1	3.5	2,934
Total (% of CEE states)	1,059 32.8%	105.5 (28.3%)	39.1 (54.3%)	8.6 (96.5%)	6,066 (41.2%)
EU15	3,232	372.5	72.0	8.9	14,724
3rd circle states [3] not yet requesting EU membership	263	24.4	13.5	2.7	1,277
4th circle states [4] 'European states' of the CIS	848	66.6	22.4	3.3	5,386
Total	2,170	196.5	74.9	17.7	12,730

1   Estonia, Hungary, Czech Republic, Poland and Slovenia (members of NATO and candidates for EU entry)
2   Bulgaria, Romania, Latvia, Lithuania and Slovakia (acknowledged candidates for NATO and EU membership)
3   Albania and the four states to emerge from Yugoslavia, Bosnia, Croatia, Macedonia and Montenegro
4   The three 'European' states of the Russian Federation, Byelorussia, Moldavia and the Ukraine.
Sources: compiled by the author from statistics of the Population Reference Bureau and the Food and Agriculture Organization

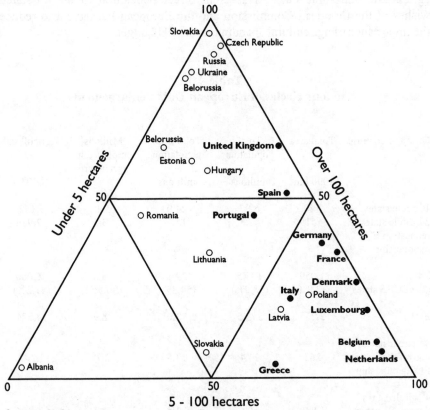

Figure 4.5
Farm structures in Europe

Source: Author
Sources: OECD (1996) 'Politiques, marché at échanges agricoles dans les pays en trasition pour les PECO et les NEI, OECD, Paris.Eurostat (1996) Structure des exploitations en 1963 pour l'Europe de l' Ouest, Luxembourg, Office for Official Publications of the European Community

Farming models

A third series of questions for the future, that are closely linked to the arguments presented above, concerns appropriate models of agricultural development. The current agricultural structures within greater Europe (EU, CEE and other ex-Russian states) reveals considerable variation (Figure 4.5). On the one hand, the original six EU Member States are closely associated with medium-sized farm units (defined as being between 5 and 100 ha.). The UK is immediately distinguished in this regard by its large average farm size, with Spain and Portugal also having some large farm units, owing to the continued existence of southern latifundia. Very small farm units (under 5 ha) were strongly under-represented within the EU when it had nine Member States, for farms of this size never exceeded 20% of the agricultural area of any one country. Only with the accession of Greece, was this figure surpassed, in this case to 30%.

On the other hand, if we consider the 39 countries of an enlarged Europe, the structural profiles diversify considerably. First, there are countries with a concentration of very small farms. These cover more than 20% of the agricultural land in eight countries. Second, there are nations with very large numbers of farms with more than 100 ha. (in nine states these cover more than 20% of the land area). A third category can be recognized, in which certain countries contribute to both groups. Thus, in Bulgaria, Estonia, Hungary and Romania, 'medium' farm sizes (5 - 100 ha) account for less than 20% of the total farm area. As Figure 4.4 brings out, a hitherto unknown issue is now being placed high on the EU agenda; namely, how to assure, without explicit derogation to the rules of the internal market, the coexistence of farm structures that differ so massively within states (such as Hungary) and between states (for example, Albania and Slovakia)? Must the total number of farms in Poland (where the farm structure is perhaps closest to the West) be reduced from two million to 600,000 in the shortest time possible, as political leaders have recently claimed? Who, knowing current levels of farm worker unemployment and levels of non-agricultural rural employment, would take the risk of advocating such a policy, particularly as the peasantry in Poland was a key element in the downfall of the communist state. Conversely, how do policy-makers reconcile concentration that is well advanced in a number of candidate states, with legal ceilings placed on agrarian concentration in states such as France? How to encourage new societal forms of farm holding on a grand scale while retaining the classic European model of family farming?

Sustainable development

The fourth and last issue to be raised concerning the significant problems that are raised by the prospect of EU expansion eastwards is that of the emerging notion of sustainable farming. New social demands and concerns, not only for sufficient food requirements (Hervieu, 1996) but also for traceability, food quality and environmental protection, have strongly influenced recent agricultural policies. The introduction of measures designed to encourage environmentally sound farming techniques as part of 1992 CAP reform are one testament to this.

However, environmental preoccupations have also been present for several years within the 'second' Europe. These concerns emerged first in Poland, which has long maintained a tradition of scientific exchange with the West.

Already in the 1970s, the level of environmental degradation was considered alarming, particularly in the industrial regions of Silesia and along the German/Polish/Czech frontier. Studies carried out by the Academy of Sciences, amongst others, identified serious breaches in existing regulations that had major environmental consequences. Denied, kept secret or suppressed by the authorities, these studies never percolated outside an essentially academic community, despite the efforts of academics, including geographers, to attract public attention to them. As one illustration, in 1985, Kasenberg and Rolewicz produced a map of the 27 environmentally threatened regions of Poland (Plit, 1991; Potrykowska, 1991).

For all East European states, in the absence of coherent or precise public information on contamination levels, the Chernobyl catastrophe created panic reactions amongst local populations, including the non-harvesting of agricultural produce many miles from the danger zone. Ecological movements, such as the Bulgarian *Ecoglasnost*, were among the first to use the accident to organize themselves and speak publicly in the face of the monopoly control still exercised by the communist and workers parties in power. With political change following 1989, research and public interest multiplied. This exposed two principal situations: first, pollution levels were linked to poor practices in industrial development, as seen in soil degradation (notably the presence of heavy metals) in and around major manufacturing sites; and, second, the quality of surface and underground water was alarming, as well as often being over-used and polluted by farming, manufacturing and urban activities. With respect to agriculture, different issues have emerged according to the country concerned. In Bulgaria, badly managed water extraction was critical. In East Germany, it has been heavy concentrations of animal waste in and around large-scale animal farms. Common to all states is the over-use of fertilizer and other entrants. Since 1989, disorganized water management structures, plus the abandonment of many state animal farms, have led to a reduction in certain aspects of pollution. However, due to lack of investment in environmental management or restitution, it is difficult to claim there has been any real improvement (Kostova and Giordano, 1997).

Nevertheless, for observers of changing social attitudes, the growth of environmental concern is first and foremost a phenomenon of the younger generation (as it is in many countries; Clark and Hoffmann-Martinot, 1998). The notion that the visible degradation of the environment should be the price society must pay for its comforts, its economic development and its technological progress, is still present in Central and East European public opinion. Within agriculture, calls for landscape protection and the development opportunities that organic farming represents are emerging. Gorlach (1993, p.16), for example, anticipates for Poland at least:

... a third and unusual possible scenario [that] could be described as so-called 'ecological family farming'. This would involve limited intervention by the state in the concentration of land ownership and the reduction of family farming to a relatively small number of commercial farms. In this situation, farms would cover less than 20 ha. and would not use fully industrial forms of production. They would compete with West European agriculture by the quality and not the quantity and hence the price of their products...

Such calls find a ready public, with the sample of farmers polled by the Polish public opinion body CBOS placing 'ecological farming' amongst their top four preferred scenarios for the future of Polish agriculture (quoted in Gorlach, 1993). Amongst the new farm business people she recently studied, Zrinscak (1996) describes the growth of organic farms offering farm tourism in the Czeck-Moravia uplands, although she notes the comparative rarity of such enterprises. In the Romanian Carpathians, the production of local goat's cheese takes place amongst the asbestos fumes of a nearby cement plant, while the project of setting up regional nature parks along the French model, linking rural development with environmental protection, has only gained a handful of supporters to date. In the rural and agricultural domains, environmental sensibilities are still relatively diverse and weak.

Here too, the obligations of contractual forms of farming and the cross-compliance of subsidies with environmental protection measures are likely to be misunderstood by those most immediately concerned. Preoccupied by making farms viable and by improving yields and productivity, a future of having to respect restrictive environmental regulations without any tangible advantages, and of having to depend upon what are likely to be low level Structural Fund allocations, is more likely to encourage active Euro-scepticism that a necessary reorientation towards more sustainable farming.

Conclusion

Because it places at its centre the full re-establishment of private property, the restoration of capitalism in the Central and Eastern Europe can be interpreted as the intentional re-creation of a property owning middle class (Dontchev, 1997). This class is likely to become the chief protagonist of economic development and the backbone of a new civic society. In agriculture, however, the exhumation of a class of numerous small landowners (a sort of 'Polandization' on a larger scale), is likely to become at one and the same time both the most remarkable expression of a political project and the clearest obstacle to its actual realization. The advocates of this new agrarian policy have naively believed that from private land reappropriation and the capitalist market economy a small and medium size farmer class will 'naturally' emerge. It further seems to be assumed that this class will be capable, as in the Western model, of assuring its own extended reproduction.

In spite of the political, ideological and financial support from which it has benefited, this peasantry remains a minority; it is even embryonic. The result of the restitution policy has been the emergence of a class of small peasant landowners, who are little able to invest and develop their agricultural enterprises, but who are politically legitimated by their capacity to ensure their own subsistence. From a half-century of major agrarian enterprise, two other models have ultimately emerged. These are large-scale capitalist farms, similar to their Western neighbours and neo-collective structures, which bear witness to the unexpected persistence of former socialist models, albeit under new forms. Following the collapse of these former structures and their partial splitting up, a new cycle of agrarian concentration has begun. The open competition between landowners and farmers, and between different forms of land ownership, will undoubtedly bring solutions, perhaps some genuinely innovative, to the old problem. But it is difficult to anticipate the final result. That said, in the light of what we know of the history of the European Union's agricultural policy, it seems most likely that in an enlarged Europe competition between producers, between regions, and between nations, will have major social costs, particularly in the newer states.

From the radical nature of recent fundamental changes in the ownership, organization and use of over half of the European continent, a new concept could have emerged. From the dismantling of an entire system, a new development strategy could have been drawn up. But, since the outset of these changes, ideological objectives and political assumptions have done away with much needed reflection and, in doing so, have considered the problem largely solved. History has not, however, finished. Let us hope that the integration of the two Europes will open the way to a more profound interrogation that is capable, in the West as in the East, of revealing new ways forward for rurality and for farming.

Notes

1   The current 15 Central and East European (CEE) states referred to in this chapter are: Albania, Bosnia, Bulgaria, Croatia, the Czeck Republic, Estonia, Hungary, Latvia, Lithuania, Macedonia, Poland, Romania, Slovakia, Slovenia and Yugoslavia. The historical analysis presented here takes into account the German Democratic Republic, which has since been reunited with formerly 'western' Germany and alludes to the current Russian Federation states of Byelorussia, Moldavia and Ukraine, which lie outside the CEE states.

2   Following established conventions (for example, Maurel, 1994b, Rey, 1996a, 1996b), the states considered here are referred to as 'socialist' or 'formerly socialist' states. As 'socialist' states, many were ruled by communist or workers parties. Hence the word 'communist' is used here strictly in political terms.

3   The Commonwealth of Independent States or CIS was set up in 1991. It includes Armenia, Belorussia, Kazakhstan, Kyrgyzstan, Moldavia, Russia, Tajikistan, Turkmenistan, Ukraine and Uzbekistan.

4   The Cairns Group is a group of exporters of agricultural commodities from both the 'North' and the 'South'. It has sought to mediate between the USA, Japan and the European Union in trade talks. Australia, Canada and New Zealand are among its leading members.

5   The 'fourth circle' states are Belorussia, Moldavia and Ukraine.

References

Billaut, M. (1996) Les campagnes bulgares: le grand chambardement pour quels résultats?, in V. Rey (ed.) *Les Nouvelles Campagnes de l'Europe Centre Orientale*, CNRS Editions, Paris, pp.121-152.

Blaas, G. (1993) 'Agriculture in Slovakia', unpublished paper to the Annual Convention of the Hungarian Sociological Association, Miskolc.

Blanchet, J. and Revel, A. (1997) L'intégration des PECO à la nouvelle PAC: une double révolution inachevée, *Economie Rurale*, 240, pp.49-57.

Civici, A. and Lerin, F. (1997, eds.) Albanie, une agriculture en transition, *Options Méditerranéennes*, Série B, 15, pp.1-318.

Clark, T.N. and Hoffmann-Martinot, V. (1998, eds.) *The New Political Culture*, Westview, Boulder, Colorado.

Conte, E. and Giordano, C. (1997) Sentiers de la ruralité perdue. Réflexions sur le post-socialisme, *Etudes Rurales*, 138/140, pp.51-59.

Dawson, A.H. (1986) Agrarian reform in Eastern Europe, in M. Pacione (ed.) *Progress in Agricultural Geography*, Croom Helm, London, pp.149-166.

Dontchev, D. and Lenormand, P. (1993) L'agriculture bulgare à l'épreuve des réformes, *Cahiers Agricultures*, 2, pp.131-140.

Dontchev, S. (1997) La transition en Bulgarie, in C. Durand (ed.) *Management et Rationalisation: Les Multinationales Occidentales en Europe de l'Est*, De Boeck University Press, Louvain, pp.65-76.

Duval, L. (1997) 'Etude de la Viabilité des Exploitations Privées en Moldavia', unpublished DEA Memoire, Montpellier.

Gerbaud, F. (1996) L'Allemagne des nouveaux Bundesländer: une transition agricole sous toutelle?, in V. Rey (ed.) *Les Nouvelles Campagnes de l'Europe Centre Orientale*, CNRS Editions, Paris, pp.33-83.

Gerbaud, F. (1997) Enjeux de la privatisation foncière en ex-RDA, *Etudes Rurales*, 138/140, pp.143-145.

Gorlach, K. (1993) 'Between "farmerization" and "fossilization": rural restructuring in Poland', unpublished paper to the Annual Convention of the Hungarian Sociological Association, Miskolc.

Halamska, M. (1992) Les cadres de la mutation fonctionnelle de l'exploitation famililale sous la contrainte du marché en Pologne, *Economie Rurale*, 214/215, pp.71-75.

Halamska, M. (1995) La difficile reconversion de l'agriculture étatique en Pologone, *Revue d'Etudes Comparatives Est-Ouest*, 26(3), pp.91-118.

Hervieu, B. (1996) *Du Droit des Peuples à se Nourrir Eux-Mêmes*, Flammarion, Paris.

Hirschausen, B. (1996) Les campagnes roumaines: la force des lieux, in V. Rey (ed.) *Les Nouvelles Campagnes de l'Europe Centre Orientale*, CNRS Editions, Paris, pp.153-198.

Jaruga-Nowacka, I. (1998) Interview, *Regards*, February, 8.

Kostova, D. and Giordano, E. (1997) Bulgarie, une réforme agraire sans paysans, *Etudes Rurales*, 138/140, pp.157-171.

Lacquement, G. (1993) *La Décollectivisation dans les Nouveaux Lander Allemands: d'un Modèle à l'Autre*, Montpellier, *Espace Rural*, 31, pp.1-134.

Lavigne, M. (1979) *Les Économies Socialistes*, Colin, Paris.

Lavigne, M. (1985) *Economie Internationale des Pays Socialistes*, Colin, Paris.

Lenormand, P. (1996) Relations sociales et acteurs sociaux dans les campagnes de l'est Européen, in Espaces Marx (ed.) *Relations Sociales et Acteurs Sociaux à l'Est*, L'Harmattan, Paris, pp.115-145.

Lenormand, P. (1997) 'Privatisation et Investissement Étranger dans l'Agriculture et l'Industrie Agro-Alimentaire Hongroises', unpublished working paper for Espaces Marx 'Pays de l'Est' Group.

Lhomel, E. (1996, ed.) *Transitions Économiques à l'Est (1989-1995)*, Les Etudes de la Documentation Française, Paris.

McIntyre, R. (1988) *Bulgaria: Politics, Economics and Society*, Pinter, London.

Maurel, M-C. (1992, ed.) *Les Décollectivisations en Europe Centrale, Volume 1*, Montpellier, *Espace Rural*, 30, pp.1-257.

Maurel, M-C. (1994a, ed.) *Autopsie d'un Mode de Production, Volume 2*, Montpellier, *Espace Rural*, 33, pp.1-189.

Maurel, M-C. (1994b) Terre, travail, capital: vers de nouveaux rapports sociaux en Europe centrale, *Cahiers Internationaux de Sociologie*, 96, pp.7-32.

Maurel, M-C. (1995, ed.) Décollectivsations agraires en Europe centrale et orientale, *Revue d'Etudes Comparatives Est-Ouest*, 26(3), pp.1-244.

Morgan, W.B. (1987) Productivity and location in private agriculture around Warsaw, Poland, *GeoJournal*, 15, pp.375-385.

Plit, F. (1991) La dégradation de l'environnement en Pologne, *Strates*, 6, pp.7-18.

Potrykowska, A. (1991) L'environnement en Pologne: Etat des lieux, *Strates*, 6, pp.19-38.

Pouliquen, A. (1996) Dynamiques et compétitivités agro-alimentaires dans les PECO: implications pour l'élargissement européen, *Economie Rurale*, 240, pp.37-48.

Rey, V. (1996a) Les nouvelles campagnes de l'Europe de l'entre deux, in J. Bonnamour (ed.) *Agricultures et Campagnes dans le Monde*, Sedes, Paris, pp.163-192.

Rey, V. (1996b, ed.) *Les Nouvelles Campagnes de l'Europe Centre Orientale*, CNRS Editions, Paris.

Simon, F. (1994) La transition dans le secteur agro-alimentaire tchèque: de la propriété publique à la propriété privée, *Economie Rurale*, 223, 46-52.

Streih, M. (1997) Cultivateurs du Mecklembourg: survie d'un savoir faire, *Etudes Rurales*, 138-140, pp.185-194.

Zrinscak, G. (1996) Les campagnes thcèques: dynamique du changement et latences des territoires, in V. Rey (ed.) *Les Nouvelles Campagnes de l'Europe Centre Orientale*, CNRS Editions, Paris, pp.85-119.

5 The impact of state deregulation on agriculture and the food chain: lessons from Russia

Larisa Mokrushina

Question: I am in a desperate, hopeless and impossible situation, what
               should I do?
Answer: We do not discuss agricultural questions on this programme.
               [attributed to the mythical Radio Armenia; quoted in
                   Chadwick *et al.*, 1972, p.63]

The requirements of a world economy that is in the process of globalization pushes local and national economies toward integration into a world-wide economic organism with a dominant regulatory system called the 'market economy' or the 'system of freedom enterprise'. Acting on the 1992 advice of the International Monetary Fund (IMF) and the World Bank, reformers in the Russian Government accepted the internal application of economic liberalization policies. Associated with a substantial foreign loan to help transitional arrangements, these policies were intended to foster long-term economic growth and integrate the Russian economy smoothly into the dominant world order. The concept of liberalization that lay at the base of IMF programme of stabilization was oriented toward the destruction of the former state monopoly over the national economy. Under economic liberalization, the regulation of production decisions was given over to mechanisms of market competition. As Abalkin (1997, p.4) noted: "The common meaning of this concept is that liberalization and freedom of self-organization are good and that state regulation is evil". He then goes further in noting an underlying implication in early commentaries on economic liberalization. These put across the view that: "The example of Russia will be included in all world textbooks on economics as a bright illustration of ousting of the state from the economic sphere or as an example of state deregulation". As this chapter shows, so positive an imagery is highly questionable, with the consequences of liberalization having serious negative implications for the short- and long-term development of the Russian economy, and especially for its farm sector.

The general impact of economic reform

Capturing the trauma that is now the Russian economy is not difficult. If the shock of rapid liberalization from the rigidities of tight state control was not enough, the political disintegration of the USSR provided an added twist. This resulted in the loss of primary markets for Russian products, as well as disengagement from the principal suppliers of inputs into Russian production processes. In terms of where the 'blame' lay, Shmelev (1996) argued that, during the first stage of reforms in 1992/93, the rupture in normal economic connections with the former republics of the USSR caused half the GNP fall in Russia. A further 20-25% drop came from connections being disrupted with countries of the Council for Economic Mutual Assistance. Only 25-30% of GNP decline was ascribed by Shmelev to Russia's market reforms. Whatever the precise impacts of different sources, the end-product was the virtual collapse of the Russian economy. The national agro-industrial complex provided a ready exemplar of this collapse, with the result that material and institutional structures required for food security have been severely disrupted. It is little surprise to find similar messages of economic trauma being written about for other nations in Eastern Europe (e.g. Agócs and Agócs, 1994; Pata and Osmani, 1994). This is because the Soviet system of production was imposed on satellite nations; even if in somewhat different form across nations (e.g. see Dawson, 1986, on the uneven imposition of farm collectivization). Understanding why economic liberalization has been so traumatic is a simple task. A primary feature of Soviet production systems was the maximization of output, while maintaining full-employment, so as to persuade the working population of the 'superiority' of the Soviet system over capitalism (Bleaney, 1994). As with other Soviet Bloc countries this often led to an emphasis on high production levels, whatever the cost (e.g. Bicik, 1998). The rapid transference from this ethos to one that prioritizes profit not unnaturally induced economic turbulence (highlighting this for one industry, that benefited from significant financial support from the German Government, see Marshall, 1996). Production units and even whole industries whose rationale was previously seeped in the dictates of Communist Party ideology, national security considerations and the strategic goal of integrating the economies of the USSR with its satellites, suddenly found they had to work with a markedly different *modus operandi*. Had this shift occurred in a gradual, planned manner, the resulting traumas might have been less severe. However, the rapidity of shift after the IMF agreement heightened production problems (an indication of the scale of transference is that more than 95% of state and collective farms were reorganized by the end of 1993; Gidadhubli, 1996). As in many East European countries, the political considerations that propelled the government toward a rapid assertion of capitalist principles and practices, frequently led to state action aggravating economic problems (e.g. Agócs and Agócs, 1994; Abrahams, 1996; Szyrmer and Reiner, 1997). That said, even had governments wished to cushion the impact of economic trauma, high inflation and widespread production collapses left little freedom to manoeuvre (Morgan, 1992; Agócs and Agócs, 1994; Bleaney, 1994).

Signifying the scale of economic fallout from liberalization measures, International Monetary Fund data show that Russia's GDP is now less than that of California, and stands at some 10-15% of the 1990 Russian level (Mostovskoi, 1997). During the years of 'reform' since 1992, Russia has come to outdistance Brazil in per capita debt, with the Russian model of economic development taking on clear tones of Latin American neo-colonialism (Mostovskoi, 1997). Most critical here has been the impact on consumption, especially as this affects the quality of food products, and so the health of the population. The share of the population that is now living below the poverty line is 40% of the total. Real income had halved before the crisis of 17 August 1998 and consumption stood at 40% of its 1991 level (Rimashevskaiya, 1997). After the crisis of 17 August,[1] when devaluation of the rouble occurred and the government defaulted on debt repayments, the exchange rate for the rouble against US dollars fell fourfold, with prices for imported commodities correspondingly rising to three or four times their former level, albeit wages, pensions and other payments were kept at the same level. The share of the population that might be regarded as being of middle income, that is those who can offer a base giving some stability in market relations, has shrunk alarmingly. Today Russia has huge inequities in incomes. Indeed, compared with other countries in Eastern Europe, income differentiation shows such an unusual pattern that it may be unprecedented (as Pockney, 1994, notes that the re-stratification of the Russian economy occurred very rapidly after 1992, with about 5-10% of the population becoming very rich, and the remainder suffering). Even according to official figures, only 3-5% of the population has an income of $3,000 or more a month, with 15% in the $1,000-$3,000 range, 20% having between $100 and $1,000, another 20% receiving from $50-$100, and a startling 40% having to live on a monthly income of less than $50 (Rimashevskaiya, 1997). Providing a further insight on the situation, Abalkin (1998, p.12) has charged that:

> The liberalization of the economy has led to changes in the structure of society; to social and property stratification. The average income of the

wealthiest 10% of citizens was 13.2 times greater than that of the poorest 10% in 1997. The wealthiest group, that constitute 1.5-3.0% of the population, have in their hands practically all the economic potential of the country and operate outside the democratic exigencies of governmental structures. The middle class are absent today in Russia and the mass strata of poor people make up 60-65% of the population; 9-12% of this strata are socially unprotected in the zone of real risk and 7-9% are pauperized, de-socialized citizens.

Associated with the crippling economic problems that have beset Russian governments and enterprises, the practice of non-payment, whether for bills, wages, pensions or allowances, now embraces the whole country. This has aggravated social problems. Indeed, Glasiev (1997) has argued that the destructive consequences of economic reform have exceeded the combined losses suffered by Russia's productive units during the Second World War (also Pockney, 1994). Putting this devastation in an international context, we can set figures for change in the Russia economy against those used by the United Nations to indicate a critical level for socio-economic (and political) stability (Table 5.1). According to the UN, a 'catastrophic state' is reached when five of its key indices record worse scores than the critical level. As can be seen in Table 5.1, on this basis Russia easily merits a 'catastrophic' label.

Table 5.1
Critical and Russian levels of performance on key UN indicators

Indicators	Critical level	Russian level
% fall in GDP	30-40	38
% of food imported	30	39
% of high technology products	10-15	1
% state expenditure on science	2	0.32
Income ratio for richest and poorest 10% of population	10:1	15:1
% of population on/below the poverty threshold	10	20-40
Ratio of minimum to average wages	1:3	1:10
Ratio of number of deaths to births	1.0	1.63
Number of crimes per 100 persons	5-6	6-6.5
Consumption of alcohol in litres	8	14-18

Source: Korovkin (1997)

To provide some indication of why the label 'catastrophe' is merited, it is worth noting that in the first five years of 'reform' from 1992 to 1996 natural decrease in the country's population equalled three million people (2.3% of the total). If we simply look at population totals, part of the excess of deaths over births is hidden (Table 5.2), for the new geopolitical and economic situation resulted in a flood of return migrants from former Soviet satellites. As a consequence of these arrivals, absolute population change in Russia has not been great. It follows that outside observers might not pick up that the mortality rate amongst men is alarmingly high. In terms of average life expectancy, for example, in 1991 this was 63.5 years, yet just four years later it had fallen to 58, with a value of just 56 for rural areas. Special alarm has been raised over a sharp increase in the rate of suicide (which stood at 45 persons per 100,000 people in 1995), as well as a high level of child mortality. Today, the number of people dying surpasses the number born by 60%. The destruction of social and economic infrastructure, a fall in GDP, growing unemployment, the spread of poverty, consumption decline, deteriorating health and depopulation of the country, are shared consequences of Russian market reforms (see Nickolsky, 1994).

Table 5.2
Population change in Russia, 1950-1995

Year	total	Population size (millions) urban	rural	Per cent rural
1951	102.6	45.9	57.0	55
1961	120.8	66.1	54.7	45
1971	130.1	81.0	49.1	38
1981	139.0	97.7	41.3	30
1986	143.8	104.1	39.7	28
1990	148.0	109.2	38.8	26
1991	148.5	109.8	38.7	26
1992	148.7	109.7	39.0	26
1993	148.7	108.9	39.0	27
1994	148.4	108.5	39.9	27
1995	148.3	108.3	40.0	27
1996	148.0	108.1	39.9	27
1997	147.5	107.8	39.7	27

Source: State Committee for Statistics (1997)

Further problems arise on the environmental front, as current economic policies leave little room for concerns about ecological reconstruction (which are badly needed, as environmental concerns were given restricted attention under the Soviet system; Kluev, 1996). Most industries and enterprises also lack the reserves that would enable them to respond positively to the wear and tear of material resources; even less to the socio-psychological pressures workers face owing to the instability and uncertainties of contemporary Russian society. As a consequence, accidents are practically a constant feature of coalmines, manufacturing plants, aircraft journeys and much else, with resulting deaths for hundreds of people. Ecologically, the threat posed by the current situation exists not only for Russia but for the biosphere as the whole. Chernobyl might simply be the tip of the iceberg, as many atomic and military enterprises are operating with virtually no state supervision (often in conditions where pay and essential raw materials do not arrive). Providing an indication of the scale of the previously 'hidden' problem, Lappo and Polian (1997, p.21) note that 47 towns and settlements with a combined population of about 1.5 million people were 'closed' (officially unacknowledged) before 1994. Of these 47, 10 belonged to the Ministry of Atomic Energy and 37 to the military-industrial-complex (viz. the Ministry of Defence). These towns tend to be near space bases and other high-prestige and secret military units. They had the best facilities, the most modern technical equipment, the most qualified workers, engineers and scientists, and a high quality of life. Today, owing to the lack finance for such activities, a lot of these enterprises have been closed, with unemployment and outmigration increasing significantly. Such places have been deprived of previous privileges but are now on the brink of disappearing.

It comes as little surprise to find that the Russia people do not see the 1990s as an era of transition but rather as a time of severe trouble. The people cannot understand the nature of the catastrophic changes that beset them, nor do they comprehend why they are forced to live through them (let alone whether they will be able to survive). Corruption, racketeering and organized crime have achieved such a grip on everyday affairs that the majority of people doubt it is possible to return again to a 'normal' life. Capturing the mood, Hoffman (1999, p. 1) recently referred to:

> ... a whole panoply of abuses that have plagued Russia in recent years. These include the exploitation of government money for private gain, the use of secretive, offshore shell companies to hide cash and the helplessness or complicity of high-level officials in such schemes.

Similar points about economic liberalization fuelling criminal and anti-social activities have been reported for Hungary (e.g. Agócs and Agócs, 1994).

Transforming and traumatizing agriculture

While the Russian economy as a whole has been traumatized, this experience has been more intense for agriculture and rural economies (for a similar view on Poland, see also Ingham *et al.*, 1998). By 1995 rural commodity enterprises accounted for about 60% of unprofitable enterprises in the Russian economy. Just one year later this figure had risen to more than 75% (Zeldner, 1997). By this year, profit in the Russian agro-industrial complex was reported to be *minus* 6% (compared with a 1991 value of *plus* 43%). Recognizing the grave circumstances of the sector, in the 10 April 1997 Resolution of the State Duma (Parliament), on the catastrophic situation in the agro-industrial complex of Russian Federation, it was acknowledged that the course of reforms that had been followed had a primary role in generating the disastrous conditions of the agrarian economy. By this time, state regulation of the agro-industrial complex, whether related to prices, production or the provision of technical services, was effectively non-existent. The price disparity between the manufactured products farmers require and farm-gate commodities had grown to such an extent that it led to the bankruptcy of more than 70% of agro-organizations. Faced with (actual or potential) bankruptcy, farm organizations stopped buying fertilizer, pesticides, machinery, technical support services, or other factors needed to ameliorate land degradation problems. As an illustration, purchases of tractors fell to one-fourteenth of their previous level, lorries to one-eighteenth, and farm combines to one-eighth (a companion example is provided by Szyrmer and Reiner, 1997, for Ukraine, when noting that the official wage in agriculture was 5% above the national average in 1990 but had fallen to 43% below that average by 1996).

Soil degradation, and a decrease in soil fertility, was a notable consequence of these cuts (albeit there were problems of this kind before the reforms; see Breburda, 1990). Also of importance is the abandonment of farmland. Since 1992 more than 15 million hectares of arable land have been taken out of production. In the absence of seeds, machinery and fuel, much farmland, especially in wooded zones, has become overgrown with shrubs and trees. Even where efforts are made to keep production up, labour productivity has fallen (by 40% over the period 1992-1996, so it stood at the same level in 1996 as in 1971). Major programmes of agricultural scientific research and extension were closed, with the result that programmes to improve seed growing and pedigree stock-breeding have been wrecked. Not surprisingly, while the share of total capital investment that went to agriculture was 18% in 1991, by 1996 it was just 4%. Similar paths were followed elsewhere in Eastern Europe (e.g. for Hungary, the 1992 figure of 5% was down from

Table 5.3
The dynamic of Russian agricultural production, 1950-1995

Year	Gross grain harvest (million tons)	Total head of cattle (millions)	Meat production (million tons)	Milk production (million tons)
1950	46.8	31.5	2.6	21.4
1955	54.7	29.4	3.4	24.6
1960	72.6	37.6	4.5	34.5
1965	66.3	44.9	5.2	40.1
1970	107.4	49.4	6.2	45.4
1975	72.4	56.5	7.5	46.8
1980	97.4	58.6	7.4	46.8
1985	98.6	60.0	8.5	50.2
1990	116.7	58.8	10.1	55.7
1991	89.1	57.1	9.4	51.9
1992	106.9	54.7	8.3	47.2
1993	99.1	52.2	7.5	46.5
1994	81.5	48.9	-	-
1995	65.4	39.2	-	-
1996	63.0	-	-	-

Source: Paliev (1996)

14.4% five years earlier; Agócs and Agócs, 1994; see also Morgan, 1992, on Poland; Chapter Four). The outcome for total output is predictable (Table 5.3). Comparing average annual output for 1991/95 with 1986/90 reveals that total production fell by 35% (with a further 7% fall for 1995/96). With a grain harvest of 63 million tonnes, output for this commodity was at the same level as 1963. Accompanying this, the cattle population fell by 16.4 million head, so animal numbers now stand at the 1961 level. Not surprisingly, the average annual output of milk and dairy products was 46% lower in 1991/95 than in 1986/90, while meat output fell by 41% (Gidadhubli, 1996). The picture is the same for other animals. For pigs the fall was 13 million head, which brought the stock back to its size in 1958. A 28.3 million fall in sheep and goat numbers had an even more dramatic effect, for this shrank the stock by 80% and returned the sector to its position in 1933. According to Kurbatov (1998, p.28):

> All the improvements in gross agricultural output that had been made in the previous 20 years were lost during the three years of 1990-1992. From 1990-1997 the total number of cattle fell by 44%, cows by 29%,

pigs by 27%, meat by 51%, milk by 39%, eggs by 33%, and wool production by 74%.

Again, the general trend is one that is repeated in a variety of other East European nations, such as in the Czech Republic, which saw a 20% farm output fall from 1989 to 1996 (Bicik, 1998). Moreover, we should note that agrarian decline brought severe social consequences. Thus, as Kurbatov (1998) has noted, many schools, clubs, libraries, services, and hospitals were closed in rural places. Work stopped on road-building, on connections to gas supplies and on electrification. As one measure of these cuts, more than two million children of school age were denied the opportunity to attend school.

One structural result of the agricultural crisis has been an expansion in the use of personal 'subsidiary' plots and holdings (one symbol of the magnitude of this movement is that between 1992 and 1995 the number of farm enterprises tripled in Russia; Scott Leonard and Szyrmer, 1997). The inhabitants of towns felt an urge to visit rural localities in search of cheaper food, with some city dwellers relying on food supplies from relatives in rural areas (see also Creed, 1995). All those who had access to a small land plot began to cultivate potatoes and other vegetables to meet this new demand (as well as to help meet household needs). By 1996 these small plots were responsible for 88% of potato production, 67% for vegetables, 42% of meat output, and 39% of milk yield. The share of the animal stock in these small private plots began to rise, with cow and pig shares increasing from one-fifth (in 1991) to one-third, while the proportion of sheep and goats on such holdings rose to half the national population (Nefiodova, 1997).[2] For some commentators this might all have a familiar ring, as small privately-owned plots were seen to be the backbone of much East European agriculture, when the collective, cooperative and state farms of the Communist era proved inefficient and ineffective in meeting national food requirements (e.g. Hedlund, 1990; Klodzinski, 1992; Abrahams, 1994; Agócs and Agócs, 1994; Creed, 1995). However, what also has to be stated is that the warnings that accompanied commentaries on private farm production under the Communists are equally valid today. In the main these landholdings are associated with production methods that, in an international context, are inefficient and labour intensive. They are heavily dependent on inadequate marketing mechanisms, and the inadequacy of supply systems for farm inputs makes their capacity to expand severely limited (e.g. Pockney, 1994; and see comparable commentaries on Poland by Morgan, 1987, 1990, 1992). In Russia, spare capacity on these small private plots was reached quickly (Pockney, 1994). They have few labour reserves to call on and their primitive production practices offer little prospect that greater yields will be forthcoming (especially given difficulties paying for and even obtaining farm inputs like fertilizer).

Table 5.4
Growth of food imports in Russia (in thousands of tons)

Product	1992	1993	1994	1995	% change 1992-1995
Chilled meat (not poultry)	288	85	358	505	190.9
Chilled poultry meat	46	74	496	797	1732.6
Butter	25	70	103	167	688.0
Alcohol and non-alcoholic beverages (mln. decalitre)	203	199	695	1048	518.8

Source: Korovkin (1997)

Food security

Before 1991 Russia was a world leader in the production and consumption of food products. At this time it held fifth or sixth place in the world in per capita consumption terms. By 1995 its rank position had fallen to 40th (Gidadhubli, 1996). Today food consumption per capita is 2,350 kkal a day, having stood at 3,200 kkal in 1990. As with elsewhere in Eastern Europe (Morgan, 1992; Agócs and Agócs, 1994), a significant element in this change has been soaring price levels, with the cost of 19 staple products rising 45-fold over the period January 1993 to December 1995 (Gidadhubli, 1996). Of notable concern is the fact that the maximum fall in consumption occurred for products that contain protein and vitamins. Thus, over this period, the Russian population saw a reduction in consumption of 32% for meat and meat products, 35% for milk and milk products, and a 40% fall for vegetables and fruit. Only bread-products and potatoes saw increased consumption (by 13% and 10%, respectively). In combination, these changes resulted in a reduction in protein averaging 30%, with a fall in vitamin intake of 50% (see Korovkin, 1997; Rimashevskaya, 1997).

Even with this fall in consumption, the sharp decline in agricultural production led to increased reliance on imported food. In truth, Russia (or more broadly the former USSR) had imported food for a long time, with economic crises in the early 1990s reducing imports from former satellite countries, which further destabilized their economies (e.g. Morgan, 1992; Abrahams, 1994). But the devastating impact of agricultural reform in Russia has led to greater commodity imports (Table 5.4). With troubled farm sectors in key East European suppliers, serious questions are being raised about the quality of imported food (e.g. Agócs and Agócs, 1994). Serious concern is also being expressed about the security or future stability of food supplies. Here the UN uses a critical figure of 30% to indicate a nation that is in a dangerous food supply position. For Russia the volume of imported food is now more than 50% of total consumption, with the share in large towns rising to 70-80%, and with imports rising (Korovkin, 1997).

Import dependence discriminates against domestic farm producers, who have to combat the hazards of internal economic reform pressures, as well as see part of the domestic market given over to external suppliers (Paliev, 1996; Korovkin, 1997; Miloserdov, 1997; Shutkov, 1997). The expression 'given over' is deliberately chosen here, for home producers do not compete with imports on a level playing field, for the purchase price of wheat and other grain crops grown in Russia is 30-35% less than that for imported supplies. Trade Liberalization it seems is designed to force Russia farmers to conform to a production environment that is more hostile than that faced by producers in (many) other countries. With borders open to imports (as reported for other Eastern European nations; e.g. Unwin, 1997), the message that underlies Russia's IMF-inspired trade and subsidy policies are that rapid liberalization, like that experienced in Chile and New Zealand, is justified because brings long-term farm benefits (at least for those whose businesses survive the immediate disruptions of deregulation). However, this picture raises two doubts over its veracity. The first is that farm economies in nations like New Zealand are better placed to adapt to economic trauma (more resources, larger units, more experience of free markets, etc.). These countries also have broader support systems (like welfare systems and pension schemes) that help those who wish to leave the sector (e.g. Valdés, 1994; Cloke, 1996). (The contrast with Russia is stark, with the absence of other jobs encouraging a reversion toward subsistence or barter systems; Pockney, 1994). Secondly, the unwillingness to raise internal farm commodity prices to the world trade level has an odour of (urban) appeasement, which carries tones of Lipton's (1977) urban bias hypothesis. Set against this, city dependence on imported food is accompanied by many registered cases of food imports being of dangerous hygienic quality, which has led to people being poisoned and becoming ill. Indicative of the potential hazards that exist, in 1996, spoiled articles constituted 58% of meat products, 57% of canned foods, and 36% of butter supplies (Paliev, 1996).

Agricultural policy and reform

The agrarian sector in Russia, which includes a quarter of the national productive capacity and 27% of the population, has undergone a deep socio-economic transformation. Most *kolkhozes* and *sovkhozes* (which comprise 67% of the 25,600 state and cooperative farms) have been reformed as joint-stock companies, private enterprises or (private) cooperatives. In addition, since 1992, more than 280,000 private peasant farms have been created.

According to the State Committee on Land Management and Reform, 49% of the farmland in Russia has shifted into civil ownership.[3] Yet up to this point there is no land market in the country. The 'land code' that was worked out during first four years of economic reform forbids the buying and selling of land, so there is no opportunity to create a land market. On this, the President of Russia has vetoed any change. Moreover, land reform moves forward only under Decrees of the Russian President. Thus, it was the 1996 Presidential Decree, *On the realization of the constitutional rights of citizens concerning the land*, that gave members of *kolkhozes* and *sovkhozes* their agricultural land share (the size of land given differs across regions from two to eight hectares). Although many rural people have documents of land ownership that extend to periods before collectivization or other forms of state take-over, few have gained ownership of land.[4] In this regard, it is clear that the chair of agricultural production units, the so-called 'local tsars', are trying hard not to hand back land (as reported for other former Soviet territories, such as Estonia; Abrahams, 1994, p. 357). In many cases these 'local tsars' have become the real owners of the land.[5] Yet, given the extreme poverty that exists in many rural zones, it is the case that the grassroots population cannot afford to cultivate any land that does receive. Indeed, data for individual districts shows that about 70% of those who do gain ownership of land make this available for leasing to agricultural enterprises or joint stock companies, on condition they receive services like the ploughing of their kitchen-garden or the ability to collect wood. As well as this 70%, a further 15% have not decided how to use the land they had been given, while 5% have turned this land over to another private farm. Just 2% have commenced farming themselves. Despite the reorganization of farm and landholding structures through Presidential Decrees, the management of most farm production is in same hands as before. Significantly, attempts to restructure the large-scale state-associated farms of the Soviet era have singularly failed to increase productivity or output through an infusion of free market, entrepreneurial values. The picture is 'the same as before but much worse'.

Rural migration

What can be asked in this regard is whether this despair has resulted in rural residents leaving the countryside for (potentially) better prospects in larger centres. Rural-to-urban migration flows were certainly the norm under the Communist regime. Indeed, processes of de-ruralization have long prevailed in Russia; most especially in regions with historically important urban centres, and in regions in close proximity to Russia's capitals (Moscow and St. Petersburg). In the Soviet period the trend in government policies carried notable negative tones for rural areas, with 'scientific methods' being used to demonstrate that certain rural areas were not suitable for cultivation, so out-migration by local residents was promoted. In this era, many villages were decreed to have no future prospects. The rural population decreased as migration volumes were higher than rates of natural increase. Thus, between 1979 and 1988, 9.1 million people or 1% of the population migrated out of rural areas each year (Zaionchkovskaya, 1997). One consequence of this trend is that, since 1940, thousands of villages and roads have been abandoned, while about 20 million hectares of former agricultural land are now covered by shrubs and forests. On average the land area devoted to farming fell by 30% over this period. In some regions losses were more severe. For example, in Vologodskaya oblast the loss was 63%, in Novgorodskaya it was 55% and in Tverskaya 40%. Compact villages, with a relatively high population density, and villages near to urban centres, tended to survive, but many, many others declined or disappeared altogether (for a commentary on these processes, including the emergence of subsidiary farm plots, see Shaposhnikov, 1990).

It is a significant therefore that, since 1991, official statistics show a slight increase and then sa tabilization in the size of the rural population (for elements of changing attitudes towards the countryside, even before farm reforms took hold, see Kaplan, 1990). A key reason for this growth has been the arrival in the countryside of town-dwellers, refugees and settlers.[6] For example, for 1991-1994 the population increment in rural localities that resulted from in-migration amounted to 855,000 people. This was more than the migration increment for urban settlements (which was 650,000 people). In some of the sparsely populated regions of Nechernozemiya (in the central European part of Russia) the growth in the rural population from 1991-1994 that came from settlers alone amounted to 5-7 % of all rural dwellers. Such migration flows are closely connected with labour market conditions and more widely with means of livelihood. Zaionchkovskaya (1997) points out that a reversal in the direction of migration away from urban centres, at a time when conventional models suggest the Russian process of urbanization is not yet complete, is a visible sign of how deep-seated the current socio-economic crisis is. For Zaionchkovskaya, the strength of rural in-migration reflects the very forceful jolt to people's conceptions of their country and themselves that the disintegration of the USSR and the new geopolitical position of Russia has engendered. What has accompanied this rural-ward movement has been an increase in subsistence-type farm plots. For Russia as a whole, these personal plots have increased in number by 19% since 1992. Many town dwellers have became farmers or now use personal subsidiary plots to grow food (see also Creed, 1995). However, this process of farm formation really attained it peak in the period 1992 -1994 and has since diminished sharply. This is not a continuing source of farm output growth. Many urban residents bought rural houses simply for access to small growing plots in the summer season. Their output is small, and little of the material grown comes onto the open market. In addition, many of these plots are in zones with ready access to large urban centres (like the south Novgorod and Pskov regions and other zones within the immediate sphere of influence of Moscow and St. Petersburg), with little room for further expansion. Set against this, these summer residents help fill the 'rural desert'. In some villages with a history of population loss it is only thanks to these summer residents that the settlement remains on the map. In this regard the views of the rural population might be expected to reveal complex reactions to post-1992 reforms.

Perception of reform by rural people

Adding to this complexity, and perhaps mitigating the perceived impact of economic trauma in the 1990s, Russian peasants have been through many, many years of suffering and poverty. Serfdom was only abolished in 1861 and hunger was a common companion of life for the majority of the Russian population for long after that. Yet after the abolition of serfdom, up to the First World War, the agricultural economy developed significantly, such that even during the war years of 1913-1917 farm commodities were exported. Following the disruptions surrounding the 1917 Revolution, alongside crop failures and hunger soon after, from 1921 vigorous growth in agricultural production began and continued until the 'great change' of collectivization in 1929. In effect, the collectivization of peasant farms and the compulsory taking of them into *kolkhozes* meant a return to serfdom for workers, with complete indifference over the impact of collectivization amongst those who managed the new holdings (see also Abrahams, 1994). Hence hunger returned in 1933 and there were chronic food shortages for some time following. During the Soviet period growth in the effectiveness of agricultural production was limited. Agricultural development was subject to constant government attention but food provision for the general population improved slowly. Yet, looking back from the late 1990s, there is no doubt that production and consumption under the Soviet regime was the peak of Russian achievement (e.g. Table 5.3). Set against this, the bias in Soviet development strategies was toward manufacturing and the cities. Rural people suffered a great deal under the Soviet regime, so it might be thought that they welcomed democratizaton and capitalist market relationships, given that these held the promise of greater economic and political freedoms. But in elections to the State Duma in 1993 and 1995, and in the election of the President in 1996, rural residents voted for representatives from the Communist and other opposition parties (the same is reported for Bulgaria; Creed, 1995). What makes this understandable is research showing that rural residents opposed market reforms and privatization more vigorously than their urban

96

counterparts (Velicki, 1996; Mokrushina, 1997; Orlov and Uvarov, 1997). This is not a phenomenon that is restricted to Russia, for the pain of 1990s economic reform has made many East European farmers sceptical about the real benefits of 'capitalist' production relations (e.g. in Hungary only 1.9% of farm cooperative members expressed an interest in tryng private farming; Agócs and Agócs, 1994). Economic transformation has been realized by shock therapy, which has inflicted a painful blow on farmers, by reducing incomes, increasing the chances of non-payment, and raising the costs of inputs (especially machinery, fuel-lubricants and fertilizer). Hardly surprising that, amongst those who have responded to questionnaire surveys on economic reforms, more than 60% of rural Russian respondents believe their quality of life has deteriorated. In this regard, as with elsewhere in Eastern Europe, with rural dwellers having started with lower incomes than their urban counterparts, the 'forced march' toward free-market capitalism is believed to have brought greater benefits for city dwellers than for country residents (e.g. Unwin, 1997).

Strengthening negative rural sentiments surrounding reform programmes, are fears for rural identities and lifestyles (as reported for Bulgaria as well; Creed, 1995). In this regard, there is little doubt that predilections favour the old order of things in Russian rural society. This is perhaps not unexpected, as change brings uncertainty, and the majority of rural people believe that control over their quality of their life is not in their own hands. Thus, in opinion poll surveys, 30% or rural residents report that their quality of life is in the hands of the President, with a further 25% placing primary emphasis on the national government. Only amongst those aged under 30 years is there a strong sentiment in favour of the view that life chances are dependent upon the individual's actions (42%) (Orlov and Uvarov, 1997). Compared with other settlement zones, however, this perspective is less potent, as rural zones are distinctive social-demographically, in that they have a high share of pensioners in their population, as well as a high proportion with low levels of formal education. That said, there are notable regional differences in views on the economic reform process. In some cases, such as the 'red belt' of the Chernosem zone, we find a rejection of the reforms, whereas in southern regions, where the attractiveness of the territory has drawn many resettlers, views are more favourable (even if, on the whole, the rural population adopts a more conservative stance than their urban counterparts). Even so, the vast majority of rural peasants favour the preservation of Soviet *kolkhozes* and *sovkhozes* structures (support for this view is as high as 96% in the North-West Region and 91% in the Central Chernozem Region). Associated with such views, in the country as a whole, more than 50% of respondents do not support the free buying and selling of land.

As sociological research shows (Velicki, 1996; Orlov and Uvarov, 1997), the priorities of Russian peasants are not a consequence of their conservatism as such, nor do they arise from an aspiration to preserve old traditions in invariable form. Rather the Russian rural population favours a healthy traditionalism in which change is accepted if it fosters an improvement in the quality of life. The post-1992 economic reforms are not disliked simply because they have brought change, nor on account of increased poverty. In fact, it is inequality that outrages rural people more than poverty (which they have had to endure for long periods in the past). In this regard, economic reform is distrusted, with this sentiment turning to a stronger negative sentiment on account of reform having a destructive influence on practices that were deemed to work, alongside evaluations that find few grounds for acknowledging positive results from reform.

Issues of state regulation and rural development

The majority of Russian commentaries point out that the main cause of the difficult situation that agriculture is facings is state deregulation. Analysts argue that the continuation of the economic crisis provides ready evidence that there cannot be self-regulating markets without state participation in rural commodity production. Within these messages, commentaries imply or assert that the current strategy of privatization, and the manner in which land is being disposed from state-related farms, have destructive impacts (Paliev, 1996; Korovkin, 1997; Mostovskoi, 1997; Shutkov, 1997). However, set against this view is another interpretation, which holds that the crisis of agriculture has more to do with the economic situation in Russia as a whole, rather than reform in the farm sector (Chernichenko, 1997; Nefiodova, 1997). Those who take this stance hold that the communist economic system cannot change quickly, but that if there is hesitation or a marking of time in removing its vestiges, this will lead to a catastrophic economic collapse.

But in reality state policy towards agriculture is not well worked-out. There are a number of key documents that purport to define agricultural policy, but as Vetoshkin (1996) notes, to a large extent these only offer a framework for action, rather than a plan or a regulatory schema. This applies to the 1997 Law of Russian Federation on *State Regulation of Agro-industrial Production*,[7] to *Federal Programmes of Stabilization and Development of Agricultural Production in Russia, 1996-2000* and to its companion *Federal Programmes for the Development of Peasant Farming Enterprises and Cooperatives, 1996-2000*. All these articulations of good intention need additional legislative mechanisms for strengthening performance and articulating responsibility for carrying-out specified obligations that support the agro-industrial complex. Unfortunately, the absence of a clear specification of responsibility is not unexpected. Across a broad range of issues, commentators have long recognized that questions related to the responsibility of authorities bring into highlight a key problem in Russian society. As Belocerkovski (1997, p.4) put it: "In Russia the authorities are of such a low quality and ruling oligarchies are so egotistical and predatory that very great political activity by the people is needed in order to change their life for the better". Putting this comment in a realistic, cautionary framework, Belocerkovski (1997, p.4) goes on to lament that "... it is terrible that there is no will or ability amongst the people to engage in political struggle". There is lethargy in this regard, hat is a result of the tragedy of Russian history. This has seen pain being inflicted on the ordinary citizenry through serfdom to cruel wars, to revolutions, to collectivization, then industrialization and now capitalism. To explain the behaviour of people simply in terms of a servile psychology is not sufficient, for the traumatic events of Russian history have demanded colossal exertion from the populace just to survive. One result has been the 'premature' exhaustion of politically-active and rebellious traits in the people (with the propensity for rebellion being very evident before the Communist Regime, when economic uncertainty beset agricultural regions; Cox and Demko, 1969; Jenkins, 1982). For Shmelev (1996), Russian history has generated in people a sense of disgust toward violence and revolt; with this sentiment particularly apparent in rural areas. But if strong public reaction against the traumas of today is not to be expected, what of responses from governmental institutions?

The conditions of economic liberalization that so dominate Russia today exist in a framework in which there is little state regulation or local self-government. At a local level, administrative structures are weak, with little others would recognize as a semblance of democratic society. In fact, discussions on local self-government have only just begun. The stated intention might be to broaden the participation of rural people in decision-making, but the Law on Local Self-Management does little more than enable local elites from the Soviet era (the 'local tsars') to enrich themselves by selling the best and most valuable lands to high-ranking officials and other wealthy people. What we see here, as in other segments of current Russian society, is the exercise of uncontrolled criminal business activity, alongside legal forms of anti-social cooperation between officials and private enterprise. These are growing in stature at the cost of devastation to the national economy. Faced with this situation, local 'self-government' offers nothing to represent citizen interests, nor does it offer a vehicle for resolving local problems. The organization of society at the local level has not changed in structural, economic or administrative relations since the Soviet period.

Capturing the sense of the situation, it is pertinent to note the thoughts of the social geographer Ioffe (1997, pp.143-144), who used to live in Russia and work at the Institute of Geography in Moscow, but who has lived for the last six years in the USA:

It seems that the USSR was a fine state that had more meaning than each of its independent parts .... [however] It was a country of socially protected sufferers. Such everyday illnesses as having an inferiority complex, envy, sexual dissatisfaction, and the thirst to give orders, could all be ascribed to the state and the [Communist] Party. Now ... it is impossible to hide them [these 'passions' or 'vices'] under mask of a righteous social anger .... The [country's] misfortune was not in converting to the postulates of what was, for Russia, an alien Marxist ideology, but in the mean souls and deepest corruptibility of its leaders. Under socialism Russia had rapid economic development, and the rate of improvement in living standards was as high as in the West, although perhaps initial living standards were much lower in the USSR. These improvements did not result from an indulgence in Marxism or communism but emanated from organization and state regulation.

These thoughts do not simply reflect a sense of nostalgia that widespread in Russian people today. State regulation in the Soviet period did have a lot of shortcomings (with insufficiency and undependable food supplies being a common trait, even if not at today's levels; e.g. Nove, 1977; Brada, 1986; Jones *et al.*, 1996). The personal life of people was under rigid controls (even down to small-scale subsidiary farm plots). The penetration of the state into all spheres of life irritated the people exceedingly, and state regulation did not induce communal awareness or the sense of common society. Perhaps contradictions exist between the individual and society in any nation, so the more important and difficult question is how to achieve sustainable development that has a balance between liberalization and state regulation? At this point in time, it has to be concluded that Russia's liberal reforms, which are being enacted without effective state regulation, are not generating economic development. The current economic chaos that dominates life in Russia, alongside the mood of the people, should remind us of the Fellini film 'The Rehearsal of the Orchestra' - where the disharmony is so terrible that it threatens all.

Notes

1 This crisis is associated with the replacement of the Government of Kirienko by that of Primakov. From this time, the larger part of what was owed in wages and pensions were paid, with these payments being made more or less regularly. However, expressed in US dollars, payments

diminished in scale by more than four times. At the same time prices rose, not only for imported commodities but also for Russian products, as well as for transport and other kinds of services (for electric power, for instance, there was a two-fold cost increase and for food products a three-fold rise). For survival, it became necessary to have two or three jobs. The practical sensation for the overwhelming majority of the population is one of survival rather than living. After the crisis of 17 August it became clear to many people that it will take a generation at least before life will return to anything approaching 'normality'.

2   A note of caution should be sounded about Nefiodova's figures as these refer to personal subsidiary plots (that the state allocated to those working on larger operations, such as the former *kolchozes* and *sovchozes*), for which no official statistics exist. Indeed, virtually nobody has counted the crop output from private peasant enterprises. All the agricultural statistics for the Soviet period and for today include measures of output from the agro-industrial complex (the *kolchozes* and *sovchozes*), with no data on private small plots. Two short notes by Hochuikina (1999) and Butusova (1999) have recently appeared concerning research conducted by Teodor Shanin of the University of Manchester and the Russian Agricultural Academy on holdings in Orlovskaiya Oblast, some 300-400 kilometres south-west of Moscow. This survey shows that 96% of rural residents have personal subsidiary plots, 95% have at least one but not more than four cows, 86% have between three and ten pigs, and all keep some poultry and have an aviary. Hochuikina (1999) points out that it is a distinctive feature of rural society that many people have little money but have adapted to live outside the cash economy. Many of these people had previously worked on collective farms, but have become individual farmers. However, these private agricultural holdings defy registration and taxation controls (Butusova, 1999, pp.16-17). Indeed, peasant farmers reveal a rare case of unanimity in their efforts to conceal their property. In stimulating these efforts, they are helped by a sense of disgruntlement built on the lack of social protection for peasant farmers. If they are not a member of a peasant association, farmers are not covered by social welfare protection. Peasant farms might work from morning until night, but they provide only for themselves and (in part) for their town relatives. Officially they are counted as unemployed, without medical insurance, with few everyday amenities and their pension is commonly of the most minimum kind.

3   There is uncertainty over the exact share of land that has been transferred into private ownership. Miloserdov (1998, p.28), for example, gives a 1997 figure of 62% for all the farmland in the former *kolchozes* and *sovchozes*. This was a result of 11.6 million farm workers receiving a land share. Inevitably there is uncertainty owing to the position of personal subsidiary plots. These plots were always near dwelling houses in more densely

populated rural areas and were held on long-term lease or even as life-legacy leases, even during the Soviet period. Such houses were always legally held to be private property, but if an owner wanted to sell a house its price was determined by the size of its associated land plot. These plots are now legally held in private ownership, but in effect they were always private in a latent form. However, this market was really one for housing alone, without any organizing market structures. The first commercial mediating institutions for land transactions only began to appear recently. Technically, in the USSR, as in Russia today, there were (and are) a number of main categories of land: those in populated areas; land for agriculture; land for forestry; land for transport; plus protected and other lands. It was the practice to require a local government decision before allowing land to pass of one class to another. Under this system, someone could build a house or plant potatoes in any land category provided they had permission. But the selling or purchase of land could only take place in the populated areas category. During the period of state deregulation (which included land reform) local municipal governments were granted greater authority. In some regions there have been auctions of land of little value. For example, the mayor of Moscow decided to sell-off waste ground and dust-heaps to willing buyers. Outside these special land categories and circumstances, there is officially no land or property market. However, even prior to land reform, a potential seller could place an advertisement on a notice board in a well-visited place or even in a newspaper. This is no different from what is happening now.

To clarify this complex situation somewhat, technically there is no 'buying and selling of land' in Russian Law. However, in Presidential Decree 337 of 7 March 1996 (*On the realization of the constitutional rights of citizens concerning the land*), the State Land Committee of the Russian Federation (currently named the State Committee on Land Management and Reform) could give certificates of private ownership to citizens who had a plots of land in active use (these plots of land were attached to a rural house, were a collective farmer's personal subsidence plot, were plots of land associated with a 'horticultural and vegetable association', or were a country house with a plot that was used as a summer residence). All these plots have an average size of less than one hectare.

4   For further reports on the difficulties that have accompanied the return of land to former private owners, and for insight on the rise of questionable practices (and opposition from local populations) associated with the privatization of land, commentaries on a number of East European nations are available (e.g. Abrahams, 1994; Verdery, 1994; Vogeler, 1996; Szyrmer and Reiner, 1997).

5   In reality, most of those who have received land already held a privileged position in the 'corridors' of the administration or government (especially in

the suburbs of larger city). Perhaps the exception to this 'rule' is those people who wanted to become individual farmers in distant rural places, without access to roads. Yet, when someone only has a spade for cultivation, even a minimum of two hectares is too large an area to cultivate. Statistical data issued by the Land Committee show that 70% of new land owners put their land share up for lease to large agricultural enterprises (the former *kolchozes* and *sovchozes*, which are today farm associations). Usually this is done on the condition of receiving services, like having their personal subsidiary plot ploughed, obtaining wood from the association, etc. Add to this 70%, 15% who have not decided how to use their land share and 5% who have made their land available for leasing to a private farm. Only 2% of new landowners are developing the land as their own farm. The majority of these farmers possess an average of 7-10 hectares, with only 6% having a holding of 50 hectares and more. Most of these farmers produce for their own consumption.

6 The politics of the former USSR led to the intermixing of people of different nationalities (mixed marriages, inter-regional migration, etc.). As one example, after university many young specialists were sent from Russia to the different republics that made up the USSR. This was an obligatory condition on those attending university, who received accommodation and work in the area they went to. With the break-up of the USSR, many of returned to their home nation. In Russia, many moved to rural areas.

7 This covers issues as broad as the formation and functioning of markets for agricultural inputs and outputs, credit, insurance and favourable taxation for farmers, protective measures for domestic commodity-producers in the face of external economic actions, scientific development, and the provision of finance for development in the agro-industrial complex.

References

Abalkin, L. (1997) The role of the state in taking root and the regulation of the market economy, *Questions of Economics*, 6, pp.4-12 [in Russian].

Abalkin, L. (1998) Social priorities and mechanisms of economic transformation in Russia, *Questions of Economics*, 6, pp.10-67 [in Russian].

Abrahams, R. (1994) The re-generation of family farming in Estonia, *Sociologia Ruralis*, 34, pp.354-368.

Abrahams, R. (1996) Some thoughts on recent land reforms in Eastern Europe, in R. Abrahams (eds.) *After Socialism: Land Reforms and Social Change in Eastern Europe*, Berghahn, Oxford, pp.1-22.

Agócs, P. and Agócs, S. (1994) Too little, too late: the agricultural policy of Hungary's post-communist government, *Journal of Rural Studies*, 10, pp.117-130.

Belocerkovski, V. (1997) It is terrible, when the upper strata cannot and the lower strata cannot, *New Newspaper*, 14(April), 7 [in Russian].

Bicik, I. (1998) Czech agriculture 1989-1996: towards sustainable development, in R. Epps (ed.) *Sustaining Rural Systems in the Global Context*, University of New England School of Geography, Planning, Archaeology and Palaeoanthropology, Armidale, pp.375-380.

Bleaney, M. (1994) Economic liberalisation in Eastern Europe: problems and prospects, *World Economy*, 17, pp.497-507.

Brada, J.C. (1986) Harvest failure in Eastern Europe: planners' responses and their implications for world grain markets, in J.R. Jones (ed.) *East - West Agricultural Trade*, Westview, Boulder, pp.61-97.

Breburda, J. (1990) Land-use zones and soil degradation in the Soviet Union, in K-E. Wädekin (ed.) *Communist Agriculture: Farming in the Soviet Union and Eastern Europe*, Routledge, London, pp.23-39.

Butusova, L. (1999) From then life of the individual peasant, *Moscow News*, 14-21 February, 16-17 [in Russian].

Chadwick, J.W., Houston, J.B. and Mason, J.R.W. (1972) *Ballina: A Local Study in Regional Economic Development*, Institute of Public Administration, Dublin.

Chernichenko, G. (1997) Thieves must be in prison, *Moscow Komsomolets*, 20 June [in Russian].

Cloke, P.J. (1996) Looking through European eyes?: a re-evaluation of agricultural deregulation in New Zealand, *Sociologia Ruralis*, 36, pp.307-330.

Cox, K.R. and Demko, G.J. (1969) Agrarian structure and peasant discontent in the Russian revolution of 1905, *East Lakes Geographer*, 3, pp.3-20.

Creed, G.W. (1995) The politics of agriculture: identity and socialist sentiment in Bulgaria, *Slavic Review*, 54, pp.843-868.

Dawson, A.H. (1986) Agrarian reform in Eastern Europe, in M. Pacione (ed.) *Progress in Agricultural Geography*, Croom Helm, London, pp.149-166.

Federal Law of Russian Federation (1997) About the state regulation of agro-industrial production, *Economics of Agriculture of Russia*, 9, pp.9-14 [in Russian].

Gidadhubli, R.G. (1996) Agriculture: problems of transition, *Economic and Political Weekly (Bombay)*, 25 May, pp.1245-1248.

Glasiev, C. (1997) Russian reforms and the new world order, *Russian Economic Journal*, 7, pp.3-18 [in Russian].

Hedlund, S. (1990) Private plots as a system stabilizer, in K-E. Wädekin (ed.) *Communist Agriculture: Farming in the Soviet Union and Eastern Europe*, Routledge, London, pp.215-229.

Hoffman, D. (1999) As Russia pleads for aid, big bank scandal erupts, *International Herald Tribune*, 12 February, 1.

Hochuikina, A. (1999) The undead, *Moscow News*, 14-21 February, 17 [in Russian].

Ingham, H., Ingham, M. and Weclawowicz, G. (1998) Agricultural reform in post-transition Poland, *Tijdschrift voor Economische en Sociale Geografie*, 89, pp.150-160.

Ioffe, G. (1997) Reminiscences and reflections, *Issues of Settlement Geography: Today and in the Past*, pp.141-145 [in Russian].

Jenkins, J.C. (1982) Why do peasants rebel?: structural and historical theories of modern peasant rebellions, *American Journal of Sociology*, 88, pp.487-514.

Jones, J.R., Li, S.L., Devadoss, S. and Fedane, C. (1996) The former Soviet Union and the world wheat economy, *American Journal of Agricultural Economics*, 78, pp.869-878.

Kaplan, C.S. (1990) The emergence of new attitudes in the Soviet countryside, in K-E. Wädekin (ed.) *Communist Agriculture: Farming in the Soviet Union and Eastern Europe*, Routledge, London, pp.56-71.

Klodzinski, M. (1992) Processes of agricultural change in Eastern Europe: the example of Poland, in K. Hoggart (ed.) *Agricultural Change, Environment and Economy*, Mansell, London, pp.123-137.

Kluev, N. (1996) *Ecological-Geographical Location of Russia*, Russian Academy of Sciences Institute of Geography, Moscow [in Russian].

Korovkin, V. (1997) Economic and social crisis in the agro-industrial complex of the Russian Federation, *International Agricultural Journal: Land Relations and Land Management*, 4, pp.21-25 [in Russian].

Kurbatov, Y.(1998) Development of the agro-industrial complex of Russia and ways out of the crisis, *International Agricultural Journal: Land Relations and Land Management*, 5, pp.27-30 [in Russian].

Lappo, G. and Polian, P. (1997) Closed cities in semi-open Russia, *Issues of Settlement Geography: Today and in the Past*, pp.20-29 [in Russian].

Lipton, M. (1977) *Why Poor People Stay Poor: A Study of Urban Bias in World Development*, Temple Smith, London.

Marshall, N. (1996) *Vehicles of change: Socio-Spatial Change in the Automobile Industry and the Post-Socialist Transformation of Eastern Germany*, PhD thesis, King's College London, University of London.

Miloserdov, V. (1997) Food security of Russia, *International Agricultural Journal: Land Relations and Land Management*, 1, pp.30-35 [in Russian].

Miloserdov, V. (1998) Land relations: formation and necessity for adjustment, *International Agricultural Journal: Land Relations and Land .- Management*, 6, pp.28-33 [in Russian].

Mokrushina, L. (1997) Opinion poll of Nevel district about ownership and using of land plots: resources and paths of development in conditions of self-government, *Nevel*, pp.33-38 [in Russian].

Morgan, W.B. (1987) Productivity and location in private agriculture around Warsaw, Poland, *GeoJournal*, 15, pp.375-385.

Morgan, W.B. (1990) Some aspects of recent improvements in the productivity of private agriculture in Poland, *Geographia Polonica*, 57, pp.99-110.

Morgan, W.B. (1992) Economic reform, the free market and agriculture in Poland, *Geographical Journal*, 158, pp.145-156.

Mostovskoi, G. (1997) International financial organizations: a help to economic reforms in Russia, *Public Sciences and Contemporaneity*, 4, pp.37-46 [in Russian].

Nefiodova, T. (1997) Russian agriculture: social infrastructure and other risk factors, *Issues of Settlement Geography: Today and in the Past*, pp.54-63 [in Russian].

Nickolsky, S.A. (1994) Radical reform of the Russian village: a route to the destruction of Russian agriculture?, in D.J. Symes and A.J. Jansen (eds.) *Agricultural Restructuring and Rural Change in Europe*, Wageningen University Press, Wageningen, pp.162-166.

Nove, A. (1977) Can Eastern Europe feed itself?, *World Development*, 5, pp.417-424.

Orlov, G. and Uvarov, V. (1997) The village and Russian reforms, *Sociological Research*, 5, pp.43-53 [in Russian].

Paliev, S. (1996) Foodstuff security, *International Agricultural Journal: Land Relations and Land Management*, 5, pp.28-34 [in Russian].

Pata, K. and Osmani, M. (1994) Albanian agriculture: a painful transition from communism to free market challenges, *Sociologia Ruralis*, 34, pp.84-101.

Pockney, B.P. (1994) Agriculture in the new Russian Federation, *Journal of Agricultural Economics*, 45, pp.327-338.

Rimashevskaiya, N. (1997) Social consequences of economic transformation in Russia, *Sociological Research*, 6, pp.55-64 [in Russian].

Scott Leonard, C. and Szyrmer, J. (1997) Agrarian transition in the former Soviet Union, *Bulletin de la Société Géographique de Liège*, 33, pp.31-36.

Shaposhnikov, A.N. (1990) The problem of developing independent peasant initiative in Russia, *International Social Science Journal*, 42(124), pp.193-207.

Shmelev, N. (1996) Economy and society, *Questions of Economics*, 1, pp.17-32 [in Russian].

Shutkov, A. (1997) About the necessity of correcting economic policy in Russia, *International Agricultural Journal: Land Relations and Land Management*, 1, pp.15-20 [in Russian].

State Committee for Statistics (1997) *Russian Statistics Yearbook*, Moscow [in Russian].

Szyrmer, J. and Reiner, T.A. (1997) Ukraine's agriculture 1990-1996: an incomplete transition, *Bulletin de la Société Géographique de Liège*, 33, pp.25-30.

Unwin, T. (1997) Agricultural restructuring and integrated rural development in Estonia, *Journal of Rural Studies*, 13, pp.93-112.

Valdés, A. (1994) Agricultural reforms in Chile and New Zealand, *Journal of Agricultural Economics*, 45, pp.189-201.

Velicki, P. (1996) Rural reality, *Sociological Investigations*, 10, pp.35-46 [in Russian].

Verdery, K. (1994) The elasticity of land: problems of property restitution in Transylvania, *Slavic Review*, 53, pp.1071-1109.

Vetoshkin, G. (1997) State regulation of the agro-industrial complex of Russia, *Economics of Agriculture of Russia*, 9, 3 [in Russian].

Vogeler, I. (1996) State hegemony in transforming the rural landscape of eastern Germany: 1945-1994, *Annals of the Association of American Geographers*, 86, pp.432-458.

Zaionchkovskaya, J. (1997) Population migration in Russia: brand-new trends, *Issues of Settlement Geography: Today and in the Past*, pp.30-37 [in Russian].

Zeldner, A.(1997) State regulation of the agro-industrial sector of the economy, *Questions of Economics*, 6, pp.83-90 [in Russian].

6 Agricultural development and environmental regulation in Ireland

Hilary Tovey

What form can agricultural development take in a post-productivist rural Europe? From the point of view of farmers, agribusiness and food industry interests, and proponents of economic growth generally (if not environmentalists), this is surely the central problem posed by the growth of environmental regulation in the EU. This chapter looks at some of the ways in which the agricultural community in Ireland has been trying to solve the problem.

The Irish case is interesting because of the continuing importance of agriculture to the Irish economy, as a source of foreign exchange earnings and a supplier of raw materials to a rapidly expanding and increasingly transnationalized food processing industry. Countries which are closer to the European core, not just in geographical but also in socio-economic terms, may be more sanguine about proposals to move their agriculture beyond productivism; but in Ireland the continuance of farming as a productive activity is still seen as a key element for economic growth. Different states in the EU, and indeed the global system, respond differently to productivism and to the opportunities created by post-productivist movements. In some core states in Europe, public objections may reach a level where it is no longer possible to continue intensive, productivist forms of farming. This might simply encourage its continuance or exportation elsewhere, where objections are less intense or controls are not so severe (Portela, 1994; or see Yearley, 1991, for a discussion of regulation flight in industry). Investigating the way in which agriculturalists in Ireland are responding to increased environmental regulation of their activities may help us understand the direction that environmental policy in general is taking in Europe. In turn, this may help to advance the environment versus development debate a little further.

Productivism, post-productivism and agricultural development

First we should clarify some of the terms used above, particularly productivist and post-productivist. That EU policy is moving towards a strategy for managing rural areas that is in a sense post-productivist, or beyond productivism, has been widely accepted in rural studies (Marsden, 1992; Shucksmith, 1993; Ward, 1993; Veerman, 1994; Winter, 1997; Ilbery *et al.*, 1997; O'Hara and Commins, 1998). Yet the term itself has been relatively little discussed. A central feature of a post-productivist regime appears to be increased environmental regulation of agriculture, but how we should interpret the recent inclusion of environmental concerns into the Common Agricultural Policy (CAP) remains open to question. It may signal the start of a genuine move away from productivist orientations towards farming, or alternatively, an attempt to create consent around the continuance of productivism.

As a concept developed specifically within rural studies, post-productivism reflects broader debates in social science around the characterization of contemporary society as post-Fordist, post-industrial or post-modern. Theories of post-productivism can be seen as the form that macro-sociological theorizing about post-modernity has taken in rural studies. They should therefore be theories about the specific way in which post-modernity unfolds itself in rural societies. In practice, however, discussions of post-productivism tend to say more about the productivist era that is supposed to be being superseded than about the new one coming into existence. The same point is frequently made about attempts to theorize modernity and post-modernity in sociology more generally:

> The 'post' of post-modernity is ambiguous. It can mean what comes after, the movement to a new state of things, however difficult it might be to characterize that state in these early days. Or it can be more like the post of *post-mortem*: obsequies performed over the dead body of modernity, a dissection of the corpse. The end of modernity is in this view the occasion for reflecting on the experience of modernity; post-modernity is that condition of reflectiveness.... (Kumar, 1995, pp.66-67)

Ward's (1993) development of the post-productivist thesis could be considered a post-mortem. Despite the reference in his title to agriculture in the post-productivist era, the paper is primarily a reflection on productivism, on how that has been appraised and understood in the sociology of agriculture from the 1950s to the 1980s. But that reflection is very useful. Ward suggests that we can think of productivism as operating on two distinct levels. First, as a logic of production found at farm level; as a set of assumptions or values held by farmers about how to farm. Second, as the regime of accumulation involving specific relations between the state and leading economic actors that was institutionalized in the aftermath of the Second World War and lasted up to at least the mid-1980s. I suggest below, following Scott (1995), that there is also a third way in which we might understand the concept.

Productivism as an on-farm logic of production appears to result from working within a productivist regime (that is, if it is not simply a definition of farming). The idea of a productivist regime therefore seems the more useful one to follow up. Central to productivism as a specific regime of accumulation, according to Ward (1993), is that it involves a process of technological intensification in agriculture. But it is also more than this. The concept of regime points us specifically towards investigating ways in which the state is implicated in bringing about technical and social change in farming. That is, how the state provides appropriate institutional and normative frameworks to encourage farmers to take up new technologies or stabilize opportunities for capital to secure profits within a particular socio-historical context (Friedmann and McMichael, 1989). Regimes, then, are distinct periods or stages in the development of capitalism, guided by distinct modes of regulation in which state sponsorship, if not state intervention, plays a formative part (see also Friedmann, 1993).

Ward (1993) linked productivism, as the core feature of the post-war agro-food system, to the evolution of industrial Fordism. As a regime of accumulation based on continuous growth in output and consumption through technological innovation, Fordism requires the progressive adoption of mass consumption by the industrial working class (Ward, 1993, p.353). Agriculture's role within the Fordist regime was to provide cheap food to a largely urban workforce. In turn this freed large proportions of household income to be spent on mass-produced non-food goods. For food to be produced cheaply, industrial capital had to identify possibilities for accumulation in the agro-food system, though strategies of appropriationism or substitutionism (Goodman *et al.*, 1987). At the same time, primary producers had to accept a falling share of the consumer price of food, as agricultural input manufacturers, food processing companies, as well as packing and retailing concerns, expanded their share. This pushed farmers to produce more and more, simply to maintain an existing level of income. The productivist regime, then, was characterized by an alliance between the interests of the state, agro-industrial capital and science (Ward, 1993, p.354). All benefited from promoting a model of agricultural production and development that centred on the adoption of intensive, technology-driven production methods. Agricultural research, often directly funded by government, targeted the development of technologies to save labour and boost yields. Under the CAP, capital grants and input subsidies were made available to farmers to encourage them to adopt these new technologies.

Ward (1993) dates the end of the productivist era to the mid-1980s, although he sees it starting to go into decline 15 years earlier. The productivist model was undermined by a series of concerns. These include global and EU concerns around the burden of financing the productivist regime, rising public concern over food quality and, critically, rising public concern about environmental impacts. These produced a critical change in the role of the state in relation to agricultural development:

> By the mid-1980s ... states were no longer prepared to underwrite capital accumulation in the agro-food system, or at least, not to the same extent as previously. In effect, the state lost interest in maintaining the technology/policy model that had been established in the 1940s, leaving the global food system, and the production practices of the farm sector in particular, exposed to a crisis of legitimacy. (Ward, 1993, p.357)

Yet, for Ward, the full impact of the shift to post-productivism remains obscure, because the policy goals to underwrite it have not yet emerged in a coherent form. Only one trend emerges in Ward's account to differentiate the regime of productivism from that of post-productivism in a definitive way. This is enhanced concern about, and attempts to restrict, environmental damage resulting from agricultural production.

Ward is clearly right in directing our attention to increasing environmental regulation and in suggesting that this constitutes a significant change in contemporary European agriculture. It is not certain, however, that it constitutes a new regime of accumulation. To identify a transition to a new regime, we would need to identify new and different coalitions of interests that support it and, perhaps, different mechanisms of accumulation, new technologies, or new orientations to technology. Otherwise, the same criticism as has been made of the concept post-Fordism can be made of post-productivism: that it is simply a new round of industrial capitalism that essentially carries on the key feature of Fordism. That is, the systematic application of new techniques - social as well as scientific in the technical sense - to the organization of production in all its spheres (Kumar, 1995, p.60). Indeed, increased environmental regulation may coincide with undiminished support for agricultural productivism. Much environmental management, it might be argued, is actually concerned less about halting pollution, or the destruction of landscapes and so on, than about trying to determine what is an acceptable level of damage. From this perspective, the key role played by the state is that of securing legitimation for and consensus around acceptable environmental damage. In effect, this suggests that the role of the state in a post-productivist regime differs little from its role in the productivist era. A key state activity is still to construct consensus around technological innovation and industrial growth, virtually regardless of social costs. Viewed in this light, the state can be expected to organize and promote the same coalition of interests in both eras (the scientific community and agro-industrial capital), in an effort to manage the conditions (including popular consent) under which capital accumulation continues.

That agri-environmental regulation does not lessen productivism, and even perhaps intensifies it, is one of the claims made by Scott (1995) in her critique of the concept of development that is articulated through EU policies for regional, rural and agricultural development. She offers another way of thinking about productivism and post-productivism. Scott (1995, p.107) analyses the CAP, and particularly its price support system, as based on a specific rationality. This rationality equates progress in farming with efficiency. It understands efficiency in purely economic and technical terms, as the production of more at less cost through rapid exploitation of technological innovation (Scott, 1995, p.130). In Scott's view, the concept of agricultural development underpinning the CAP is a thoroughly productivist one. It has pushed European farming towards continuous expansion in the scale and intensity of production. This has consistently marginalized those producers who are unable to exploit this development model, particularly those with smaller holdings and those from less favoured regions, where natural features give rise to higher production costs.

> It is apparent that the price support mechanism which has come to dominate the CAP is an instrument of agricultural development and structural transformation in substance, if not in name. It has ushered in an era of capital, machine and energy intensive agriculture and promoted concentration and specialization of agricultural production. It is a policy which denies the diversity of the origins and cultural associations of food production and which invents a single rationality with respect to agriculture, a rationality which is 'functional, business-like and unsentimental' and deeply imbued with the modern accounting problem of equating more with better. In that it undermines the contribution of agriculture to the social, cultural and environmental well-being of the 'lagging' regions, it is a policy which might be said to be profoundly antithetical to real development. (Scott, 1995, p.122)

In going on to discuss the 1992 reforms of the CAP, particularly the introduction of agri-environmental measures, and the policies directed under the Guidance section towards structural change in Objective 1 Regions, the key question Scott poses concerns the rationality these embody. If the rationality on which the CAP is centred is that of productivism, do other policies introduce a different, non-productivist rationality into the system, or go some way towards recognition of the diversity of the origins and cultural associations of food production? Do they operate as a point of resistance to the premises and parameters of this system, or are they employed as a means of confirming the underlying principles and assumptions (Scott, 1995, p.102)? Productivism and post-productivism in European agriculture become a matter, not of a historical break between one regime of accumulation and another, but of changes within a regulatory system which open it up to the play of new, different and even counterposing rationalities.

On the agri-environmental measures that were part of the 1992 reforms, Scott's answer to such questions is a clear negative. Particularly because the funding for these is so meagre (around three ECU per hectare of agricultural land in the Community), they do little to challenge the dominant productivist price support system. They are inadequate as a means of buying off more intensive producers. Other producers continue to experience the same pressures to intensify and expand production as before. It has simply become even more difficult for them now to succeed.

Scott's analysis of Objective 1 Region policies, on the other hand, is more optimistic. These consist of three types of structural interventions. First of all there are attempts to provide the conditions under which farmers in lagging regions can catch up with those elsewhere and compete more effectively in the market constructed by the rules of the CAP. Then there are attempts to promote economic diversification on farms and in rural regions, so as to encourage a form of growth that does not lead to the production of agricultural commodities already in surplus. Finally, there is the provision of direct income supports that are detached entirely from farm outputs (for example, payments for landscape management or welfare supports intended to maintain minimum population levels in remote rural regions). Scott's argument is that the first two simply reproduce the productivist rationality of the CAP as a whole, although the third does offer some challenge to this. At least implicitly, it acknowledges the inherently limited capacity of the other two measures to make small producers in disadvantaged regions agriculturally viable. Disengaging farm income supports from price supports indicates a growing recognition that agricultural development implies more than an expanded productive capacity (Scott, 1995, p.129). Such a disengagement starts to challenge the expectation that the model of agriculture promoted by price support systems is universally feasible and/or desirable while offering alternative sources of support to farmers who remain outside the mainstream productivist rationality (Scott, 1995, p.129). It thus represents a step towards a development policy that is not be premised upon the reward of measurable efficiency but rather upon the preservation of lifestyles, social relations and relationships with nature, which would have no place in a purely competitive market environment (Scott, 1995, p.130).

Scott's argument is extremely interesting but her conclusions need more debate. It is not clear yet whether the detaching of income support from agricultural production, for farmers in disadvantaged regions, represents the sort of creative freeing of alternative rationalities which Scott applauds, or whether it is becoming a new form of social welfare or farmers' dole, with all the problems of poverty, dependency and humiliation that can imply. Moreover, the impact of arrangements for such payments may actually erode, rather than revitalize, the cultural diversity of farming. On the other hand, Scott may conclude too quickly that the agri-environmental measures of 1992 do not represent any new or non-productivist rationality penetrating the CAP system. It may well be, as she suggests, that these measures are more about supply control than environmental protection, but in practice the two may not be easily disconnected, as I argue below.

In the Irish case, there is little evidence that the state has lost interest, to borrow Ward's phrase, in supporting either accumulation in the food industry or technological development in farming. Nevertheless, this chapter argues that a new rationality around farming has developed in the course of implementing agri-environmental measures in Ireland, and suggests that this increasingly provides a basis for the re-orientation of intensive commercial farming. My argument is that the new rationality is still concerned with efficiency, in the sense of reducing cost, but not with expansion and intensification of production; and that attempts to reduce costs, as an expression of concern about reducing waste, can be categorized as environmental as well as economic innovations. As I illustrate below, agricultural scientists and advisors in Ireland, as well as farmers, have responded to the 1992 CAP reforms by developing a discourse around agricultural development that incorporates both dimensions; it embodies a new rationality which is non-productivist but is not anti-production. There is no move to a new regime of accumulation; nevertheless it is not simply business as usual (Winter, 1997, p.370).

The Rural Environment Protection Scheme: implementing 2078/92

My focus here is on the implementation in Ireland of EU Regulation 2078/92, through the Rural Environment Protection Scheme or REPS. REPS was introduced in 1994. It is a voluntary scheme that is open to any farmer to join, on condition that they produce a satisfactory agri-environment farm plan. It provides to those accepted onto the scheme a specified level of payment per hectare, up to a maximum of 40 hectares on any given farm. REPS is only one element in a broader package of management strategies for agriculture-environment relations in Ireland. This includes the Arable Area Payments Scheme (set-aside), a complex set of area designations or listings, such as

National Heritage Areas (see Tovey, 1994), Special Protection Areas (see below), and Special Areas of Conservation (see below). An Integrated Pollution Control Licensing Scheme has also been developed by the Environmental Protection Agency (EPA), to identify and enforce acceptable levels of emissions from production plants. This latter Scheme is being progressively applied not only to industry but to intensive forms of agriculture. Other interventions also impact on agriculture, such as legislation in relation to water pollution.

Not all environmental intervention affecting farmers derive from policy-making groups or institutions in which agricultural interests are represented. The Special Area of Conservation (SAC) scheme, for example, comes under the EU Habitats Directive (over 200 such areas have been designated, mainly along the western seaboard; see O'Hara and Commins, 1998). The Special Protection Area (SPA) scheme likewise comes under the EU Directive on Conservation of Wild Birds. As with the EU Habitats Directive, this is administered in Ireland by the National Parks and Wildlife Service of the Office of Public Works. The relevant Minister here is not the Minister for Agriculture but the Minister for Arts, Heritage, the Gaeltacht and the Islands. The Environmental Protection Agency (EPA), on the other hand, answers to the Minister for the Environment, who is also the Minister responsible for enacting legislation on water and air quality issues. While the administrators of the SPA and SAC schemes articulate a philosophy of environmental conservation or preservation (Buttel, 1994) in regard to the rural, and appear to work fairly closely with leading conservation NGOs, the Department of the Environment and the EPA have committed themselves publicly to a discourse of sustainable development (Department of the Environment, 1997). The Department of Agriculture has no publicly articulated position on environmental matters. In general it continues to talk about Irish agriculture in terms of a discourse of economic development - increasing output, increasing export markets, raising competitiveness and so on. This background is important in understanding the shaping of REPS, which can be understood as the agricultural lobby's response to the largely urban-generated environmental discourses which dominate other schemes (Tovey, 1993).

Do these in some ways fairly specific features of the Irish case affect our capacity to generalize from it to European farming and agri-environment relations more broadly? Member states responses to 1992 agri-environmental policy innovations are commonly said to have been quite diverse (Whitby, 1996; Billaud et al., 1997). Certainly there are some features of the Rural Environmental Protection Scheme (such as its requirement for the production of a farm plan) that commonly would not be found in other EU states. The diversity may however be over-emphasized. Thus, the Jokinen and Nieme-Iilahti (1997) study of the implementation of Regulation 2078/92 in Finland suggests that there are considerable similarities between the Finnish and Irish

116

schemes, despite them being directed toward arable farmers in one country and cattle farmers in the other. At any rate, the way in which agri-environmental management is elaborated and instantiated in the text of Regulation 2078/92 can be seen to permeate the discourse of Irish state agents charged with its implementation, as I suggest further below. Thus, while it is premature to try to identify a unified agri-environmental policy regime across Member States, there do seem to be commonalties in the ways EU policies are discursively framing and reframing the ongoing discourse on rural society, agriculture and environment at the national level (Billaud *et al.*, 1997, p.9).

In this context, it is pertinent to note Baldock and Lowe's (1996) summarizing of EU Regulation 2078/92 in terms of seven main measures. The first three are concerned with reducing the intensity of agriculture. These include reducing inputs of fertilizer and pesticide, reducing stocking rates, and generally extensifying farm production. The other four are directed toward encouraging farmers to undertake activities that maintain or enhance the countryside. They are concerned primarily with landscape, nature conservation and public access to the countryside, as well as a rather vague reference to '... protection of the environment and natural resources' (Baldock and Lowe, 1996, pp.20-21). I have outlined the main elements and objectives of REPS elsewhere (Tovey, 1997), but they follow a very similar pattern. The key element is the development by each participating farmer of an agri-environmental plan, centred in particular on waste management and the management of grassland:

> The plan shall ... by reference to the soil analyses reports, soil type, stocking intensity, farming enterprise, efficient use of nutrients and the environmental sensitivity of the area, prepare a nutrient management plan that specifies limits to Nitrogen from animal and other wastes, chemical fertilizer Nitrogen and Phosphorus from all sources. The tonnage of lime to be applied each year shall also be set out. (Department of Agriculture, Food and Forestry, 1994, p.8)

Secondly, the farm plan must list all features - watercourses, wildlife habitats, valued landscapes, items of historical or archaeological interest, etc. - that are to be protected, maintained or managed (Department of Agriculture, Food and Forestry, 1994, p.8).

Like 2078/92 itself, then, REPS uneasily combines two distinct strands: a preservationist strand, re-orienting farming towards the production of countryside goods, and an efficiency and waste-reduction strand. The preservationist strand has attracted most attention among conservationists and within the mass media generally. It has also generated the most hostile reaction among farmers and within the farming media, particularly since the statutory establishment of the SAC designation scheme in early 1997, and its official attachment to REPS a year and a half later. Farmers who have been designated as having a Special Area of Conservation on their land do not have to join REPS. However, as I show below, it is quite difficult for them to avoid doing so, which is a source of contention among those who are not interested in accepting REPS restrictions on their activities. If they are participating in REPS, they get flat rate top-up payments on their REPS payments, which brings these up to some 330 ECUs per hectare, for a maximum of 40 hectares of farm land (even if the SAC-designated area is less than this). Farmers who remain outside REPS must negotiate their own compensation arrangements with the Department of Arts and Heritage. They can expect to be paid only on the basis of actual losses incurred as a result of designation. Signifying the manner in which farmers are drawn into REPS, 78% of state funding allocated to cover the costs of the SAC scheme in 1997/98 went for top-up payments to participants in REPS.

However, the campaign of resistance to the SAC scheme which started particularly in the Connemara region in the west of Ireland over the winter of 1997/98 is not only, or even centrally, about compensation issues. It is provoked much more by rules regarding commonage (inherited use rights to common land) and by the management of stock movements. Many farms in this area consist of very small acreages of private land, with extensive commonage rights. No private land has been given a SAC designation, but most commonage land has been, on the grounds that it is overgrazed. However, affected farmers cannot get compensation for designation unless they already have at least 10 acres of fenced land (i.e. privately owned land). Thus the SAC scheme encourages the privatization of agricultural resources in the area. The rules also state that sheep or cattle dosed against parasites must be kept off SAC-designated land for seven days, in case residues enter into rivers or watercourses. In an area where farmers have few sheds and little fenced land, but have ewe flocks of up to 300 head, with very high parasite levels, farmers see this as an attempt to destroy the local way of farming. Effectively, farmers believe they are being told they cannot dose at all, so they might as well emigrate (*Irish Farmers Journal*, 6 December 1997, p.7).

Another campaign of resistance, using similar tactics of local meetings, generating publicity and political lobbying, has been developing in the west and midlands against restrictions on cutting turf from SAC-designated raised bogs. These restrictions are estimated to affect around 3,000 farmers. Again what is in question is the traditional right (turbary) of local farmers to take turf from a local bog that may not be part of their own holding. Cutting turf - the day on the bog - is a much celebrated element in Irish rural life. Farmers opposing the SAC scheme in this case oppose it on both economic and cultural grounds. Commonage and turbary are residues of an earlier agrarian society in which farming was less privatized and local relationships less individualized than today. In both cases, the introduction of income payments to farmers for landscape management or for refraining from productive work, far from supporting or facilitating alternative rationalities and cultural understandings of farming, seem to have the opposite effect. Through these schemes farmers are being brought into a system of bureaucratic controls on farming. As Weber (1978) predicted, this leads to cultural uniformity and impoverishment.

The attention that has been focused on the struggle around preservationist environmentalism has had the effect of obscuring the unfolding of the other, equally interesting, strand in REPS. It is this other strand which is the really important innovation of the scheme, and it is one which is now spreading into mainstream farming discourse. Briefly, this is an attempt to develop Irish farming, rather than to de-develop it in the interests of environmental conservation. A senior official in the Department of Agriculture, for example, who had been involved in the development of the REPS scheme, described it to us in an interview in March, 1996 in the following terms:

> [REPS] ... is all about nutrient management. The main focus of REPS is the soil management plan, and soil analysis interpretation linked to precise recommendations for each farm situation. The ultimate objective being the *efficient* use of plant nutrients on that farm. And the more efficiently they use them, the less likely they are to leak into surface and ground water. (emphasis added)

In this and similar interviews, it became clear that Department of Agriculture officials regarded the obligation to develop an agri-environmental scheme under the 1992 CAP reforms as an opportunity to bring more money into Irish farm localities, particularly those that had not benefited much from core CAP policies. Effectively, it is seen as a way of using money to strengthen farming in these areas.

A similar perspective on the scheme has been presented by an agricultural advisor from Teagasc (the state-sponsored agricultural research and advisory institute), who has responsibility for overseeing the operation of REPS in an area in the north west of the country. In an interview in the *Irish Farmers Journal* (14 May 1998, pp.23-24), this Teagasc advisor held that there is no antagonism between efficient farming and REPS. Rather, they are complementary. The main problem is that the scheme does not help small farmers enough. Payments are on a flat rate per area owned, so smallholders receive a relatively small total payment. On this account, this Teagasc advisor would prefer to see tiered payments. Despite its inadequacies, in a peripheral, vulnerable area like north west Ireland, which has a short grazing season and difficult farming conditions, rural development has to involve REPS if people are to be kept in villages, instead of emigrating. This advisor accepted that diversification of economic activities - such as agri-tourism and local crafts -

is important but saw farming as the core of rural life, so REPS should do more for developing farming. This does not mean intensification, or increasing the scale of production, for farmers in peripheral areas cannot afford to buy more land or to use more inputs so as to farm more intensively. What REPS is about, from this point of view, is reducing costs. It is about becoming cost conscious, reducing farm stocking rates, and getting a better stock performance, without increasing the costs of production.

Although REPS is a national scheme, the sort of farmers and farming areas with which this agricultural advisor routinely deals constitute a significant element within it. It is widely admitted that the level at which REPS payments have been set, while attractive to small to medium producers, are not attractive to the top tier of commercially successful, intensive producers, who currently account for some 70-80% of total farm output in Ireland (Leavy, 1997). These farmers are increasingly concentrated in the south, south east and eastern parts of the country (Commins, 1996). This means that farmer participation in REPS has a clear geography. In early 1998, 33,000 farmers, with around a quarter of the total agricultural land area, participated in REPS. The counties with the highest proportion of their land in the scheme were those in the north and north west. These are areas in which there has been a widespread withdrawal from farming, if not from landholding, in the last 20 years (Frawley and Commins, 1996). This withdrawal is sanctioned by the state, which in recent years has been moving closer to the view of the food processing industry. This is that Ireland needs a raw materials production sector organized tightly around a small number of quite large-scale producers who can meet the demands of the industry in terms of regularity, scale and quality of supplies. In that vision of Irish farming, up to three-quarters of farmers, and up to half of the agricultural land area, is surplus to requirements. Yet these same farmers are offered, through REPS, support for a particular type of farm development. How can we make sense of this contradictory and ironic trend?

Ecological modernization in Irish farming

Alongside environmental preservationism, what we find developing in REPS seems to be a discourse of ecological modernization (Spaargeren and Mol, 1992; Weale, 1993; Hajer, 1995, 1996). As a policy programme, ecological modernization is described as involving a switch away from end-of-pipe approaches to combating pollution (compensating for environmental damage, combined with the introduction of additional technology to minimize any recurrence). Instead the approaches that are favoured emphasize changing production processes themselves (through the use of cleaner or more intelligent technologies), so pollution or waste occurrence is prevented in the

120

first place. This new strategy is promoted as a positive-sum game (Hajer, 1995), which sees environmental protection not as a burden on the economy but as a precondition for future growth: it both stimulates industrial innovation and guarantees future competitiveness on world markets (Weale, 1993, p.207).

A very significant feature of ecological modernization policy is that it indicates the possibility of overcoming the environmental crisis without leaving the path of modernization (Spaargaren and Mol, 1992, p.334). It involves what Beck (1992) has called the further modernization of modernity, and as such is a political programme attractive to a range of political and socio-economic interests in Western Europe. For Hajer (1995, p.33) this means that ecological modernization is firmly associated with modernity:

> It is a policy strategy that is based on a fundamental belief in progress and the problem-solving capacity of modern techniques and skills of social engineering ... There is a renewed belief in the possibility of mastery and control, drawing on modernist policy instruments such as expert systems and science.

Ecological modernization policy assumes that the environmental crisis can be overcome by technical and procedural innovation. In eco-modernist discourse, environmental pollution is framed as a matter of inefficiency, and producing 'clean technologies'. 'Environmentally sound' technical systems, it is argued, will stimulate innovation in the methods of industrial production and distribution (Hajer, 1996, p.249).

Under-scoring the key ideas of ecological modernization are three principles. The first is the closing of substance cycles, so the chain from raw material via production process to product is undertaken in a manner in which waste and recycling contains as few leaks as possible. Secondly, the conserving of energy and improving the efficiency and utility of renewable energy sources is seen as critical. The third principle is that the quality of production processes and of products themselves is improved (Spaargaren and Mol, 1992, pp.339-340). In REPS discourse, each of these principles emerges as a key issue. Here too we find an emphasis on efficiency, and on reducing the cost of production inputs, which points toward an emerging conception of environmental protection as a positive-sum game for farmers. If the attempt to re-orient farming towards the production of environmental goods is what helped to sell REPS to the mass media and the urban conservation lobby, ecological modernization seems to be what sold it to the farming lobby. For this lobby, eco-modernization discourse, which presents environmentally cleaner production practices as economically more efficient, is both intelligible and attractive.

The result is that, through REPS, strategies to increase efficiency in production and to avoid waste, are focused on farmers who are regarded, in wider policy terms, as largely irrelevant producers. But perhaps the real function of REPS was to be a pilot ground for testing out such strategies - a sort of Trojan horse, which would carry the discourse of ecological modernization behind the lines of commercial, productivist farming? This may exaggerate the degree of deliberate manipulation involved. It may be more accurate simply to note that, since the early 1990s, a number of agricultural experts in the state advisory services, the farming media and the Irish Farmers Association have been engaged in reconstructing the ideal of the vanguard farmer along the lines of cost competitiveness (related to a switch from the British to the New Zealand model of dairy farming). REPS, if it provided the wrong sorts of experimental subjects on whom to target the new discourse, provided the first opportunity to set out this reconstructed ideal in any detail.

Farmers who are not in REPS - generally the larger and more intensive producers - appear at first sight to be outside the scope of agri-environmental regulation. Even though the licensing system operated by the EPA (itself an excellent example of eco-modernist thinking) is starting to be applied to intensive agriculture, to date this includes only the rearing of poultry or pigs in installations where the capacity exceeds 100,000 broilers, 50,000 layers (turkey or other fowl), 700 sows or 7,000 pigs. Intensive farming on this scale is very exceptional in Ireland (by early 1998, 11 license applications had been received by the EPA, of which only one had been fully processed). This still leaves a large number - between 30,000 and 60,000, depending on the definition used - of commercial family farms who effectively seem to be unregulated (except in being, as any citizen is, subject to general anti-pollution legislation). The main policy approach to these farmers has tended to follow what Jokinen (1997, p.54) terms informative agri-regulation rather than economic or legal constraint. In other words, farmers are encouraged to change their practices through the provision of information, exhortation and persuasion, by farm organizations, agricultural extension agents, and the farming media (see also Izcara Palacios, 1998).

Increasingly, what farmers are being exhorted to do, by these agents and in these media, is to find more efficient forms of production. They are being asked to increase profits by reducing costs rather than increasing output. This is particularly evident in dairy farming, which would be widely regarded as the most productivist of all specializations within Irish agriculture. From the, 1960s up to the last few years, the state strongly supported a high-input high-output model of dairy farming (Leeuwis, 1989). This involved the maximum possible use of purchased inputs in order to realize the maximum volume of outputs. This was presented as the only modern way to farm, as the best way to improve farm incomes, the best way to maximize the flow of price supports from Brussels, and as essential to the development of a large-scale food processing industry.

In the last few years attitudes have changed remarkably. Now the emphasis is on reducing purchased inputs and reducing stocking rates. Over the winter of 1997/98, for example, the *Irish Farmers Journal* ran frequent articles comparing the end-of-year profits of farmers on intensive and (relatively) extensive production systems, consistently claiming that those on the new low-cost systems made higher profits. The experience of small dairy farmers inside REPS, whose returns remained high despite extensification because of their enforced lower inputs, were discussed in a number of farming media. The national dairy advisory programme launched by Teagasc early in 1998 set farmers the target of producing milk with a 3.5% protein level at a cost of 40 pence a gallon. This is to be achieved by managing grassland better and reducing concentrate feeds. A new research programme has been instituted at Moorepark, the main state-supported agricultural research centre, to develop very low-cost ways of producing high quality milk from cows calving to grass, by improving grazing management, and (in a dramatic reversal of previous policy) by shifting the emphasis away from winter milk and early calving which is not possible on grass alone in the Irish climate. Lively debates are ongoing in the farming media about breeding, and how best to breed a cow which is cheap to run but very high yielding. Dairy farmers seem to be going through a new round of re-skilling - recovering earlier skills in grassland management from the pre-productivist period - and learning new, particularly business, skills in the search for the most cost-efficient forms of production.

Of course this change must be seen in context. Within the agricultural media, advice about low-input cost-efficient forms of production is a tiny element in a sea of items that carry the opposite message (e.g. advertisements for new machines, articles on the latest developments in chemical aids, reports of successful intensive and high-tech farms). The new policy direction is a response to recognition that under the current EU milk quota regime, expanding production is an option that is less and less available to farmers who want to improve their income. Dairy farmers, moreover, deal with a globalized food industry (most of the Irish milk processing industry today can source supplies on a global or at least international level; see Tovey 2000). This industry is one that is increasingly likely to take the cost of its raw materials into account in arranging supplies. What we are seeing, then, is not only, or not even very much, a response to environmental concerns. Nevertheless this new direction in policy is promoted from time to time by the state as a movement within Irish agriculture towards sustainability. As Hajer (1995) argues, ecological modernization provides the conditions for the development of discourse coalitions, whose members have very diverse interests but can separately recognize how their interests are furthered by this discourse.

Ecological modernization, food and rural society

I have argued that regulation of Irish farming shows signs of the emergence of a new rationality. This presents a new understanding of agricultural development. This understanding is about production, but is not productivist. Eco-modernist discourse provides farmers and agriculturalists with a way of reconciling agriculture and environment in terms which support continued agricultural production. It also provides grounds for refusing to see marginal farming as only or even primarily a form of landscape management, a refusal that many people in Ireland, even some environmentalists (for example, people in the organic farming movement) welcome. It expresses an optimistic, 'modernist' belief in the capacity of human intelligence and skill to solve production problems, which appeals to many people beyond just the agricultural lobby.

However it does have serious limitations. One is that it recognizes as environmental problems only those problems that have to do with nature as a resource or sustenance base. It has nothing to contribute to problems around nature as experienced in everyday subjectivity (Spaargaren and Mol, 1992). This is a particular failing when it appears as a discourse about agriculture, as issues like animal welfare or the aesthetic impact of an intensive pig farm, cannot be addressed. Another is that it makes claims about connections between environmental protection and economic competitiveness which may be effective in mobilizing coalitions of policy elites (Weale, 1993), but are unproven.

More important for my purposes are the concerns raised by Hajer and by Redclift. They suggest that ecological modernization pays no attention to distributive and equality issues that are intertwined with environmental ones, whether (as so often in the South) as a cause of environmental degradation or (more familiar in the North) as the consequence of attempts at environmental conservation and regulation (Redclift, 1997, pp.41-42). Moreover, eco-modernist discourse encourages the discursive closure of environmental problems in ways which disqualify non-(technical-)experts from any role in environmental management (Tovey, 1994; Hajer, 1995). Through its capacity to depoliticize technology, or to technologize politics, it closes down democratic debates around social development (the new problems concerning social justice, democracy, responsibility, the preferred relation of people and society, the role of technology in society, or indeed what it means to be human; Hajer, 1996, p.265). These are debates that the environmental movement did so much originally to open up. Problems in social organization, it implies, can be resolved through technical change alone.

An illustration of these limitations can be found in the way the concept of sustainability is developing in Irish policy discourse. As an official policy discourse, sustainable development has gained rapid popularity in Ireland but its meaning remains vague. The more a meaning is supplied for it out of ecological modernization discourse, the more narrowly technicized it becomes. Compare, for example, the understanding of sustainable agriculture which emerges from the organic farming movement in Ireland (see Tovey, 1997) with that found in official policy documents (for example, Department of the Environment, 1997). The organic and alternative agriculture movements challenge existing models of development for agriculture on the basis of concerns about their sustainability deriving from social and cultural, as well as ecological, conditions. From this point of view, a sustainable agriculture involves a great deal more than just reconsidering productivism in farming. Conventional food is seen to be produced not just under conditions that damage nature. It is also processed and commoditized in ways that damage both nature and social relations, and which create a gap between food producers and food consumers, which in turn helps to generate political support for Fordist, productivist types of food policies. Creating a sustainable food system must include not only finding new methods of on-farm production, but also finding ways to shorten the distance between producer and consumer, organizing more localized food production-consumption systems and encouraging less processing of food. In particular, it must include trying to alter the processes within contemporary food production that encourage inequality and poverty among farmers, the concentration of capital, land and other production resources on a smaller and smaller group of producers, and the creation of large farm population surpluses.

But the emerging official discourse around sustainable agriculture in Ireland is quite different. It is a discourse of quality food. Quality food is food that is produced with minimal damage to the physical environment, which is safe to the consumer, and is high in nutritional values. It is food that is monitored, recorded and subjected to bureaucratic traceability controls at every stage of its evolution. It is, in other words, food that meets certain technical criteria; how its production affects the animals and human workers involved, or the rural neighbourhood in which it takes place, are treated as irrelevant. They embody social and not just scientific or technical criteria. (What goes unrecognized in this, of course, is that quality food is not necessarily eatable food, since food consumers often find that social issues affect their enjoyment of what they are eating; see, for example, Beardsworth and Keil, 1992, 1996.) In the organic movement discourse, sustainable development means bringing about social and structural change in contemporary agriculture. In the quality food discourse, sustainability is

125

defined technically, in terms of the impact of agriculture on natural resources and of nature's capacity to absorb this. In this way, it becomes a rationale for keeping social change at a minimum, replacing it with technical change. Agri-environmental schemes like REPS end up asking small dairy farmers to cut their costs and become more efficient milk producers - to survive by cutting costs - instead of mobilizing them, for example, to demand from the state a more equitable distribution of milk quota.

Conclusion

This chapter has argued, against Scott (1995), that the agri-environmental measures introduced into the CAP in 1992 are providing the opportunity for a new and different rationality to penetrate into the regulatory system for agriculture. I have identified this new rationality as a version of ecological modernization. What does this mean for the claim that European agriculture is today post-productivist?

Ward (1993) describes post-productivism as a new regime of accumulation in which the state has withdrawn from underwriting capitalist accumulation in the agro-food system. But as I have argued, Irish agriculture does appear to be still being managed by the state, on behalf of dominant economic interests. The emphasis is on continuing production and developing forms of production that enhance profitability, in the food industry as a whole, if less obviously in farming. Ecological modernization is widely understood, as Weale (1993) emphasizes, as a force for industrial innovation that supports and advances accumulation in capitalist industry. In many respects, this looks like a productivist regime of accumulation, even if the manner in which it is managed, and the problems of legitimacy and consent involved, are somewhat different from before.

It may be objected that the discourse of low-input, low-cost food production, which I have called eco-modernist, discourages farmers from buying industrially manufactured farm inputs, and to that extent constitutes a withdrawal of support by the state from capitalist accumulation in the agri-food system. However, what is happening seems to be less a blanket withdrawal than a restructuring of state support for agribusiness. Certain input manufacturers, such as chemical fertilizer companies, are losing business as a result of the new production rationality. Others, particularly those who control inputs of seed and breed (the global semen companies who own the bull who can produce the low-cost high-yield cow, the seed companies who sell the white clover mix which can replace chemical nitrogen fertilizer) find their business increasing. In an increasingly concentrated agribusiness world (Bonanno et al., 1994; Goodman and Watts, 1997), the companies which lose and those which gain are often owned by the same capital.

The rationality is changing but the regime of accumulation remains largely as before. So what can we conclude about the notion of a post-productivist rural Europe? Perhaps that the concept confuses more than it enlightens. My analysis of change in Irish agriculture suggests that what we are dealing with is simply the continuance of capitalism. Agri-environmental regulation seemed at first to endanger this, but through projects like REPS a way of reconciling environmental management and agricultural production, and creating a new consensus around technical development in farming, appears to have been found. One other thing we can safely conclude is that contemporary agriculture is not becoming post-modern. Ecological modernization is a discourse firmly rooted within modernity. It implies that solutions to the problems of industrial and risk society must be sought in the further modernization of modernity, not in attempts to transcend or disavow it. Agriculture may be moving beyond (simple) productivism, but what post-modernity might mean for rural societies remains to be theorized.

References

Baldock, D. and Lowe, P.D. (1996) The development of European agri-environment policy, in M.C. Whitby (ed.) *The European Environment and CAP Reform*, CAB International, Wallingford, pp.8-25.

Beardsworth, A. and Keil, T. (1992) The vegetarian option: varieties, conversions, motives and careers, *Sociological Review*, 40, pp.253-292.

Beardsworth, A. and Keil, T. (1996) *Sociology on the Menu*, Routledge, London.

Beck, U. (1992) *Risk Society: Towards a New Modernity*, translated by M. Ritter, Sage, London.

Billaud, J-P., Bruckmeier, K., Patricio, T. and Pinton, F. (1997) Social construction of the rural environment. Europe and discourses in France, Germany and Portugal, in H. de Haan, B. Kasimis and M.R. Redclift (eds.) *Sustainable Rural Development*, Ashgate, Aldershot, pp.9-34.

Bonanno, A., Busch, L., Friedland, W., Gouveia, L. and Mingione, E. (1994, eds.) *From Columbus to ConAgra: The Globalization of Agriculture and Food*, University of Kansas Press, Lawrence.

Buttel, F.H. (1994) Agricultural change, rural society and the state in the late twentieth century: some theoretical observations, in D. Symes and A.J. Jansen (eds.) *Agricultural Restructuring and Rural Change in Europe*, Wageningen Agricultural University, Wageningen, pp.13-31.

Commins, P. (1996) Agricultural production and the future of small-scale farming, in C. Curtin, T. Haase and H. Tovey (eds.) *Poverty in Rural Ireland*, Oak Tree Press, Dublin, pp.87-126.

Department of Agriculture, Food and Forestry (1994) *Rural Environment Protection Scheme - Farm Development Service: Agri-Environmental Specifications*, Dublin.

Department of the Environment (1997) *Sustainable Development: A Strategy for Ireland*, Government Stationery Office, Dublin.

Frawley, J.P. and Commins, P. (1996) *The Changing Structure of Irish Farming: Trends and Prospects*, Teagasc Rural Economy Research Series #1, Dublin.

Friedmann, H. (1993) After Midas Feast: alternative food regimes for the future, in P. Allen (ed.) *Food for the Future: Conditions and Contradictions of Sustainability*, Wiley, Chichester, pp.213-233.

Friedmann, J. and McMichael, H. (1989) Agriculture and the state system: the rise and decline of national agricultures, 1870 to the present, *Sociologia Ruralis*, 29, pp.93-117.

Goodman, D., Sorj, B. and Wilkinson, J. (1987) *From Farming to Biotechnology: A Theory of Agro-Industrial Development*, Blackwell, Oxford.

Goodman, D. and Watts, M.J. (1997, eds.) *Globalizing Food: Agrarian Questions and Global Restructuring*, Routledge, London.

Hajer, M.A. (1995) *The Politics of Environmental Discourse: Ecological Modernization and the Policy Process*, Clarendon, Oxford.

Hajer, M.A. (1996) Ecological modernization as cultural politics, in S. Lash, B. Szerszinski and B. Wynne (eds.) *Risk, Environment and Modernity*, Sage, London, pp.246-268.

Ilbery, B.W., Chiotti, Q. and Rickard, T. (1997) Introduction, in B.W. Ilbery, Q. Chiotti and T. Rickard (eds.) *Agricultural Restructuring and Sustainability*, CAB International, Wallingford.

Irish Farmers Journal (1997, 1998, various issues), Irish Farm Centre, Bluebell.

Izcara Palacios, S.P. (1998) Farmers and the implementation of the EU Nitrates Directive in Spain, *Sociologia Ruralis*, 38, pp.146-162.

Jokinen, P. (1997) Agricultural policy community and the challenge of greening: the case of Finnish agri-environmental policy, *Environmental Politics*, 6(2), pp.48-71.

Jokinen, P. and Niemi-Iilahti, A. (1997) 'The greening of agri-environmental policies?: the Finnish response to EU regulation 2078/92', paper presented to the XVII Congress of the European Society for Rural Sociology, Crete, 25-29 August 1997.

Kumar, J. (1995) *From Post-Industrial to Post-Modern Society*, Blackwell, Oxford.

Leavy, A. (1997) The Rural Environment Protection Scheme (REPS), *Farm and Food*, 7(1), pp.12-15.

Leeuwis, C. (1989) *Marginalization Misunderstood: Different Patterns of Farm Development in the West of Ireland*, Wageningen Agricultural University, Wageningen.

Marsden, T.K. (1992) Exploring a rural sociology for the Fordist transition: incorporating social relations into economic restructuring, *Sociologia Ruralis*, 22, pp.209-230.

O'Hara, P. and Commins, P. (1998) Rural development: towards the new century, in S. Healy and B. Reynolds (eds.) *Social Policy in Ireland*, Oak Tree Press, Dublin, pp.261-283.

Portela, J. (1994) Agriculture is primarily what?, in D. Symes and A.J. Jansen (eds.) *Agricultural Restructuring and Rural Change in Europe*, Wageningen Agricultural University, Wageningen, pp.32-48.

Redclift, M.R. (1997) Frontiers of consumption: sustainable rural economies and societies in the next century?, in H. de Haan, B. Kasimis and M.R. Redclift (eds.) *Sustainable Rural Development*, Ashgate, Aldershot, pp.35-50.

Scott, J. (1995) *Development Dilemmas in the European Community*, Open University Press, Buckingham.

Shucksmith, M. (1993) Farm household behaviour and the transition to post-productivism, *Journal of Agricultural Economics*, 44, pp.466-478.

Spaargaren, G. and Mol, A.P.J. (1992) Sociology, environment and modernity; ecological modernization as a theory of social change, *Society and Natural Resources*, 5, pp.323-344.

Tovey, H. (1993) Environmentalism in Ireland - two versions of development and modernity, *International Sociology*, 8, pp.413-430.

Tovey, H. (1994) Rural management, public discourses, and the farmer as environmental manager, in D. Symes and A.J. Jansen (eds.) *Agricultural Restructuring and Rural Change in Europe*, Wageningen Agricultural University, Wageningen, pp.209-219.

Tovey, H. (1997) Food, environmentalism and rural sociology: on the organic farming movement in Ireland, *Sociologia Ruralis*, 37, pp.21-37.

Tovey, H. (2000) Milk and modernity, in H. Schwarzweller and A.P. Davidson (eds) *International Perspectives on Dairying*, JAI Press, Greenwood, Connecticut.

Veerman, C.P. (1994) Agriculture at a turning point: from agricultural policy towards rural policy, in D. Symes and A.J. Jansen (eds.) *Agricultural Restructuring and Rural Change in Europe*, Wageningen Agricultural University, Wageningen, pp.311-323.

Ward, N. (1993) The agricultural treadmill and the rural environment in the post-productivist era, *Sociologia Ruralis*, 33, pp.348-364.

Weale, A. (1993) Ecological modernization and the integration of European environmental policy, in J.D. Liefferink, P.D. Lowe and A.J.P. Mol (eds.)

129

European Integration and Environmental Policy, London: Belhaven, pp.196-216.

Weber, M. (1978) *Economy and Society*, G. Roth and C. Wittich, eds., University of California Press, Berkeley.

Whitby, M.C. (1996) The prospect for agri-environmental policies within a reformed CAP, in M.C. Whitby (ed.) *The European Environment and CAP Reform*, CAB International, Wallingford, pp.227-240.

Winter, M. (1997) New policies and new skills: agricultural change and technology transfer, *Sociologia Ruralis*, 37, pp.363-382.

Yearley, S. (1991) *The Green Case*, Harper Collins Academic, London.

7 European processes of environmentalization in agriculture: a view from Spain

Angel Paniagua

Since the mid-1980s, the dominant trend in capitalist agriculture has seen a move toward a so-called post-productivist era (Ilbery and Bowler, 1998). This has coincided with substantial modifications to the 'social contract' between society and farmers, which previously gave rise to the flourishing convention of a protected agriculture. The new scenario stemmed from factors internal and external to the sector. Amongst these we may single out changes in environmental attitudes, increased demand for consumption-oriented environmental services in rural areas, lower valuations of food production and supply, the high cost of agricultural surpluses, the excessive budgetary impact of the Common Agricultural Policy (CAP) and improved farm incomes. In combination, these gave rise to institutional change and the emergence of new instruments for intervention in the sector (Deverre, 1995; Guglielmi, 1995). These changes in turn converted environmental issues in agriculture into complex phenomena, with far-ranging physical-ecological, social, economic and politico-institutional aspects (Deverre, 1995, pp.228-229). The issues involved not only concern environmental problems associated with agriculture, but relate to modifications in consumption patterns, alongside increased population mobility and broader opportunities for leisure and outdoor recreation. Perhaps without exaggeration, the post-productivist turn may be viewed as a triumph of society over farm production.

Yet manifestations of post-productivism are not uniform across Europe. For Spanish agriculture, increased concern for and sensitivity toward the environment (i.e. environmentalization) is complex; perhaps even exceptional in Europe. The national peculiarities that underlie the Spanish response draw on: the uniqueness of Spanish environmental problems, which are often linked to the peculiar climatic and biogeographical variety of the country; a weak tradition of implementing environmental measures; the expectations of the urban population regarding the countryside; the existence of less intensive farm operations compared with north-central Europe; the immature development of environmental groups; rural depopulation; and the complex allocation of administrative, agricultural and environmental authority across governmental tiers and units.

Set against this backcloth, this chapter explores how the post-productivist turn has impacted on Spanish society in three particular ways. It explores how social change has resulted in a new social relationship between agricultural producers and the rest of Spanish society, especially in terms of growing concerns about environmental conservation. These changes will be shown to be associated with an idealization of farmers' environmental role, although this imagery sharply contrasts with farmers' evaluations of environmental considerations in agricultural policy. Through an examination of public opinion surveys and the discourses of farmers and farm organizations, the second segment of the chapter lays the foundation for the last section which examines reasons for the laggardly implementation of agri-environmental policies in Spain. In order to place the value stances and issues that surround agri-environmental policy in Spain, the first part of the chapter explores the peculiarities of Spanish (agri-)environmental problems in a European context.

Agriculture, rural areas and environmental problems in Spain

Change in Spanish agriculture since the 1960s initially saw an evolution from rather traditional productive practices into a 'modern' sector, as conventionally seen in farming systems in north-central Europe. Associated with this has been the introduction of production changes with very evident environmental repercussions. In general terms, 'modernization' has led to decline in the agricultural population, which has been matched by an increase in the area farmed per person, increased mechanization, the greater utilization of fossil energies and a marked rise in pesticide use. Illustrating the trend, during the 1980s the mean average area cultivated per farmer increased by 38.7% (from 3.3 to 4.6 hectares). This fact alone brought landscape change associated with the loss or modification of traditional jobs and types of cultivation, by altered field boundaries and new farm structures, and by a deterioration in rural housing consequent upon depopulation. As one illustration, on the Mediterranean coast, more than half the terracing is in a state of dereliction, which has led to increasing degradation of the landscape as well as heightened soil erosion (Commission of the European Communities, 1992).

Intensified farm production has also seen expression in a rise in energy consumption. At the end of the 1980s absolute consumption levels stood at 2,420 million tonnes of oil equivalent (toe), which placed Spain in third place behind France and the Netherlands in an EU context. This figure was significantly higher than that recorded in the mid-1970s, with a 63.5% rise in energy consumption per hectare from then until 1986 (Economic Commission for Europe, 1992, p.268). This increase was associated with the use of machinery that permitted working with soil qualities and on slopes that were hitherto inaccessible. Indirectly these changes increased the threat of soil erosion, with an added threat from the replacement of traditional agricultural systems, as they were more energy efficient (Economic Commission for Europe, 1992).

A further environmental impact of intensification arose from a gradual increase in the use of fertilizer and pesticides. Today, consumption of pesticides in Spain is a little over six kilograms to a hectare of Utilized Agricultural Area (UAA). However, application is concentrated in the Mediterranean provinces, where consumption may reach 20 kg/ha. (e.g. Tout, 1990). Pesticide usage is especially high for fruit and vegetables (Secretaria General de Medio Ambiente, 1990, p.151 et seq.).[1] For fertilizer, consumption is just over 2 million tonnes a year, which represents 100 kg/UAA ha. Again there is unevenness in application, with concentrations leading to the greatest risk of fertilizer pollution in market gardening areas on the Mediterranean coast, in extensive irrigated areas along river basins (where fertilizer use can contaminate surface and ground water supplies) and in areas of intensive livestock farming. A productivist ethos creates a further significant problem through the dominance of agriculture in Spanish water consumption. Some 65% of national water use is destined for the farm sector, with over-irrigation as a major cause of the salinization of soils (Szabolcs, 1991), as seen in some 99 Spanish aquifers now suffering from over-exploitation problems. But again we need to note the geographically focused impact of such effects, for, unlike many north-central European countries, 60% of cultivable land in Spain is under extensive cultivation, with low-intensity dry (*seco*) farming widespread (Donazar *et al.*, 1997, p.118).

The magnitude of environmental problems associated with agricultural practices is evident in soil erosion. This is especially problematical given dominant environmental conditions within the country (topography, climate, etc.), even if these conditions are significantly attenuated by human practices (Dirección General de Medio Ambiente, 1989). In all, 44% of the country is affected by soil erosion above tolerable levels (Palacio, 1993, p.44). The mean soil loss is 23.4 tonnes/ha/year. Of this, 73% takes place under dry-cultivation, whether for tree products, vines or arable crops, with almost 11% occurring on land that is uncultivated or covered with brush and scattered trees (Secretaria General de Medio Ambiente, 1991, p.160). In all, more than 15 million hectares of dry farming land (30% of the Spanish total) requires soil conservation treatment. With desertification closely linked to soil erosion, it is no surprise that one million hectares of Spanish territory have already been labelled 'desert', with a further seven million potentially coming under this heading in the near future (Dirección General de Medio Ambiente, 1988). Under post-1992 CAP regulations, the volume of unproductive land has risen, as has the area under forestry. Both trends are prevalent in southern Europe, with each encouraging lower rural population densities. In itself this is an influence on rural environmental degradation (Paniagua, 1997a).

Adding to these problems are farmland losses resulting from urban development. It is true that the built-up area in Spain covers barely 3.9% of the total land surface, which is small compared with other European countries (the figure is 15.4% in the Netherlands, 13.5% in Germany, and 5.4% in France; Economic Commission for Europe, 1992). Nevertheless, land under agricultural uses or with natural vegetation is gradually being lost. This tendency is apparent in practically every European country (Commission of the European Communities, 1992, p.41). In Germany, for instance, the mean loss of agricultural land has been 6.9 m² per person per year since 1981. In Belgium the figure is 8.9, and in Luxembourg 16.3. To set beside these, there are no reliable statistics on land-use conversion in Spain. We only have rough estimates to base judgements on. If we take the non-agricultural land area in the *Anuario de Estadística Agraria* (Ministerio de Agricultura, Pesca y Alimentación, annual 1980-1994), then between 1980 and 1994 this increased by 192,600 hectares (10.4%). This puts the mean consumption of land by non-agricultural activities at 3.2 m² per person per year. Most losses were at the expense of farmland, which declined by 5,170,400 hectares. However, numerical losses hide much of the impact of land conversion, because development processes tend to take place on the best land, much of which is irrigated, where the topographical features - notably the flatness of the land - are more suited to building.

Of all environmental problems arising in Spanish rural areas, one of the most visible is the proliferation of forest fires. This phenomenon is connected with increased erosion and desertification (Medalus Office 1993, 1996; Garrido and Moyano 1996). Over the last 30 years there has been a steady increase in the number of fires, although there is considerable variation across years, with 1981, 1985, 1989 and 1994 seeing the area burnt reaching exceptional levels. Nonetheless, the increasing significance of fires must be noted, not simply in terms of economic losses but also as regards environmental impact. This is understandable when it is noted that 9,031 fires broke out in the five-year period 1965/69, whereas the figure was 58,516 for the period 1985/89, and 74,836 for 1990/94 (Ministerio de Agricultura, Pesca y Alimentación, annual). This sustained increase was accompanied by a six-fold rise in the area burnt, which has exceeded a million hectares over the last five years. Significantly, the loss of primary product and amenity benefits is well above the increased incidence of fires or the land area affected. Thus, figures in the *Anuario de Estadística Agraria* indicate that since 1965/69 primary product losses have increased more than thirty-fold (by value), whereas losses in environmental services or benefits have gone up sixty-fold (Ministerio de Agricultura, Pesca y Alimentación, annual). This is indicative of the ever-growing seriousness of the fire problem, for it commonly affects woodlands in a better state of conservation, which contain highly appreciated species in biological and social terms. At the same time, drought conditions since the beginning of the 1990s have seen an increase in pests and disease affecting woodlands, so the nation's forest resources have suffered considerable deterioration. Illustrative of this, the estimate for 1990 was that 4.6% of the trees in Spain were in a damaged condition. This compared with the EU figure of 15.1%. But by 1994 the Spanish figure had risen to 19.4% compared with an EU level of around 16% (Ministerio de Agricultura, Pesca y Alimentación, annual).

In the various ways the rural environment is directly or indirectly connected with agriculture, there is considerable scope for the generation of environmental problems. For the most part, the causes of such problems are interrelated, which makes analysis of their political and socio-territorial implications complex. The singular nature of environmental problems in Spanish agriculture provides a particular twist to the incidence of environmental problems. This peculiarity is apparent in the breadth of incidence, as well as in the nature of the processes that generate environmental problems (compared to other European countries).

The impact of economic and social change on environmentalization

Alongside the increased incidence of ecological problems, growth in environmental concerns in Spain have been fuelled by changes of a socio-economic and demographic nature (Hoggart et al., 1995, pp.235-236). An important consideration in this regard is modification of consumption habits. For several generations now, citizens have had confidence in their food supplies. This is despite the fact that, according to the Instituto Nacional de Estadística's (INE) annual family budget survey, *Encuesta de Presupuestos Familiares* (EPF), the proportion of the average family budget devoted to food has fallen from 38% in 1973/74 to 23.9% in 1994. Added to this, links between food plate and farm commodities have become more indirect, as consumption of processed foodstuffs has increased sharply. In 1973, processed foods accounted for 21.3% of the family food budget, whereas the latest EPF (1993) puts the figure at 45.8% of spending (Abad Balboa et al., 1994, p.86). Changes in food consumption have had two main consequences. First, they have reduced the importance of farm products in the final food commodity, with the post-farm processing accounting for a greater share of food prices. Additionally, there has been a growing 'artificialization' of food, with food consumption more removed from the produce that leaves the farm. One consequence has been greater food variety (this effect being enhanced by reduced transport costs increasing the availability of non-local foods), which has increased consumer power in food purchasing decisions (Mili, 1997).

Table 7.1
Percentage of total household expenditure on food in the EU in 1984, 1988 and 1992

	1984	1988	1992
Austria			19.1
Belgium	22.2	19.8	17.3
Denmark	24.6	22.3	20.7
France	21.3	19.6	18.3
Finland			23.2
Germany	18.0	16.4	15.0
Greece	42.5	38.2	36.4
Ireland	42.4	40.6	34.8
Italy	29.1	22.7	20.1
Luxembourg	21.3	21.1	18.2
Netherlands	19.8	18.7	14.6
Portugal	37.0 *	37.1	32.1
Spain	31.0	26.1	20.0
Sweden			19.9
UK	19.9	17.1	20.7
EU12	23.7	21.6	19.9
EU15			19.7

Note: * data for 1982
Source: Eurostat (1996)

As a consequence of these changes, the share of Spanish consumer spending devoted to food is practically at the European average, and is below the level in other southern European countries, such as Greece and Portugal. In this respect the situation of Spain lies mid-way between these southern European countries and those of north-central Europe, occupying a similar position to Italy (Table 7.1). This trend in food consumption is linked to increases in per capita income, as well as changed life styles, with a growing appreciation of leisure time, which involves increased enjoyment of nature, amongst other things.

A second change is increased transport mobility, as revealed by the latest reports on this matter (e.g. Ruiz Olabuenaga, 1994). Associated with this, there is improved accessibility to the countryside and demand for outdoor activities is continually increasing. This phenomenon is accompanied by two processes with marked socio-territorial implications. First of all, we should note the importance of second home ownership in rural municipalities (i.e. those with a population of under 2,000). Today 38% of dwellings in these municipalities are second homes (e.g. Barke 1991). This is partly a consequence of former out-migrants retaining ownership of a dwelling and making seasonal returns (e.g. Mansvelt Beck, 1988). It also results from an increased desire to utilize the natural resources and values associated with rural areas (peace and quiet, relaxation, etc.). This phenomenon is important in coastal districts and in such inland regions as Castilla y León, where the proportion of second homes is 38.3%, or Castilla-La Mancha, where it stands at 46.7% (Nomenclator, 1994). Secondly, in certain inland areas there has been considerable expansion in rural tourism establishments and hotel bed spaces. As a specific example, in Castilla y León, there were 40 establishments offering 319 beds in 1994, which had risen to 105 establishments with 865 beds within a year (Junta de Castilla y León, 1996). Rural tourism growth is seen in many parts of Spain, with recent EU initiatives like LEADER having a substantial effect in encouraging its promotion (e.g. Barke and Newton, 1994). Both these processes mean that the social demands on agriculture and rural areas have changed. Less importance is attached to the productive function of agriculture, with more emphasis on its recreational and environmental functions.

A third change is the rise in standards of living. This has impacted on the income of farmers. Traditionally, one of the pillars supporting the age-old 'classic social contract' was the disadvantageous position of the farming community with regard to amenities and services (García Fernández, 1995). This was linked to their living environment, and to the fact that farm incomes were below those in manufacturing. Nowadays, household amenities and services in agriculture are still below the national average (Cuadrado and Tio, 1992),[2] even if this is largely due to the age of rural dwellings and to a system of access amongst agricultural workers that emphasizes inheritance and the purchase of existing (old) dwellings. In addition, according to the comprehensive review of services provided in the *Banesto Market Yearbook* (Banesto, 1989), communal services and business licenses were significantly lower in municipalities with a population of less than 3,000 than in those exceeding this figure. Illustrative of this, with the national index value at 100, these settlements recorded a value of 61 for business service licenses and 72 for pupils enrolled in compulsory secondary education. Accessibility has improved considerably, however, and today it is often harder to traverse a large city than it is to reach a district capital from a small village (Ruiz Olabuenaga, 1994).

Moreover, if we consider unemployment and earned income, the trend is more favourable for the agricultural community than for the population as a whole. Thus, unemployment in the primary sector is significantly lower than in the other sectors. In 1993, just 6.1% of the working farm population was unemployed - albeit this figure might have been lowered by outmigration - whereas for manufacturing it stood at 14.9%, with 31.8% in service industries (INE, 1994). Add to this a recent study conducted by the Instituto Nacional de Estadistica and the University of Alcalá de Henares, which shows that the average income of farm households has risen rapidly in the last 10 years. At constant 1986 prices, the 1980 income of a farm household was 1,839,455 pesetas, compared with the average net figure for the country of 2,121,453 pesetas (viz. 86.7% of the national average). By 1993, the average income of Spanish households had risen to 2,351,162 pesetas, whereas for farm households it now amounted to 2,362,988 pesetas (100.5%, *El Pais*, 6 July 1995). According to these figures, in the last 15 years the income of farm households has risen four times more rapidly than for the rest of the population. Although this situation might partly be a consequence of decline in the agricultural working population, so productive income is shared over a smaller number, this improvement has been noted by the general population. Some 47% of those questioned in opinion surveys have indicated that they think those who work in the countryside live better today than 10 years ago (*La Tierra*, 141, 1997, p.14). Consequently, the image that the agricultural community is relatively deprived has gradually faded. There is little doubt that this change owes much to accession to the EU, and the impact of CAP support on farm income (Etxezarreta and Viladomiu, 1989; San Juan Mesonada, 1993). But we must again note regional differences, for EU accession had its most positive effects on regions specializing in crops like fruit and vegetables, olive oil and wine (Mykolenko *et al.*, 1987).

A fourth change is decline in the number of people employed in agriculture and the reduced importance of agricultural workers in rural townships. According to *Encuesta de Población Activa* (INE, annual), the number of farm employees fell by 445,700 between 1989 and 1996 (30.9%). During this period, the agricultural sector saw its share of the working population slip from 14.6% to 7.9%. Although decline has affected all European countries, it has had a special impact in southern Europe. In part this is due to the high share of their population in farming at the start of the 1980s (Hoggart *et al.*, 1995, p.59), alongside significant changes in the sector since 1980 (Abad Balboa *et al.*, 1994). For instance, between 1980 and 1993, the agricultural population in Spain fell by 46%, in Italy by 48% and in Portugal by 53%, compared with a drop of 37% for the EU15 as a whole. This sharp decline has meant a loss of social and political weight in policy determination. It has changed the balance of political weight for social groups concerned with the rural environment. Even in municipalities with fewer than 2,000 residents, by 1991 only 33.4% of the working population worked in agriculture. Today the figure is much less.

This set of circumstances, which originate in socio-economic and territorial processes with different origins, but which coincide in inducing a particular pattern of change in the rural environment, make clear that the exchange of interests between citizens and farmers has been modified. Critical to this change has been the decisive introduction of environmental considerations that require a new social legitimation for agriculture and for farmers. Although these processes of change are inter-national in nature, they display special features in southern Europe that affect the rate of environmentalization. These stem, in part, from the 'start-points' of the southern Europe nations. These 'start-points' are quite different from those in north-central Europe, especially as regards consumer habits, expectations about the utilization of the countryside, and the social and political influence of farmers in rural affairs.

Public opinion on agriculture and environmental problems

As shown by various opinion polls,[3] major environmental problems in agriculture are little recognized by the general public. Thus, in a survey conducted by the CIRES Foundation in 1994, only 1.8% of the Spanish population believe that finding a solution to the problems caused by the use of pesticides in agriculture is a national priority. Just 4.3% thought it should be a local priority. Likewise, desertification, an issue of extreme gravity in Spain that is connected with increasing agricultural intensification, is rated even lower than pesticide usage as an issue meriting attention. Indeed, most of those interviewed in opinion surveys believe that agriculture is neither detrimental to the environment nor to nature (51.8%), or only has slightly negative effects (26.9%, both figures are from the CIS-96 survey).

The same tendencies have been recorded in other European countries. However, it is worth noting that Spain is second only to Greece amongst European countries in attaching little importance to pollution of an agricultural origin (Table 7.2). Relatively speaking, the agricultural sector in Spain enjoys a relatively favourable environmental rating. Two main factors explain this. First, agricultural pollution is a secondary item on the agendas of environmental groups in Spain. Second, farming systems that use low levels of fertilizer and pesticide are widespread in Spain, as seen in large tracts of open pasture land. These are regarded as the stereotypical rural landscape.

Table 7.2
Public beliefs about the environmental consequences of agriculture in the EU

% believing that

	Excessive consumption of fungicides, herbicides and insecticides have a serious effect on the environment		The economic sector with the greatest environmental consequence is agriculture
	1992	1995	1995
Belgium	29	33	22
Denmark	27	46	23
France	36	36	28
Germany	30	35	19
Greece	20	31	10
Ireland	37	35	24
Italy	45	49	22
Luxembourg	32	29	32
Netherlands	40	31	34
Portugal	32	16	26
Spain	21	26	15
UK	32	32	16
EU12	32	33	23

Source: Commission of the European Communities (series)

Public opinion on farmers and rural areas

For 77% of Europeans, farmers contribute to the conservation of the environment through their professional activities. This view is more widely held in southern than in north-central Europe, and is especially prevalent in Portugal and Spain (Commission of the European Communities, 1988). Spanish surveys undertaken by the Fundación General de la Universidad Complutense (1993) and CIRES (1992), as quoted in De Miguel (1994, p.666 et seq.), show that farming is one of the highest rated professions. This not simply due not to a farmer's food producing function, but also because of the supposed direct relationship farmers have with nature, alongside an idealization of the farmer's way of life. The CIRES-92 survey shows that small-scale farmers are seen to have a more direct relationship with the natural environment, and this group has the highest social rating of any occupation (small-scale and large-scale farmers were distinguished as occupational groups in the CIRES-92 survey). The CIRES-92 survey enables us to address another aspect of public opinion on the countryside, for it asked how the rural environment is rated as a place of residence. Here it was found that 43.3% of people would like to live in a village, with a population of 5,000 or less, compared with only 21.8% who would rather live in cities with a population of half a million or more. This idealization of small, necessarily rural places of residence, reflects the geographical identification of respondents with local places of residence (whether village or town). In Spain such sentiments are much stronger than those recorded for province, Autonomous Community or country (see Brenan, 1950, on the strength of local sentiments in Spain). From evidence in the CIRES-94 survey, the overwhelming majority of people who define their present habitat as a village wish to go on living in the same type of place (a village being defined as a settlement with less than 5,000 inhabitants). By contrast, 25.4% of residents of a large town/city would change their place residence to a village, if they were able to, with 30% of residents in small towns sharing this sentiment. This positive rating for villages stems from idealizations of rural life, from positive visions about contact with nature, and from the values attributed to this environment (peace and quiet, relaxation, absence of anonymity; Paniagua and Gomez, 1996). The rural environment is not rated adversely, despite its lack of services and amenities, alongside fewer opportunities for professional work, but is seen as a different environment from the urban. In-migration to such places is expected to lead to a change in lifestyle. Landscape deterioration, soil pollution, soil erosion, the deterioration of woodlands, and the destruction of traditional housing, are all visible in abundance in rural areas, but they do not appear to impact on the mental images of most respondents to opinion polls (Gomez et al., 1997).

In short, farmers, as the leading actors in the rural environment, and the environment itself, are perceived favourably by the general public. As one illustration, surveys carried out by farmers' unions signal that the Spanish population, which is largely urban in residence, view farm subsidies and EU aid for farmers favourably. They also accept the imposition of special taxes that would fund continuous support for farm production and the preservation of landscape (e.g. Ayudas, 1999). This is important for assessing new agri-environmental policies and the environmentalization of rural areas. Put simply, in southern Europe, and in Spain very noticeably, there is no groundswell of public demand for increased environmental regulation of agriculture. The general perception of the environmental effects of agriculture is favourable, as a productive activity and as a land-use.

Farmers and environmental problems

What this points to is the importance of farmers' own attitudes towards the environment. How farmers perceive and rate the problems of their local environment is of particular importance because of the voluntary nature of agri-environmental policy measures (Wilson, 1996). To consider farmer attitudes, the analysis that follows examines two aspects of farmer values. The first uses opinion surveys to identify general trends in farmers' views on the environment and, more particularly, how they evaluate problems linked to their productive activities. The second element is farmers' collective discourses, which are represented by examining the attitudes of agricultural unions toward environmental issues.

Farmers' opinions on agri-environmental problems

Compared with other occupational groups, opinion surveys reveal a low degree of environmental sensitivity amongst farmers. Illustrative of this, in the CIS-96 survey, only 18.4% of farmers attached importance to environmental deterioration, compared with 23.9% of the population as a whole. Indeed, 90% of Spanish farmers think that their productive behaviour contributes to conserving the environment. These sentiments coincide with indices in *Eurobarometer* (Commission of the European Communities, 1988), which show that European farmers have a more positive environmental evaluation of their work than the population as a whole. Yet the environmental attitudes of Spanish farmers appear to be exceptional compared with views in other southern European countries. In other southern European countries, the overwhelming view amongst farmers is that farming helps conserve the environment. This view is not held with as much force as in Spain (Commission of the European Communities, 1988). Spain's farmers are little disposed to take specific action geared toward environmental protection or improvement. Their degree of association with 'green' sentiments is very low, with only 5% of farm business owners ready to participate in environmental groups, while 95% assert that they not only do not and do not want to belong to one. Farmers see environmental associations as seeking behaviour that is contrary to the productivist objectives of farmers.

When asked about their attitude to paying higher prices for protecting the environment, farmers are the least favourably predisposed of all occupational groups, according to the CIRES-94 survey. In all, 33.3% are opposed to any such action. Similarly, farmers are the least favourably disposed to paying higher taxes in return for environmental protection (47.5% claim to be against or strongly against such a step, whereas no other occupational category recorded a value as high as 30% for this position). However, when farmers' productive interests are threatened they are more favourably disposed to raising taxes to solve the environmental problem than the population at large. Thus, 60.7% of farmers are prepared to pay higher taxes to prevent desertification, compared with 54.9% of the general population.

All these statistics, which reflect low environmental sensitivity and a slight predisposition towards action that does not carry personal benefit, are rounded-off by feelings of mistrust regarding environmental protection measures and by scant recognition of their necessity. In order to add some flesh to the sentiments expressed in these statistical indicators, an examination of farmers' agri-environmental discourses was undertaken using eight (1997-1998) focus group discussions in Castilla y León and Andalucía. These revealed remarkable similarities with discourses in national-level debates. The key components of farmers' agri-environmental discourses identified in these focus group sessions are:

• That growing concerns about the environment are associated with the existence of environmental problems and with the spread of greater ecological sensitivity from urban to rural areas. Yet, in its origins, the emphasis on environmental protection is urban. The aim of ecological ideas that lie behind conservation pressures in farming areas is to exclude certain activities and these are mainly of an agricultural nature.

• The farmer is the ecologist in rural areas, who lives in these areas and is a part of nature.

• An underlying assumption in discourses of 'agri-environmentalism' is that low productivity and low inputs are necessary for sensitive farm production. Set against this, farmers are expected to produce commodities cheaply for urban consumers. In making these demands agriculture is hardly seen as an economic sector. To attain cheap food it can be necessary to incur environmental 'damage' (as portrayed in environmental sentiments at least).

• The farmer has to oppose present agri-environmental measures as the costs they impose on farmers are too high and they cover too extensive a geographical area. In their application, agri-environmental regulations are too rigid in a temporal sense (causing conflict with the agricultural production calendar), are excessively bureaucratic and mainly offer poor economic compensations. In addition, the ideas that underlie agri-environmental measures reinforce the position of non-professional farmers, as they call for low inputs, which make it possible to farm while living in an urban centre.

Given these sentiments, and the implied advantages for urban dwellers, it is little surprise that there is hostility toward agri-environmental measures. Whether it is wishful thinking or not, of all occupational groups, farm business owners contend most strongly that environmental protection policy is just a fad (10.5% versus a national mean of 3.8%). This does not help induce their cooperation with agri-environmental measures. Indeed, farmers are much more likely to see objectives other than the environment as of greater consequence for their sector (73.7% versus a mean population figure of

53.6%). In short, there is little environmental sensitivity on the part of farmers and a low rating for environmental action. This undoubtedly affects the implementation of agri-environmental regulations. Added to which, despite a greater sensitivity to the need for positive environmental action, the public at large does not make noteworthy calls for a change in the professional conduct of farmers, not at least in Spain (or in other southern European countries).

Unions, farmers and the rural environment in Spain[4]

Given the concerns expressed by farmers toward environmentalist discourses, it is no surprise that agricultural trade unions are deeply concerned about the infusion of conservationist criteria into agricultural policy-making. For some years Spain's agricultural unions have seen responses to such concerns as integral to their action and, in a few cases, have even changed their organizational structures in order to better respond to environmental concerns.

To examine the representation of environmental problems amongst agricultural trade unions, the discourses of two Professional Agricultural Organizations (PAOs) are examined here. The first is the Asociación Sindical de Jovenes Agricultores (ASAJA) / Consejo Nacional de Jovenes Agricultores (CNJA), which represent the agriculture-as-business model (Moyano, 1993). The second is the Unión de Pequeños Agricultores (UPA), which is linked to the socialist Unión General de Trabajadores (UGT). This represents the viewpoint of left-wing agricultural trade unionism, which brings with it a neo-rural discourse. There are differences in the discourses of these two union options, but there are also two main points of agreement. Firstly, there is a shared sentiment that the imposition of the 'environmental guardian' function on farmers should be accompanied by new sources of income, to replace the loss of earnings caused by any limitation on farmers' productive capacity. In other words, both union groups see the need to associate a decrease in 'productivity bonuses' with an increase in 'conservation bonuses'. Such an alteration in the nature of farm subsidies is seen by these unions as a qualitative change in the 'social contract' farmers maintain with the rest of society. Such a change is envisaged as leading to a shift from the productivist approach which has been the norm under CAP towards a conservationist one. Secondly, there is acknowledgement that environmental problems can result from the nature of agricultural activity (albeit this is viewed in dissimilar ways by different agricultural unions as to origins, agents involved, nature and extent). No discourse is comprehensively articulated on this subject. The discourse maintained by PAOs is built around the idea that the environmental function is a key element in the process of social re-legitimation for farmers. Even so, arguments of an environmental nature, such as over the virtue of limiting the use of products that protect plant health, pesticides, soil resting, etc., barely appear in agricultural union discourses in comparison with abundant references to professional or production matters. Indeed, commentaries on the application of environmental measures reveal the complexity of the issues involved and the sense that deficits will accrue for farmers in the implementation of environmental measures owing to their social and productive consequences.

Apart from these points of agreement, the PAOs have different approaches to environmental issues. Within their 'traditional' discourse, agriculture-as-business unions contrast the rural environment with the urban, which they consider to be primarily responsible for environmental deterioration and for problems in rural areas. Their argument is that up to the 1980s there was a call for a reliable food supply at reasonable prices. Meeting these targets led to the adoption of the 'industrialized' production methods that are now criticized. For these unions, the ultimate responsibility for the pollution of the land lies not with the producers but with those who placed demands on the farm sector; by which they mean consumers, most of whom live in urban areas. In so far as specific policies and instruments of intervention are concerned, contradictions in EU guidelines are highlighted by these unions. For example, there is forthright criticism of planned lines of forestry action being associated with the so-called 'crisis of agriculture'. These groups insist that there needs to be a clear separation of agricultural policy and environmental policy, rather than confusing the two (as they see happening in forestry policy). In general, there is a critical attitude towards measures to discourage farm production (e.g. set-aside), especially given the view that such measures help non-professional (part-time) farmers and encourage emigration from (or short-term, second-home residence in) rural areas.

In contrast with other agricultural organizations, the 'left-wing' Unión de Pequeños Agricultores includes environmental concerns in its political ideology, as well as in its union practices. Despite this, the discourses of this organization have a clearly professional and business orientation, based on the expectation that more ecologically sensitive agriculture will increase the earnings of small farmers who focus on quality produce, especially in low-income or upland farming areas. For this organization, the introduction of stronger environmental requirements into farming should lessen or remove the comparative advantages of medium- and large-sized farms. As such these measures would represent a means of increasing the competitiveness of small-scale farms, which is expected to bring an increase in their earnings. This organization also believes that environmental measures and instruments should be part of a broad rural development strategy directed toward sustaining the population of rural areas. For both sets of organization, then, there is an unequivocal rejection of land abandonment policies (even in the form of set-aside), especially when applied indiscriminately (viz. not targeted in response to a specific problem). This is because land abandonment is seen to raise risks for the socio-economic and environmental sustainability of rural areas.

The politics of agri-environmental policies in Spain

Until the 1980s rural Spain was the subject of 'unintended' inputs from national economic and social policies, rather than being a focus for the implementation of specific environmental, conservationist or landscape policies. For the 'urban user of the countryside', up to that point, conflicts between agricultural production and environmental deterioration were almost imperceptible (whether in terms of soil deterioration, desertification, landscape desecration or water pollution). At the European Union level, a similar point could be made, for EU environment policy has paid greater attention to urban and industrial pollution, with those stemming from the management of natural resources on a lower plane (Secretaria General de Medio Ambiente, 1991, p.151). Agri-environmental policy can be seen to have originated through the evolution of CAP, rather than as an outcome of environmental policy deliberations (Baldock and Lowe, 1996). In particular, the introduction of agri-environmental measures, and the consequent development of such programmes, was primarily concerned with a desire to reduce farm surpluses and reduce the CAP budget, rather than to infuse farm production with environmental sensitivity (Lowe and Ward, 1994).

EU agri-environmental legislation specifies that every Member State may determine its own 'sensitive areas', zones that qualify for agri-environmental payments, as well as determining which production practices are consistent with environmental protection, alongside specifying standards and norms for production in designated areas. One result of this flexibility is that there is substantial scope for basic principles to be adapted in every country, and (in some nations) even every region. Agri-environmental regulations consequently have been adopted in accordance with the specific needs of Member States. This impedes inter-state comparisons of the effectiveness of such policies, as well as assessments of the impact of EU directives (Wilson, 1995, p.149). As underlined previously, cultural attitudes to the environment vary tremendously in Europe. This gives rise to different interests being expressed by different social actors and to varied methods of implementation for agri-environmental measures (Clark *et al.*, 1997).

The development of environmental regulation in Spanish agriculture

The development of environmental policy in Spain has been linked, on the one hand, to joining the EU and, on the other hand, to the transfer of political authority to Spain's Autonomous Communities (AACC) (Paniagua *et al.*,

1998). A similar process has taken place in other Mediterranean countries, such as Italy (Bianchi, 1992; La Spina and Sciortino, 1993). For Spain, the real process of environmental regulation began in 1986, when European legislation was adapted to the characteristics and needs of the Spanish situation. Taking the lead of the EU, and adapting to Spain's circumstances, continues to be the dominant Spanish response, practically to the present-day (Paniagua *et al.*, 1998). However, a transfer of authority for environmental matters has taken place, which has resulted in each Autonomous Community drawing up legislation in accordance with its own environmental and socio-economic circumstances. This has meant that environmental policies have been enacted in abundance, with 3,569 pieces of environmental legislation between 1986 and 1995 (a rate of 357 a year). This intensive legislative effort has affected rural areas through a welter of protection and conservation measures, with 69 national and 917 Autonomous Community regulations in the first 10 years of Spain's EU membership. However, this process of heightened environmental regulation has not been directed toward changing farmers' professional practices, but has protected and regulated the integrated use of natural spaces with proven environmental value and/or which are in high demand for leisure and recreational. The result has been a proliferation of declarations naming places and zones as protected spaces. Hence, while there were 46 protected natural spaces in 1987, the figure had risen to 518 by 1994, with an average size of these zones of 5,870 hectares. As a result, the area designated as protected natural space now occupies a similar percentage of Spain's land area to that found in other southern European countries, although the figure is below that in the Netherlands or the United Kingdom, both of whom have a longer tradition of protective environmental designation. In addition, protective designations in Spain have not been accompanied by action on agricultural practices outside specified areas of natural value.

To make this point more generally, the introduction of agricultural regulations with a noteworthy environmental component is meagre within Spain (Garrido and Moyano, 1996). Prior to EU agri-environmental regulations, the Spanish experience of introducing environmental considerations into farm production was practically non-existent. Policies on extensification and grants for environmental action in sensitive areas were either not available at all or were very limited in extent. Even recently, efforts to enhance environmental inputs into agricultural practices have met with a mixed response; partly as a result of being introduced during a period of political change. This is illustrated by the 1995 integrated strategy for nature conservation, which was introduced by the Ministry of Agriculture. Called the National Strategy for Integrated Nature Conservancy (ENCINA), this measure was marked by its rural character, and was intended to establish a frame of reference for activity by the Ministry, as well as for other agents in the agricultural sector. The document, which adopted sustainable development and environmentalist ideals of north-central European countries, aimed to orient the activities of professionals and agricultural authorities toward preserving non-renewable resources. This policy was drawn up under the Socialist Government, but has not been effectively implemented. Under the Centre-Right Government elected in 1996, the system of protected natural spaces and parks, which was the main environmental instrument of the previous Government, has been transferred from agricultural authorities to a new Ministry of the Environment. Added to which, the new Government's standpoint on sustainable agriculture combines a 'traditional agricultural ethos' (the good farmer, the farmers' knowledge of the environment, the 'eternal order of the fields') with a certain rural 'nationalism', which is associated with the preservation of the landscape and of rural values, together with introduction of suitable technological development. Embodied within the Government's approach is a disparity between strategic statements, that draw on objectives from CAP agri-environmental programmes and the conclusions of the 1992 Rio Conference, and the implementation of these sentiments in the instruments employed. At the heart of the matter is the manner in which implementation can be adapted to the special interests of social agents, alongside a lack of action coordination across the Autonomous Communities. In this setting, strategic statements commonly play a rhetorical role, rather than actually directing the implementation process.

Approaches of the agri-environmental programme and implementation process

The agri-environmental programme is the basic and single instrument for the development of environmental principles in rural areas of Spain. Despite this, there was delay in the introduction of agri-environmental measures compared with other countries. There are five main reasons for this: (1) there was concern about negative side effects that could emerge as a consequence of the special demographic, social and productive nature of the low-density Spanish rural environment; (2) there was relatively little agreement amongst the different social agents involved, both at the same hierarchical level of government and across governmental tiers, regarding the effectiveness and timeliness of agri-environmental measures; (3) there were felt to be financial difficulties entailed in the application of agri-environmental measures, especially pertaining to the prospect of EU budget cuts for the farm sector; (4) there were anticipated possible implementation problems caused by divisions in administrative authority between the national government and the Autonomous Communities, as well as between different agencies within each; and, (5) there were misgivings within the Spanish Government over the measures proposed, which saw expression in a belief that the environmental actions proposed were designed principally for north-central Europe and were not easily adapted to Mediterranean problems, such as aridity and desertification, nor to extensive or semi-extensive farming systems.

Thus, of the new CAP accompanying measures, the agri-environmental ones were the last to be introduced into Spanish agriculture. Their recent introduction reflects an institutional acknowledgement that farmers are to be asked to perform a new function for the benefit of society as a whole. In this respect, the agri-environmental programme enshrines the farmer's role of environmental guardian, at least in social terms (Secretaria General de Estructuras Agrarias, 1994). When negotiations on agri-environmental measures got underway, the view of the Ministry of Agriculture was that these measures should supplement the income of farmers, rather than primarily bringing benefits for the environment:

> This measure, which, in principle, will receive more support than other instruments, is meant to be the axis of the reform, in the sense that this measure would be a complement to the incomes of farmers. It is thus a measure that is defined in a way that different concepts can be included. (1991 memo of the Cabinet of the Ministry, 'Incidencia financiera para España de la reforma de la PAC')

In negotiations with the European Commission, the notion of an exclusive environmental function was introduced in 1991 and 1992: "The purpose of the Commission in relation to the accompanying measures is to adopt them with the aim of incorporating modifications ... the exclusive aim of the aid being compensation measures with a positive effect for the environment" (Cabinet of the Ministry of Agriculture, LEG.12009, p. 14). At this time, the aim of national policy-makers was to provide a basis for the coordination of an agri-environmental programme that was in the process of negotiation, with (small-scale) participation by the Autonomous Communities. But in the negotiation processes between the European Commission and the state, as well as between the Autonomous Communities and the state, the regional perspective grew in importance. As a consequence, for national policy-makers, the agri-environmental programme became something of a mosaic, with Autonomous Communities able to influence the phasing of implementation, as well as developing agri-environmental measures according to their own interests. This mosaic effect has contributed to the perception that agri-environmental measures have had limited environmental impacts.

The reality of Spanish agri-environmental measures is that their recent and tentative introduction has followed a complex path. This has highlighted the difficulties involved in developing policies of this type (Regina Segura, 1996). Even so, Spain is the Member State with the most agri-environmental programmes in the EU (amounting to some 66). Of these, three are horizontal measures and 63 relate to specific geographical areas. This large number does not reflect great concern for these policies. It simply shows lack of coordination in the preparation of programmes, which stems from different proposals coming forward from the Autonomous Communities, which have administrative authority for agriculture and the environment. For this reason, amongst the programmes that exist, one can find varying perspectives on and objectives for environmental action. There is no one approach to the concept of the environment. Moreover, there is unevenness in the implementation of policies affecting agricultural practices that could improve environmental sustainability. There is also variety in the groups that are targeted by efforts to improve the environment. Thus, alongside measures that seek to change professional farm practices, there are area programmes with a demographic focus, which see population retention as critical for environmental sustainability. This variety arises from the uncoordinated participation of both agricultural and environmental authorities in the drafting of agri-environmental plans. In fact, strictly environmental concerns are only combined in a coordinated manner with broader rural and agricultural viewpoints in a few programmes, with individual Autonomous Community measures enacted without regard to the possibilities of coordination across regions. Making the situation yet more complex, in the drafting of agri-environmental measures there has been little involvement by PAOs or environmental NGOs. This has led to difficulties over the adoption of programmes by farmers (Paniagua, 1997b). Along with these shortcomings, programme funding was reduced by 70% during the process of negotiation with the EU.

In the end agri-environmental measures were enacted in two stages. A horizontal package, was applicable to the whole of the country, was adopted in September 1994. This was followed by an area package, which received the green light in 1995. This was comprised of two differentiated operational facets. On the one hand, there were the national parks and environmentally sensitive areas. On the other hand, there were areas of ecological interest, as defined by each Autonomous Community (again, this led to diversity in area designations, in administrative arrangements, and in the measures adopted). The Spanish agri-environmental programme was adopted as a whole by the EU STAR Committee in January 1995. Despite the large number of programmes submitted, only two, neither horizontal, were put into effect in 1995. Compared with both France and Germany, whose programmes saw more than five million hectares covered by agri-environmental measures in 1995, Spain had just 89,802 hectares covered by designations. Even Portugal had 471,312 hectares (with the UK on 796,219 hectares), so while Spain did not have the smallest designation, its performance was noticeably inferior to many EU countries (Commission of the European Communities, 1996).

In addition, the aims and period of application of horizontal programmes are limited with regard to those proposed in Community Regulation 2078/92, as well as compared with those submitted by other countries. Of the seven types of action mentioned by Regulation 2078/92, Spain only uses two. The first is a reduction in the use of fertilizer and products designed to protect plant health. This is favoured to encourage more biologically sensitive agriculture. The second is the promotion of production practices consistent with protecting the environment and natural resources. Initiatives here include complying with conservation practices in the rearing animals in danger of extinction. In this way, the measures adopted are closely connected with actual agricultural dynamics, so avoiding diverting land into non-agricultural activities. The other five measures in Regulation 2078/92 are incorporated only in regional programmes. In terms of the horizontal or vertical emphasis, then, Spain is in a mid-way situation in implementing agri-environmental measures, for in countries like Ireland or Portugal horizontal measures prevail, while in nations like Italy regional measures dominate.

That said, in negotiations over the environmental package for Agenda 2000, the Spanish position has been to strengthen horizontal measures linked to certain commodities (like sunflowers and oil-producing crops). This position is similar to that adopted by Spain during 1991/92 negotiations over agri-environmental measures, with assistance being sought to improve farm incomes through these mechanisms. At present, horizontal programmes in Spain comprise a variety of packages. Included amongst these are the encouragement of extensive cereal production, the maintenance of rare livestock breeds, the promotion of more ecological agriculture (e.g. organic farming) and the development of environmental training programmes. The application of these programmes through area measures affects 500,000 farms and 3.5 million hectares. Of the measures used, special importance is attached to cereal extensification (receiving about 85% of total aid). This is intended to maintain production in areas that are already extensive that benefit from no other assistance under the new CAP. Compensatory grants for other arable crops are restricted to farms that exceed a set-aside rate of 10%. Most farms that fall into this category are located in Castilla-La Mancha and Castilla y León. In the case of the Autonomous Community of Castilla y León, districts that have higher yields have lower 'traditional set-aside' rates (computed from the agricultural census, based on non-cultivated areas prior to the set-aside programme). They have been allocated smaller 'mandatory set-aside' rates in accordance with the regulation of compensatory grants for arable crops. It is in this type of area that subsidies stemming from the extensification policy are focused. The logic behind this is that extensification has greater relative environmental benefits than set-aside in such areas, for in high yield areas farmers are less attracted by set-aside options. Set-aside is a more fruitful policy in zones of marginal farm production. Initially, to encourage set-aside in zones of more marginal productive capacity, higher set-aside compensatory grants were available for smaller farms. However, under pressure from farmer unions on the political right, in 1999 the zonal programme in Castilla y León was adjusted so it mainly benefits (large-scale) professional farmers. This change brought the programme into conflict with the policy emanating from Brussels, as it changed the initial purpose of the programme.

The obligation not to grow crops defines that the area affected must cover a minimum of five hectares, although this does not take into account land that is withdrawn compulsorily or voluntarily in accordance with arable crop regulations. In addition, farms that are more marginal in economic or size terms are prevented from adopting the measure (in total there are approximately 971,000 farms of less than five hectares in Spain). This minimum size limitation, together with a 20% allowance in the average premium paid per hectare for full-time farmers, highlights the bias in favour of professional farmers. As a whole, the cereal land that is likely to be affected by these extensification benefits cover some 2.5 million hectares, or 100,000 out of the 922,410 cereal farms in the country (Castillo, 1995). Yet the impact of such measures is uneven, as horizontal programmes are necessarily regulated by each Autonomous Community. In the first phase of the programme (from 1993-1997), all the Autonomous Communities regulated horizontal measures, albeit with different timing and intensity in implementation, according to the specific problems and potentialities associated with agricultural policy in each region. The Autonomous Communities with the most extensive cereal farming systems (Castilla-La Mancha and Castilla y León) implemented agri-environmental measures most quickly, as the relevant instruments added to the incomes of farmers. In Autonomous Communities like Cantabria, this measure was not implemented, for a specialization in dairy products lessened interest in this dimension of agricultural policy. By the end of 1998, effective investment under these programmes included 6,003 million pesetas spent on the horizontal measures (3,284 million on cereal extensification, 1,400 million on organic farming, 524 million on maintaining livestock breeds in danger of extinction and 727 million on training farmers). This expenditure represents just 8.5% of the initial budget (some 70,914 million pesetas), which gives one indication of the low priority Autonomous Communities have accorded such measures. This is illustrative of the inherent difficulties that surround the implementation of agri-environmental measures in Spain. Whether this will change in the second phase of the agri-environmental scheme is to be seen. This second phase runs from 1998-2001. Some changes have been implemented for this phase, with horizontal programmes seeing shifts in favour of smaller scale farms and the inclusion of more breeds in danger of extinction (Table 7.3). Yet the emphasis on extensification in the cereal sector is still strong, with 73.4% of the budget for horizontal measures (50,673 million pesetas) going on this element (affecting 1.3 million hectares).

Table 7.3
Phases in agri-environmental programmes in Spain

Programmes	First phase 1993-1997	Second phase 1998-2001

Horizontal
Budget commitments

	70,914 million pesetas	50,673 million pesetas
	. organic farming 6.5%	. organic farming 14.4%
	. endangered species 3.7%	. endangered species 5.8%
	. training 4.5%	. training 6.4%
	. cereal extensification 85.2%	. cereal extensification 73.4%

Most favoured Autonomous Communities (% total budget)

	Castilla-La Mancha 21.1%	Aragón 22.9%
	Castilla-León 19.0%	Andalucía 18.6%
	Aragón 15.3%	Castilla-León,Extremadura 16.1%

Typical beneficiaries

	Cereal farmers in the interior with larger farms than the regional average	Cereal farmers with farms of around average size for the region

	Problems	**Changes from first phase**
	Excessively bureaucratic, lack of coordination between organizations, main benefits for large-scale farms and absentee landowners, weak voluntary involvement.	Greater benefits for median sized farms, more attention to organic farming.

Vertical/zonal
Autonomous Community programmes

	42 programmes cover 2,390 million ha. Budget 97,475 million pesetas	Also 42, with 1,862 million ha. Budget 72,359 million pesetas

National parks

	Area 329 million ha. Budget 37,801 million pesetas	Area 340 million ha. Budget 57,244 million pesetas

ZEPAs and RAMSAR

	Area 79 million ha. Budget 8,369 million pesetas	Area 193 million ha. Budget 17,110 million pesetas

	Problems	**Changes from first phase**
	Fundamentally not implemented, Poor socio-economic objectives, little protection for birds, lack of coordination between Autonomous Communities.	Elimination of landscape programmes, smaller but more focused programmes, greater role for programmes on specific crops.

Source: own compilation from a variety of documentary sources

Zonal measures in the agri-environmental programme   For aid applied to specific geographical areas with special environmental sensitivities or with the aim of maintaining traditional agricultural activities, the areas selected are dominated by the national parks, the wetlands on the RAMSAR Convention list, and by more than 130 natural spaces of international ecological interest that have been declared Zones of Special Protection for Birds (ZEPAS), with the inclusion of this last group owing much to the intervention of the Spanish Society of Ornithology. In addition, a list of areas has been included by each Autonomous Community, by virtue of their special socio-economic problems, where these are aggravated by restrictions of an environmental nature (such as where farmers are restricted from changing traditional farming practices). It is estimated that 93,262 farmers may benefit from grants associated with these area-based measures, which are expected to cover more than 2.8 million hectares. The outlay for this agri-environmental measure is anticipated to be of the order of 142,000 million pesetas. This will include an allocation of 38,000 million pesetas for national parks, 11,000 million pesetas for RAMSAR Convention wetlands, 7,000 million pesetas for the ZEPAS and 86,000 million for sensitive areas selected by the Autonomous Communities (Secretaria General de Estructuras Agrarias, 1994).

The common objective of these zonal measures is to supplement and diversify agricultural incomes in order to maintain the profitability of farms and, at the same time, secure environment-friendly farming practices. The programme incorporates suggestions on new uses for abandoned agricultural land, so as to prevent the aggravation of soil erosion and the risk of fire. As may be seen from Table 7.3, the zonal programmes that have a more rural or ecological nature, as well as those devoted to the protection of bird life, have a broad scope and substantial funding. Strictly agricultural programmes, that are concerned with modifications to land-use or its non-use, are less prominent. Wildlife protection programmes in inland regions are particularly prominent in the area covered, as special programmes exist to protect the habitat of the great bustard. The agri-environmental programme, however, also contains measures of a demographic or landscape type. These confer on the programme a rural character, as they combine environmental, cultural, demographic, land-use, farm and strictly ecological factors. Yet the definition of zones is a consequence of the interplay between social agents in each region. As a consequence, precise practices over the delimitation of zones, along with their budgets and themes, are subject to variation across regions.

From the perspective of the central agricultural administrators, perceptions of the agri-environmental programme as a 'mosaic', with limited coordination between regions, limited the effectiveness of 'real' environmental elements in the programme. Viewed in this light, the regional point of view is seen to be more important than the national in the construction of the agri-environmental programme. The solution for national policy makers is seen to be to

154

incorporate agri-environmental measures into specific EU farm commodity subsidies. As a further outcome of the lack of coordination of Autonomous Community policies, uneven time frames exist for the regulation and implementation of agri-environmental programmes.

Overall, however, it is premature to make an assessment of the agri-environmental programme. It was only in 1993 that zonal programmes were introduced to provide income compensation for reduced water usage from aquifers 23 and 24 in Castilla-La Mancha and for the cereal-growing plains of Castilla y León. Since 1995 the surroundings of the Picos de Europa National Park in Asturias has been added, the hazel nut growing area in Cataluña became part of the programme in 1996, and at the end of 1996 Doñana was added, although this element has yet to be implemented. Other programmes for which regulations have been approved, but implementation has not started, include: the national parks in the Islas Canarias, traditional landscape areas in the same region, the Gallocana wetlands area in Aragón, the Albufera wetlands in Valencia, and the protected 'natural areas' of Murcia. Only five Autonomous Communities have developed agri-environmental regulations for ZEPAS (Aragón, Asturias, Baleares, Extremadura, Murcia) and only four have done so for RAMSAR wetlands (Aragón, Baleares, Murcia, Valencia). All of these are for specific areas that have limited economic connections to the surrounding rural economy. The investment between 1993 to 1998 was 27,500 million pesetas, yet the initial budget was 143,645 million. In other words just 19.1% of the 1993 budget was used. As with the horizontal programmes, the primary reason for this is the low priority that is afforded to agri-environmental initiatives by the Autonomous Communities. For the five zonal programmes that were started, we can identify different origins, although there are some common strands in their socio-economic contexts. The programme concerning aquifers 23 and 24 in Castilla-La Mancha and that for the zones near the Picos de Europa National Park in Asturias, are connected to the existence of surrounding national parks, although varying interests are concerned with their programme outcomes. For the Tablas de Daimiel Plan, which is connected with the regulation of sensitive environmental areas, the programme tries to offer a solution to a water use dispute between irrigating farmers and the needs of national park wetlands. By contrast, the Picos de Europa National Park Plan is under-scored by conflict between stockbreeders and environmentalist groups/authorities. Here the aim is to supplement the income of stockbreeders by changing their farming practices and reducing stock loads.

The hazel nut growing programme in Cataluña may be considered an outcome of socio-economic conflict arising from the lack of competitiveness of local producers, allied to a drop in hazel nut prices, which led to numerous demonstrations by agricultural unions. The most far-reaching and soundly based programme, in purely agri-environmental terms, is the so-called 'Steppe

Plan' in Castilla y León. It affects 512 municipalities and covers 1.6 million hectares, with a budget of around 30,000 million pesetas. Its prime aims are to increase set-aside, to reduce fertilizer usage, and so decrease agricultural output, and to re-introduce extensive farming practices that are consistent with the conservation of ecosystems and habitats of bird life in the area. This programme is organized through four types of contract, with each having application in areas defined according to the density of great bustards. The programme is distinguished by the first two contracts being administered by agricultural authorities and the second two by environmental authorities. This is the first case of a regulation stemming from the CAP being applied by a non-agricultural agency in Spain.

Unfortunately, the results of this programme have fallen far short of those initially foreseen. In all, only 18.3% of the intended area has availed itself of the plan. This is mainly due to problems in publicizing the programme. This is as a result of administrative division in its implementation, because of weather problems (especially low rainfall in recent years), and as a result of attractive alternative EU subsidies (subsidies from other EU programmes - such as set-aside - offer more favourable payments for some farmers). However, results have varied considerably by type of contract. Most evidently, contracts covered by environmental authorities only cover 5,250 hectares, compared with 121,000 hectares for those administered by agricultural authorities. This seems largely to result from the longer time commitments required for agreements with environmental agencies, which entail the non-use or non-marketing of produce for 20 years. In any case, as PAOs recognize themselves, the agri-environmental programme will not meet its objectives unless farmers are made aware of its objectives. As a consequence, it is recognized that considerable effort still needs to be put into publicity and training, in order to amend or remedy shortcomings in the environmental sensitivity of the farmers. Linked with this, the programme is being adjusted so it is more acceptable to farmers. Different types of agri-environmental contract are being created, with a mixing of responsibilities between agricultural and environmental agencies. One example is in the Autonomous Community of Navarra. Here, in September 1998, the Community Government developed its own agri-environmental programme, with seven different types of contract, with one part of the programme conducted by the regional environmental administration. Similar to the situation in Castilla y León, in Navarra some of the horizontal programmes, like bird-life protection areas or the RAMSAR and wetland areas, sit within broader zones of agri-environmental regulation, such as zones of cereal extensification.

What should be noted is that, at the end of 1997, important changes began to occur in the zonal programme. This did not impact on conditions affecting small-scale farm operators as such but did mark important modifications in the orientation of agri-environmental measures in each region. This reorientation was associated primarily with environmental and socio-economic demands that were specific to each region. This new phase has reinforced the regionalization of the agri-environmental programme, in that expenditure growth has been focused more on zonal than horizontal measures. The budget for zonal measures is now twice that of horizontal measures, encompassing some 146,714 million pesetas, 74,380 farmers and 2,396,003 hectares. Linked to this has been change in the nature of zonal programmes, with their objectives becoming more specific. Zonal programmes with general objectives, like maintaining traditional landscapes, are being replaced in Autonomous Communities like Andalucía and Castilla y León with specialized programmes that focus on characteristic regional products. Only in the more industrialized and higher density AACC, such as the Islas Canarias, Madrid and Pais Vasco, do agri-environmental landscape measures cover a whole region.

Problems in implementing agri-environmental programmes

Amongst commentators on the farm sector, there is broad agreement that the slight effectiveness of Spanish agri-environmental implementation is due to a number of factors: (1) there is little tradition of implementing environmental regulation measures, especially when these influence the professional activities of farmers, nor is there a strong tendency toward the integrated protection of spaces that possess special natural, scenic or environmental resources; (2) there is a lack of policy coordination, alongside a high 'density' of bodies taking part in decision-making processes, both at European and national levels; and, (3) there is scepticism and reluctance over the practicalities of implementing agri-environmental measures amongst agricultural authorities, in part on account of the necessity to integrate measures across sectors, in part because of the fragmented nature of agri-environmental actions, with these views prevalent amongst agricultural and farm organizations. Interviews with the PAOs extend the list of factors that limit the implementation of agri-environmental measures. Most evident in this regard are: (1) some farmers holding that implementation would improve if grants were awarded to professional farmers only, with recognition that programme measures, which are subject to modification, can determine the type of farmer that engages with an agri-environmental programme; (2) the long time farmers are required to sign-up for agri-environmental measures (often five years as a minimum); (3) the rigid timetable for agri-environmental practices, for which even a change in the weather can make fulfilment difficult; and, (4) competition from other CAP assistance, which can make options like the withdrawal of land more financially attractive than increasing environmental sensitivity in farm practices. Some left-wing organizations also point out that the limit of five hectares for traditional set-aside benefits

157

medium-to-large farmers in regions like Castilla y León, and discourages small-scale farmers from participating in this (and perhaps other) agri-environmental measures.

For their part, environmental organizations like the Coordinator of Environmentalist Associations of Spain (CODA) are in favour of awarding subsidies to 'integrated production systems' instead of giving specific grants according to the number of hectares or livestock affected.

Conclusion

Environmental deterioration in the rural environment went almost unnoticed by Spanish society and did not form part of the so-called 'environmental issue' until the early 1980s. Today, concern for the environmental deterioration of farmland is part of the restatement of a 'pact' between society and farmers. This pact needs restating owing to changes in rural society. Most important in this regard are the reduced dependence of the rural population on agriculture, a rise in standards of living amongst farmers, an increase in second homes, the growth of rural tourism and outdoor recreation, and less concern over the reliability of food supplies. These processes have been particularly dynamic in the last 10 years in southern Europe.

Alongside these changes, opinion surveys reveal that rural areas are highly rated in environmental terms in Spain. Farming is one of the highest socially-rated professions, as a people hold that it brings participants into direct contact with nature. For much of society, the countryside represents a refuge against the environmental deterioration they associate with towns and cities. Perhaps this is why the population in general does not blame farmers for rural environmental deterioration. The environmentalization of rural areas (and agriculture) is not taking place around a specific set of environmental problems (although such problems do exist). Instead the strengthening of rural environmental sentiments is linked to the environmental appeal of rural areas, alongside the opportunities rural areas offer for recreation.

Contrasting with the general strengthening of environmentalism, farmers have a poorly articulated environmental sensitivity and a lower inclination toward environmental action. These are important factors in explaining the difficulty of implementing agri-environmental measures in Spain (by comparison with other EU Member States).

Compared with farmers, environmental problems are more prominent in the discourses of PAOs. This has two obvious facets. The first is a denial of responsibility on the part of farmers for environmental deterioration in rural areas. This is most notably seen in the claim that farmers only meet the demands of society when they engage in production intensification. The second associates the new conservation function that is being asked of farmers with a transfer of income from society as a whole. This turns the 'environmental issue' into a new legitimation for farmers.

The process of implementing environmental measures reveals difficulties in introducing regulations that limit the productive function of farmers. Agri-environmental programmes have granted an institutional acknowledgement to the conservation function society assigns to farmers (beside their productive one), yet these measures have been delayed in preparation and enactment, compared with other CAP reforms. One good reason is confusion over the objectives of agri-environmental instruments. Thus, for the 2001-2006 period, the aim for agri-environmental policy in Spain is double-sided. On the one hand, it is to provide compensation for certain commodity sub-sectors (e.g. oil-producing crops). On the other hand, it is a regional and rural instrument, that compensates the rural population for environmental services (Sumpsi, 1999) and helps maintain people in remote, marginal and less developed areas. The first of these is best suited to more productive agricultural areas, where agri-environmental measures would essentially be a financial instrument to compensate for limiting options. The second is more an instrument for less productive agricultural areas. The possibility of using agri-environmental policy in these two ways (supporting agriculture and as an instrument for rural development) is coincident with the historical position of the Spanish agricultural administration. But this bifurcated approach, which is favoured in other countries with an unbalanced structure of agricultural production, such as those in southern Europe, represents a limited translation of EU agri-environmental legislation. This was seen in negotiations between the European Commission and the Spanish authorities in May-June 2000, when quite different interpretations of agri-environmental measures were evident. In Spain, compensation for agri-environmental measures has been seen as a payment for the extra labour of farmers, rather than as income compensation. For the Commission, Spanish actions are not introducing strong agri-environmental infusions, but rather enhance the productive position of farmers ('good farmers' are thereby not equated with 'agri-environmental farmers', with Spain being seen as giving insufficient emphasis to the latter, who are the ones who are viewed as seeking environmental improvements).

From the outset commentators have pointed out that agri-environmental measures will have limited effectiveness unless there is a change in farmers' productivist mentality. But at this time there is no real pressure on Spanish farmers to change their environmental values, for the countryside is viewed positively by the general populace. Hence actions for rural environmental improvement have been directed more toward regulating natural spaces than changing farmer behaviour. This is in keeping with the general population being more aware of the need to safeguard 'special' places. All this necessarily affects the attainment of environmental objectives and permits misgivings about environmental action amongst agricultural professionals. The standpoint in agri-environmental programmes favours practices that can be sustained by the farm population. This leads to flexibility in implementation, but means that the environmental benefits of regulation are almost non-existent, as the coordination of action is weak.

Notes

The research for this paper is part of a project entitled 'Joint vested interests and conflict between social agents at national, regional and local policy-making levels after the introduction of environmental regulation in agriculture'. This project is funded by the Spanish Ministry of Education (grant code: PB95-0076).

1   The consumption of mineral fertilizer is low in Spain compared with many other European countries. According to 1989 FAO figures, if we take as an indicator the kg/ha. consumption of nitrogenous fertilizer, which is an important measure due to its effect on ground water, and also look at phosphate fertilizer, which has environmental significance owing to the possible accumulation of heavy metals in the soil and the effects this has on the soil microflora (OECD, 1991), Spain has a low consumption level. Thus, the 48 kg/ha. of nitrogenous fertilizer were used in Spain compared with 489 for the Netherlands, 242 for Portugal, 104 for Greece and 76 for Italy. For phosphate fertilizer, the Spanish consumption was 23 kg/ha., compared with 93 for the Netherlands, 75 for France, 59 for Italy, 45 for Greece and 32 for Portugal (Economic Commission for Europe, 1992, p.276).

2   Thus, 17.6% of dwellings in towns with less than 10,000 inhabitants did not have sanitary services or only shared them, compared with a figure of 7.6% for the nation. Likewise, 8.9% did not have cold running water, compared with the national figure of 3.8%, while only 25.9% had a telephone, as opposed to 50.7% nationally.

3   Four nation-wide opinion polls of Spanish citizens aged 18 years or more have been used in this section. Each of these are digital data bases that provide the results from the surveys conducted. The four surveys are: (1) that conducted by the Centro de Investigaciones Sociológicas (CIS), which was undertaken in March 1996 (CIS-96), with responses from 2,500 interviews; (2) the 1986 Secretaria General de Medio Ambiente survey, which was undertaken by the Instituto de Estudios Socials (IDES-86), with 2,017 interviews completed; (3) the Centro de Investigaciones Sobre la Realidad Social (CIRES) study of October 1992 (CIRES-92), which

produced returns from 1,200 responses; and, (4) the CIRES study of December 1994 (CIRES-94), for which 1,200 interviews were completed.

4 In writing this section, texts have been used that appeared from January 1985 to August 1995 in the following journals of Professional Agricultural Organizations (PAOs): *La Tierra del Agricultor y el Ganadero* of the Unión de Pequeños Agricultores; *Jovenes Agricultores* of ASAJA; and, lastly, *Iniciativa Rural* of Jovenes Agricultores.

References

Abad Balboa, C., García Delgado, J.L. and Muñoz Cidad, C. (1994) La agricultura española en el último tercio del siglo XX: principales pautas evolutivas, in J.M. Sumpsi (ed.) *Modernización y Cambio Estructural en la Agricultura Española*, Ministerio de Agricultura, Pesca y Alimentación, Madrid, pp.69-126.

Ayudas (1999) Las ayudas para la pequeña agricultura, *Tierras de Castilla y León*, 46, 8.

Baldock, D. and Lowe, P.D. (1996) The development of European agri-environment policy, in M.C. Whitby (ed.) *The European Environment and CAP Reform*, CAB International, Wallingford, pp.26-42.

Banesto (1989) *Anuario de Mercado*, Servicio de Estudios-Banesto, Madrid

Barke, M. (1991) The growth and changing pattern of second homes in Spain in the 1970s, *Scottish Geographical Magazine*, 107, pp.12-21.

Barke, M. and Newton, M. (1994) A new rural development initiative in Spain: the European Community's Plan Leader, *Geography*, 79, pp.366-371.

Bianchi, A. (1992) Environmental policy, in F. Francioni (ed.) *Italy and EC Membership Evaluated*, Pinter, London, pp.71-105.

Brenan, G. (1950) *The Spanish Labyrinth*, second edition, Cambridge University Press, Cambridge.

Castillo, J. (1995) La agricultura y la conservación del medio natural: un programa de futuro, *El Boletín*, 28, pp.18-24.

Clark, J.R.A., Jones, A., Potter, C.A. and Lobley, M. (1997) Conceptualizing the evolution of the European Union's agri-environment policy: a discourse approach, *Environment and Planning, A29*, pp.1869-1885.

Commission of the European Communities (series) *Eurobarometro*, Office for Official Publications of the European Communities, Luxembourg.

Commission of the European Communities (1988) *Eurobarometro: Los Europeos y su Agricultura*, Office for Official Publications of the European Communities, Luxembourg.

Commission of the European Communities (1992) *El Estado del Medio Ambiente en la Comunidad Europea: Una Idea General - Volume III*, Office for Official Publications of the European Communities, Luxembourg.

Commission of the European Communities (1996) *La Situación de la Agricultura en la Unión Europea: Informe de 1995*, Office for Official Publications of the European Communities, Luxembourg.

Cuadrado, J.R. and Tio, C. (1992) *El Desarrollo del Mundo Rural en España*, Madrid, Secretaria General de Estructuras Agrarias.

De Miguel, A. (1994) *La Sociedad Española, 1993-94*, Alianza Editorial, Madrid.

Deverre, C. (1995) Social implications of agro-environmental policy in France and Europe, *Sociologia Ruralis*, 35, pp.227-247.

Dirección General de Medio Ambiente (1988) *Medio Ambiente en España: 1987*, Ministerio de Obras Públicas y Urbanismo, Madrid.

Dirección General de Medio Ambiente (1989) *Medio Ambiente en España: 1988*, Ministerio de Obras Públicas y Urbanismo, Madrid.

Donazar, J.A., Naveso, M.A., Tella, J.C. and Campion, D. (1997) Extensive grazing and raptors in Spain, in D.J. Pain and M. Pienkowski (eds.) *Farming and Birds in Europe: The Common Agricultural Policy and its Implications for Bird Conservation*, Academic Press, San Diego, pp.117-149.

Economic Commission for Europe (1992) *The Environment in Europe and North-America: Annotated Statistics 1992*, United Nations, New York.

Eurostat (1996) *Anuario 1995: Visón Estadistica Sobre Europa 1983-1993*, Office for Official Publications of the European Communities, Luxembourg.

Etxezarreta, M. and Viladomiu, L. (1989) The restructuring of Spanish agriculture and Spain's accession to the EEC, in D. Goodman and M. Redclift (eds.) *The International Farm Crisis*, Macmillan, Basingstoke, pp.156-182.

Fundación General de la Universidad Complutense (1993) *La Sociedad Española*, Universidad Complutense, Madrid.

García Fernández, G. (1995) Territorialización de las rentas y subvenciones agrarias, *El Boletín*, 28, pp.25-30.

Garrido, F. and Moyano, E. (1996) Spain, in M.C. Whitby (ed.) *The European Environment and CAP Reform*, CAB International, Wallingford, pp.86-104.

Gomez, C., Noya, J. and Paniagua, A. (1997) Agricultura y naturaleza: una aproximación a las imágenes y actitudes de la población respecto a las relaciones entre agricultura, medo rural y naturaleza, *Política y Sociedad*, 23, pp.97-108.

Guglielmi, M. (1995) Vers de nouvelles fonctions de l'agriculture dans l'espace?, *Economie Rurale*, 229, pp.22-28.

Hoggart, K., Buller, H. and Black, R. (1995) *Rural Europe: Identity and Change*, Arnold, London.

Ilbery, B.W. and Bowler, I.R. (1998) From agricultural productivism to post-productivism, in B.W. Ilbery (ed.) *The Geography of Rural Change*, Longman, Harlow, pp.57-84.

INE (1994, annual) *Encuesta de Población Activa*, Instituto Nacional de Estadística, Madrid.

INE (annual) *Encuesta de Presupuestos Familiares*, Instituto Nacional de Estadística, Madrid.

La Spina, A. and Sciortino, G. (1993) Common agenda, southern rules: European integration and environmental change in the Mediterranean states, in J.D. Liefferink, P.D. Lowe and A.J.P. Mol (eds.) *European Integration and Environmental Policy*, Wiley, Chichester, pp.217-236.

Lowe, P.D. and Ward, N. (1994) Agricultura y medio ambiente: temario sociológico, *Agricultura y Sociedad*, 71, pp.257-270.

Junta de Castilla y León (1996, annual) *Anuario Estadistico de Castilla y León*, Valladolid.

Mansvelt Beck, J. (1988) *The Rise of the Subsidized Periphery in Spain*, Nederlandse Geografische Studies 69, Utrecht.

Medalus Office (1993) *MEDALUS I: Executive Summary*, Report for the Commission of the European Communities DG-XII, King's College London Department of Geography, London.

Medalus Office (1996) *MEDALUS II: Executive Summary*, Report for the Commission of the European Communities DG-XII, King's College London Department of Geography, London.

Mili, S. (1997) Comportement du consummateur et demande du viande en Espagne, France et Italie, *Actes et Communications*, 14, pp.77-104.

Ministerio de Agricultura, Pesca y Alimentación (annual) *Anuario de Estadística Agraria*, Madrid.

Moyano, E. (1993, ed.) *Las Organizaciones Profesionales Agrarias en la CEE*, Ministerio de Agricultura, Pesca y Alimentación, Madrid.

Mykolenko, L., de Raymond, Th. and Henry, P. (1987) *The Regional Impact of the Common Agricultural Policy in Spain and Portugal*, Office for Official Publications of the European Communities, Luxembourg.

Nomenclator (1994) *Nomenclator de las Ciudades, Villas, Lugares, Aldeas y Demás Entitdades de Población con Especificaciones de sus Núcleos 1991*, Instituto Nacional de Estadística, Madrid.

OECD (1991) *The State of the Environment,* Organization for Economic Cooperation and Development, Paris.

Paniagua, A. (1997a) Significacion social e implicaciones para la politica agraria de la 'cuestion ambiental' en el medio rural español, in C. Gomez and J.J. Gonzalez (eds.) *Agricultura y Sociedad en la España Contemporanea*, Ministerio de Agricultura, Pesca y Alimentación - Centro de Investigaciones Sociológicas, Madrid, pp.975-1017.

Paniagua, A. (1997b) Recomposition rurale et politique agri-environmentale: el programme de 'l'outarde' en Castille-Leon (Espagne), in *Les Mesures Agri-Environmentales: Premiers Bilans des Expériences Européennes - Une Perspective Pluridisciplinaire - Conferences Plenieres er Cahier de Resumes,* Societe Francaise d'Economie, Paris, pp.90-92.

Paniagua, A. and Gomez, C. (1996) Hábitat y ocupación agraria en la definición de la base social del ambientalismo en España: un análisis preliminar, *Document's d'Analisi Geografica,* 29, pp.127-153.

Paniagua, A., Martin, L. and Hernandez, I. (1998) Análisis de la normativa agroambiental comunitaria, estatal y autonómica en el periodo de 1985 a 1997, *Revista de Estudios Europeos,* 18, pp.51-70.

Palacio, E. (1993) La lucha contra la erosión en España, *El Boletín,* 4, 12-47.

Regina Segura, A. (1996) Reflexiones sobre el reglamento agroambiental europeo y el programa naciónal español, *Quercus,* 125, pp.46-48.

Ruiz Olabuenaga, J.I. (1994) Ocio y estilos de vida, in M. Juarez (ed.) *Informe Sociológico Sobre la Situación Social en España: Sociedad para Todos en el Año 2000,* Foundation Fundación para el Fomento de Estudios Sociales y Sociológia Aplicada, Madrid, pp.1881-2073.

San Juan Mesonada, C (1993) Agricultural policy, in A.A. Barbado (ed.) *Spain and EC Membership Evaluated,* Pinter, London, pp.49-59.

Secretaria General de Estructuras Agrarias (1994) *Programas de Ayudas para Fomentar Métodos de Producción Agraria Compatibles con las Exigencias de la Protección y la Conservación del Espacio Natural,* Ministerio de Agricultura, Pesca y Alimentación, Madrid.

Secretaria General de Medio Ambiente (1990) *Medio Ambiente en España 89,* Ministerio de Obras Públicas y Urbanismo, Madrid.

Secretaria General de Medio Ambiente (1991) *Medio Ambiente en España 90,* Ministerio de Obras Públicas y Transportes, Madrid.

Sumpsi, J.M. (1999) Luces y sombras del acuerdo agrícola de la agenda 2000, *Cuadernos de Agricultura, Pesca y Alimentación,* 8, pp.21-26.

Szabolcs, I. (1991) Salinization potential of European soils, in F.M. Brouwer, A.J. Thomas and M.J. Chadwick (eds.) *Land Use Changes in Europe,* Kluwer, Dordrecht, pp.293-315.

Tout, D. (1990) The horticulture industry of Almería Province, Spain, *Geographical Journal,* 156, pp.304-312.

Wilson, G.A. (1995) German agri-environmental schemes II - the MEKA Programme in Baden-Württemberg, *Journal of Rural Studies,* 11, pp.149-159.

Wilson, G.A. (1996) Farmer environmental attitudes and ESA participation, *Geoforum,* 27, pp.115-131.

8 Is it the same animal?

Keith Hoggart

Has the world been turned upside down, or is it the way the mass media portray what is going on? Look back, in anger or in joy, at farm-related headlines of previous eras and you are confronted by messages signifying huge changes in the agricultural sector. Take the situation in the UK five to 10 years ago. At this time newspaper readers were regaled with messages that spelt money, trade and taxes. Accompanying the news that the "UK wants to scrap farmers' subsidies" (*Guardian*, 27 July 1995, p.8), critiques of state-farm regulation were common. Irrespective of whether UK citizens were expected to be haunted by the message that "EU quotas offer chilling news to sheep farmers" (*Guardian*, 24 January 1995, p.14), they were reminded of a variety of abuses perpetrated by producers in other countries. "Irish mushroom growers deny they are unfairly subsidized" (*Financial Times*, 16 April 1995, p.17), "Greek farmers cut off main trade arteries" (*Guardian*, 5 December 1996, p.13), "EU fights US on beef hormones" (*Guardian*, 22 November 1995, p.8), "EU warns French over fruit fight" (*Guardian*, 27 April 1995, p.12), "EU stops subsidies for Corsica's bogus cows" (*Guardian*, 22 November 1994, p.16), or the earlier "French kill hijacked lambs" (*Guardian*, 7 September 1990, p.2), provide a flavour of the time. At heart these messages did not appear to be embedded in nationalistic xenophobia, albeit with the UK press such conclusions are only reached with a sense of caution. Given the bounty of critiques of UK farmers, concern that something was rotten with farm policy comes across as a more prevalent sentiment. Whether you prefer "Farmer gets £1m for doing nothing" (*Observer*, 6 February 1994, p.9) or "Idle farmers reap benefit of 'bizarre' EU subsidies" (*Guardian*, 13 April 1996, p.7), the message is pretty unambiguous. Of course there were a few positive images as well, like "Farmers sow seeds for revival of forests" (*Observer*, 16 April 1995, p.5), but even these articles commonly dwelt on the funds farmers would claw-in by being environmentally 'positive'. The messages in such stories left a rather unpleasant after-taste, which was overt in headlines like "Wildlife cash for farmers" (*Guardian*, 27 March 1993, p.10) or "Farmers offered deal to save salt-marshes" (*Guardian*, 16 May 1994, p.4). The impression left was that farmers were money-grabbers, who were taking the rest of the population for a ride.

How farmers must wish for such negative commentaries today. Instead of being accused of ripping-off the public, the way they are now portrayed sends the message that they are poisoning the population on a rather grand scale. Traces of this commentary were certainly apparent in the early 1990s. Yet the headlines at that time were inclined to be relatively modest, with reports on health-scares a lot less prominent than articles on money, taxes and trade. "Farmers risk court action over residues in meat" (*Guardian*, 24 December 1990, p.2) and "Farmers warned over pollution" (*Guardian*, 22 January 1992, p.3), might seem fairly innocuous, but the pace soon quickened, and sentiments sharpened. "Food poisoning cases reach all time high" (*Guardian*, 9 January 1993, p.3), soon turned into warnings to food consumers to "Be very afraid" (*Guardian*, 29 May 1996, p.19), or to note "Intensive farming methods 'risk to health' " (*Guardian*, 12 March 1998, p.6). That food has the potential to be a lethal commodity was regularly reported, as with "Belgium removes pork from sale as new dioxin scare hits country" (*Guardian*, 24 July 1999, p.15), "Merde! EC reveals disgusting truth about French food" (*Evening Standard*, 22 October 1999, p.2), and "Chernobyl legacy lingers down on the farm" (*Guardian*, 1 May 1999, p.10). Farmers are not simply being implicated in discourses on food that emphasize the 'dangers' of food production and eating, but are castigated for turning the countryside into a danger zone. Some headlines are pointed: "Taking your children for a day at the farm? It's not worth running the risk, warns E.coli expert" (*Independent*, 22 April 2000, p.9). Added to which, there are repeated messages, stretching over a long period, warning of the dangers of farming systems to what many regard as the essence of 'the countryside' (e.g. " 'Common' birds in danger", *Guardian*, 28 January 1998, p.10). Indeed, when proposals are put forward that could limit damage to the rural fabric or even improve its environment, the media is quick to note farmer reservations (e.g. "Farmers fear EC curb on nitrates will hit land prices and production", *Guardian*, 13 June 1991, p.2). The image projected leaves a largely overt, although at times more subliminal, message that farmers cannot be trusted. Farmer activities, if the media is to be believed, are regularly portrayed as a threat to society ("Q: What causes as much air pollution as power station chimneys? A: Pig farms", *Observer*, 25 July 1999, p.4; "French defy feed ban as BSE spreads", *Independent*, 22 April 2000, p.1). Even the potential for organic food to offer a 'purified' food sanctity is maligned by reports that farmers want greater subsidies to convert to this farming form ("Organic farms' grant cash runs out", *Guardian*, 3 August 1999, p.5). All this while farmers sit on accumulated government 'hand-outs' that could buy-up their farms a few times over, with the farmer free to reap the bounties of land sales to insatiable housing and commercial development.

166

Set alongside such concerns are stories suggesting that, despite all the hype about low farm incomes, farmers are not doing badly financially. It might be that they need to change their activity sphere, but the message seems to be that they are prepared, indeed happy to make such shifts (e.g. "Old Macdonald had a farm ... but now he's letting holiday homes", *Observer*, 15 June 1997, p.6). Moreover, contrary to proclamations that they are the countryside's guardians, the media points to farmers actively forcing 'foreign' activities onto an idyllic countryside (e.g. "Farmer to fight tank-driving ban", *Guardian*, 6 June 1997, p.12). The imagery is that farmers are driven by a money interest, rather than emotive attachments to the sanctity of the countryside. Perhaps this message comes as no surprise, at least for academics. After all, the history of the UK countryside is littered with instances of shoddy accommodation, poor pay and bad working conditions for employed farm workers (Newby, 1972; Danziger, 1988; Hussey, 1997). For the UK at least, such practices appear to be largely ignored or unknown by the general public, although both TV programmes and newspaper reports are beginning to cast farmers in a poor light in this regard (e.g. "Bucolic game's up for the fat of the land", *Guardian*, 11 August 1997, p.17; "The lie of the land", *Guardian*, 14 January 1998, Society Section pp.2-3); with recent reports bringing out how current regimes are highly discriminatory toward farm women (e.g. "Plough the fields and scatter: Farming families all over Britain are anxiously awaiting a divorce ruling that could end centuries of tradition", *Times*, 8 July 2000, Weekend p.3).

A further element in recent adverse commentaries is British paranoia over illegal immigrants and asylum seekers, with the media drawing attention to the illegal employment of foreign labourers on UK farms and in agro-processing (e.g. "Harvest of fear in picking fields", *Guardian*, 9 June 1998, p.23). Of course, the 'reality' of the agricultural situation is far more complex. At one level this is signified in the subtitle of the last cited newspaper report. This reads: "Gangmasters recruit casual farm labour but it is the supermarkets that dictate terms now". The message that corporations alone pull the strings farmers dance to is exaggerated, as the state must be included in such a formulation. Yet the media has begun to portray corporate interest in the farm (and food) sector in a notably conspiratorial and exploitative light. The messages here emphasize greed, image distortion and lack of choice (e.g. "Food: the £250bn gamble", *Guardian*, 15 December 1997, p.1; "Biotech firm has eye on all you can eat", *Guardian*, 15 December 19997, p.3; "Exposed: the great organic food rip-off", *Independent on Sunday*, 6 February 2000, p.1; "More checks on healthy food ads", *Guardian*, 20 June 2000, p.11; "Plan drawn up to avert food panic if BSE found in sheep", *Guardian*, 19 July 2000, p.3). Public disquiet over the practices of food production and its sale take on almost sinister tones (e.g. "Public unease on GM crops 'not irrational' ", *Guardian*, 19 October 1999, p.5). Perhaps it has more to do with cultural purity and local farm incomes than food quality, but resistance to the

McDonaldization of France has received a warm welcome in UK media commentaries (e.g. "Carnival greets French farmer who took on McDonald's outlets", *Guardian*, 1 July 2000, p.15). In this new environment it is not just 'the little people' who can become 'heroes', for companies that are quick off the mark can capture public support by acting fast. The recent announcement that the UK retail company Iceland has bought a proclaimed 40% of the world's organic vegetable supplies for exclusive sale through in its stores offers a ready example ("Iceland makes big switch to organic veg", *Guardian*, 15 June 2000, p.8).

In reality, of course, the critical insight from this message lies in informing the public that 'over-night' a single company can secure exclusive rights to not far-off half of the world's supply of a selection of farm commodities. The signification that agriculture is buffeted by forces beyond its control is compelling. For whom it is compelling, is another matter. Certainly it is compelling for farm organizations, for it helps deflect criticism away from farmers and what some see as a long list of far from public-spirited acts (stretching from less than wholesome treatment of their workers, to domination of state policy toward rural areas that restricts opportunities for others, to self-interested moralizing to justify environmental desecration; e.g. Newby, 1977; Lowe *et al.*, 1997; Strijker, 2000). Certainly, as empirical studies show to effect, it would be incorrect to fall into the trap of bemoaning the fate of the 'poor farmer' who faces increasingly unpredictable income streams and ever-decreasing workplace autonomy. To accept so simplistic a formulation would over-sentimentalized 'the farmers' plight'. This would be dangerous on a number of grounds. For one, can we really talk about 'the farmer'? The complexity of farm organization and personnel involvement in production (and consumption) tasks is such that enormous diversity exists amongst farm units. This is hardly a new insight (Gasson, 1974; Hill, 1993). Even if we ignore over-generalized commentaries on 'the farmer', this does not justify sentimentalizing what is happening in the farm sector. Understandable though it might be, given fears of food shortage surrounding two world wars in the twentieth century (Tracy, 1989), there is no reason why farmers should be considered more sympathetically than other petit bourgeois entrepreneurs. Given the rate at which restaurants, manufacturing plants and accommodation services close, farmers get a good press, in the academic as well as the popular media. How many press articles have you seen lamenting the failure of rural non-farm businesses? How many decry the number of restaurants or hotels that go out of business? There is also a notable social class bias in sentimentalizing the difficulties farmers face. Perhaps it passed me by, but I have seen little media recognition that, while farm numbers are declining, this pales into insignificance compared with decades of farm labour redundancies resulting from the adoption of labour saving devices.[1] Farmers who are 'forced' to give up farming owing to market pressures deserve sympathy, for they not only experience job loss but also potentially experience cultural and social dislocation. But why should we sentimentalize this transition compared with the loss of other occupational groups? Did farm labourers not lose an income source and a 'way of life' when they were told their farm services were no longer required? With many academic commentators on rural areas having a country and/or farm background, there is a need to be doubly cautious over misrepresenting rural change processes. Unless they are renters, even smallholders in areas experiencing population loss possess a significant economic resource in the land they own. Analysts have shown that this land often not disposed off, but earns a desirable monetary return (e.g. for areas seeing population loss in inland Spain, see Brandes, 1975; Paniagua, 2000). This fact alone puts many farmers in a different position from the vastly greater number of labourers who saw their jobs and communities destroyed by technological change, state policy and corporate profiteering. As an occupation, farmers have been well treated by the (academic and popular) media compared with their compatriots who once fuelled European economic growth through their labours in coal mining, iron and steel or shipbuilding.

Obviously, in making this point we need to be sensitive to cross-European disparities. The comments so far have a particular UK flavour. This is not simply on account of the high price land fetches in the UK, compared with other goods, but also on account of UK farms generally being larger compared with elsewhere in the continent (Hoggart *et al.*, 1995). The pace of farm number decline is also smaller in the UK (Table 8.1), so the magnitude of farmer 'ejection' from the sector has less potential for garnering media sympathy. But the issues are not just about declining numbers but relate to difficulties of living on a reduced income (e.g. "Farm incomes at 40-year low", *Guardian*, 1 June 1991, p.4; "Farming crisis", *Guardian*, 28 May 1998, p.19; "Pig farmers face bankruptcy as prices fall", *Guardian*, 6 October 1999, p.13; "Farmer drives 600 miles to sell his lamb", *Independent on Sunday*, 6 February 2000, p.7). Attach. to this message, TV pictures of burning carcasses in the BSE aftermath. Add real fears about decline in rural services, as seen in the closure of rural banks and post offices. Further take on board active political lobbying and marching. Not here by small-scale French farmers protesting about insufficient subsidies, foreign imports or government (over)regulation (Naylor, 1994), but by a combination including high numbers of green-wellies, blue-rinses and the otherwise well-healed. They have come together because they hold that the UK countryside is 'under threat' from unsympathetic government leaders and harsh market conditions (Hart-Davis, 1997; George, 1999). The resulting picture is one of a countryside and farm sector that is at the very least being shaken rather rudely. Read some of the literature and you certainly come to the conclusion that revolutionary change is occurring in the countryside. In this sense, the question 'is it the same animal?' might be answered negatively. In this chapter, this question is posed on a somewhat broader front. Here the issue is not simply about the degree of farm sector change but also about the degree of internal coherence in the farm sector. The focus is not just on whether agriculture has been re-invented, such that the sector in 2000 is a different animal from that found in (say) 1950 or 1970, but on the degree to which the sector has become so fragmented that it no longer makes sense to discuss agricultural trends as if there is a unified entity, called 'agriculture'. In the spirit of editor's contributions to the book series that spawned this volume,[2] this chapter approaches this question by drawing on recent literature to examine evidence on the question posed.

Table 8.1
Percentage change in number of agricultural holdings in the EU,
1975-1997

	1975-1997	1987-1997	1995-1997
Belgium	-51	-27	-5
Denmark	-52	-27	-8
France	-48	-31	-7
Germany	-41	-24	-6 *
Ireland	-35	-32	-4
Italy	-13	-17	-7
Luxembourg	-52	-29	-6
Netherlands	-34	-18	-5
UK	-17	-10	-1
Greece		-14	+2
Portugal		-34	-8
Spain		-33	-5
Austria			-5
Finland			-9
Sweden			+1 *
EU9	-29	-21	-6
EU12		-24	-5
EU15			-5

Note: * data for Germany for 1995-1997 include the Länder
          of the former GDR. The 1997 Sweden figure includes
          a change of threshold, so smaller farms are included
          for that year.
Source: http://europa.eu.int/eurostat.
          Eurostat Product 5-14032000-EN-AP-EN
          (Agriculture and Fisheries News Release 35/2000, 14 March 2000)

The 'crisis' of European farming

Compared with previous post-war decades, the academic literature on farming is replete with references to the recent crisis of agriculture, or at least to a crisis for agriculturalists (e.g. Drummond *et al.*, 2000). The most recent figures put out by Eurostat appear to confirm that farm incomes are in sharp decline; if not everywhere within the EU, then at least in most venues (Table 8.2). These figures really do need to be treated with a high-level of scepticism. Perhaps in euro-land more stability can now be expected in farm receipts but until the recent past exchange rate fluctuations induced real instability in farm returns. Gilg (1999, p.84) provides a good example, using UK area payments for arable land by way of illustration. Talking 1994-1996 to illustrate the instability that exists, he notes that sums received per hectare changed from £193 in 1994, to £276 in 1995, before falling back to £247 in 1996. Amidst voluble pronouncements about a farm income crisis, how many noticed that farm incomes in 1995 were at their highest level for two decades? Even if this high was due to the currency fluctuations, such fluxes are not always positive. At the present time, for instance, the weakness of the euro against other currencies has markedly negative repercussions for EU farmers outside the euro zone. Yet even here we need to be cautious in ascribing grief and trauma to farm producers. For certain today's policy environment might have lost the fiscal feather-bedding and public support that has dominated post-war decades (Tracy, 1989). It is harder now to secure high farm commodity prices, and

Table 8.2
Percentage change in EU farm income, 1998-1999

Ireland	-35	UK	-2
Denmark	-11	Finland	-2
Belgium	-9	Austria	-1
Netherlands	-6	Greece	0
France	-4	Luxembourg	+2
Spain	-3	Sweden	+6
Germany	-3	Portugal	+16

Source: http://europa.eu.int/eurostat.
Eurostat Product 5-20032000-EN-AP-EN
(Agriculture and Fisheries News Release 36/00, 20 March 2000)

perhaps the scale of state largesse for the sector is less (or in danger of lessening at least). But then the regimes that developed in the early post-war years were designed for a quite different farm sector. Politicians and, perhaps more deliberately, farm organizations appear not to promulgate this story. As Hill (1999) notes, one result is that policy assumptions about farm income are largely unsubstantiated. Sources other than commodity sales yield a substantial share of household income, even if the farmer's main income source is agriculture. As a consequence, the imagery of the 'poor farmer' is commonly a bad misrepresentation of real income standing, given that returns from farming are not a reliable guide to household income. Hill provides his commentary with a UK focus, but the message has broader pertinence. This is seen in an array of recent publications on different parts of the EU that note growth in farm pluriactivity (Martin 1996; Damianakos, 1997; Djurfeldt and Waldenström, 1999; Eikeland and Lie, 1999; Jervell, 1999). The form, and even magnitude of such pluriactivity is nonetheless varied. It is reported to be different close to cities with abundant job opportunities and in areas with less favourable employment contexts. In the former it is more likely to reflect a grasping of opportunities to generate more income, whereas it is often a means of securing necessary income to sustain a farm livelihood or modernize farm units in the latter (Campagne et al., 1990; Efstratoglou-Todoulou, 1990; Eikeland and Lie, 1999).

Shifts in farm household economy activity are not simply the result of some immutable economic exigency. They bear significant cultural messages as well. Of particular note here are changing expectations amongst the young and for women living on farms (Moissidis and Duquenne, 1997; Villa, 1999; albeit reports of young people rejecting farm work have been with us for a long time, even in locations with a strong agricultural base – e.g. Greenwood, 1976). The literature has provided substantial notices about the defeminization of farm work for some time. In some cases, this has occurred because women hold extremely negative attitudes toward farm work (Gidarakov, 1999), seeking jobs in any other sector, if they become available (García Ramon and Cruz, 1996), with a strong desires not to see their children working in agriculture (Gourdomichalis, 1991; Navarro, 1999). In other cases prejudices within societal frameworks and practices have led to a reduced farm involvement. Repassy (1991) provided an early report on this, in noting that as jobs on large-scale farms became relatively attractive in Hungary a masculinization of the farm workforce occurred. Blekesaune (1994) identifies a similar trend, in noting how the Norwegian farm workforce has been transformed as women's farm labour has been displaced through mechanization (see also Fink et al., 1994, on female job losses in eastern Germany). In the Norwegian case, rigidity of land market regulations also plays a part, for despite changes in succession laws and the promotion of equal opportunities, property still tends to pass down the male line (Jervell,

1999; more generally Shortall, 1999). But to emphasize 'push' factors too much would be misplaced, for there is also the attraction of non-farm work (e.g. Navarro, 1999). In Brandt and Haugen's (1997) figures of 50% of Norwegian farm women now working off-farm, compared with 6% in 1969, we might not be able to read causality, merely magnitude. Look behind the figures and we see women seeking off-farm work more vigorously than in the past. This is to be expected given empirical messages in the research literature that many more women who marry or live with farmers come from non-farm backgrounds (Oldrup, 1999).

Changes in marriage partner origins owes something to the manner in which farming itself has become more professionalized as an occupation. It is true that in southern Europe this tendency might be less marked, with proportionately less farmers having a professional farm qualification, but in northern Europe more 'scientific' farming methods are common fare. This is helped by the size of the farm units. We read a lot in the literature about post-productivism, a consumption-based countryside and farmers being paid to tend the landscape, rather than farm the land. The sense the literature provides on this is over-blown. Minor tendencies are being picked up and, perhaps dazzled by their newness, commentators are drawn into exaggerating their importance. Thus, as Marsden (1999) points out, despite all the research attention given to agri-environmental schemes (and LEADER) they in fact make minor impressions on the rural scene (as Morris and Evans, 1999, note for pluriactivity). Perhaps in the current academic environment, in which novelty is inclined to secure research grants and publications, we are being besieged with writing on minutiae; being overwhelmed by publications on new trends, whose weight of numbers lulls us into ascribing substantive importance? Certainly there is much in the literature to cast doubt on the magnitude of farm production change. Reports of growing concentrations of farm production (and agro-processing), or of increased specialization in agricultural organization, are possibly not fashionable, but they are central features of the European countryside (Fanfani, 1994; Walford, 1999). In a context in which the World Trade Organization is pushing for further reductions in farm subsidies, alongside greater proximity to an idealized free trade in agricultural commodities, commentaries suggesting that European farming can 'make a go of it' through environmentalization and specialized production seem far-fetched (except perhaps at a much reduced scale of production). Bear two points in mind. First, note estimates that food-related farm production needs to double to meet global demand by the year 2025 (Vega et al., 1999). Second, note the manner in which Third World countries are already entering organic primary production in significant ways, seeking certification for their products in global consumer markers (Monk, 1999). In this context there will be ongoing pressure for farm output to expand and, even assuming European production is pushed toward more environmentally sensitive practices, they are likely to face stiff competition for high-quality goods from cheaper production sources.

Table 8.3
Percentage change in number of agricultural holdings of at least 50 hectares in the EU, 1975-1997

	1975-1997	1987-1997	1995-1997
Belgium	98	48	13
Denmark	74	19	2
France	45	22	2
Germany	188	86	6 *
Ireland	6	7	3
Italy	11	9	3
Luxembourg	127	17	-1
Netherlands	133	49	8
UK	-5	-3	-2
Greece		-17 *	-7
Portugal		30	-2
Spain		7	2
Austria			7
Finland			17
Sweden			2
EU9	40	22	2
EU12		19	2
EU15			2

Note: * data for Germany for 1995-1997 include the Länder
          of the former GDR. The fall in value for 1987-1997 in
          Greece is only apparent as it results from a change in
          the method of sampling.
Source: http://europa.eu.int/eurostat.
          Eurostat Product 5-14032000-EN-AP-EN
          (Agriculture and Fisheries News Release 35/2000, 14 March 2000)

In this context it is perhaps not so surprising to find analysts reporting a continuance of traditional high-intensity farming alongside growth in organic production (Bruckmeieir and Grund, 1994). Certainly, in the manner in which farms are increasing in size across much of Europe, the language of dominant trends continues to spell productivism (Table 8.3). In this regard the points made by Drummond and associates (2000) are worthy of broader consideration. As they charge, contemporary European farm policy is unsustainable, as there is a confusion of environmental and social goals embedded within it (also Charvet, Chapter Two). It might be that this is all part of a 'slow' process of change in the farm sector (toward a more 'social' function). Perhaps we are not seeing the sustenance of productivism, but its gradual diminution? Viewed from this perspective, continuing growth in farm output (with heightened farm specialization and farm size growth) might have more to do with letting commercial farmers down slowly than with promoting a competitive European position in global markets. Most certainly, in a context of diminishing demand for their products (Miele, Chapter Three), there are over-production problems in various European commodity markets, such as the beef and dairy sectors. Despite all the hype about 1992 CAP reforms, these did not decouple income support from production wholly. Decoupling only applied to about half of EU farm output, so farmers are still encouraged to produce more (Ingersent et al., 1998). But is it realistic to conceptualize the 'remnants' of productivist subsidies that were unaffected by 1992 reforms as 'transitional payments'? For me, this is not appropriate. Some European farms are capable of competing on world markets, others are adopting highly productivist stances aimed at capturing shares of specialized markets, while national governments and the European Commission are seeking to develop (and legitimize) regional labelling to protect 'quality' producers (Moran, 1993; Ilbery and Kneafsey, 1998, 2000). Providing a specific illustration of this, Bessière (1998) draws out how culinary heritage is a social construction that has been promoted since the 1980s by the French Government, which has sought to promote traditional treasures, through the valorization and re-creation of gastronomic knowledge and skills. As others have brought out (e.g. Perkins, 1997), the state is critical in processes of developing markets for commodities. Within the EU, there are various member states for whom such agricultural development is central to national economic strategies. Hardly surprising in this context, collectively the members states of the European Union are not disposed toward radical policy reform that will further reduce farm subsidies, or freely allow 'untaxed' imports into the Union (Grant, 1997). Indeed, for some member states, production intensification was until recently a dominant element in farm policy (e.g. France, Greece, Portugal and Spain). In these nations both sectoral opposition and domestic economic priorities make progress toward policies with an alternative logic slow (Buller, 2000).

Although the EU is under pressure to introduce key changes, at this stage all we have seen is a gentle acceleration of trends, alongside compensations that are justified on non-production grounds (like environmental improvement) but which help maintain farm incomes. For sure, the impact of the various initiatives governments have introduced to cushion farm sector change vary across sectors, just as they vary across years. Farmers are experiencing economic pressure, but they exist in a policy environment that has been less harsh on them than on many other economic sectors. Iin this context it might be reasonable to see European farmers as being under pressure but not in crisis. If it is crisis you want, look to East European farmers (Lenormand, Chapter Four; Mokrushina, Chapter Five). European Union operatives are in a much more stable financial and social environment than their counterparts to the east. Perhaps the high level of subsidies large-scale producers receive is now under (partial) threat but for these farm households this does not equate with crisis.[3]

Forces of inertia

A number of driving forces lie behind inertia in the farm sector. For one, there is the power of consumer demand. There is little doubt that preferences over food consumption have changed over time. Perhaps a new tragedy, such as a fatal virulent epidemic arising from food production practices (perhaps vCJD?; e.g. "Scientists warn of 30% rise in human BSE", *Guardian*, 18 July 2000, p.6), might alter views rapidly. But in the absence of so traumatic an event, the reality of the moment is that relatively few consumers are even vegetarians, and relatively few consume organic products. Moreover, most consumers do not appear to be willing to pay more for food in order to protect the environment (or keep farmers in comfort, or at most engaging in the husbandry of the landscape, while sitting on ever-rising potential capital returns as land values increase). Thus, in a European Commission sponsored opinion pool on the environment, only 33% of Europeans claimed they would pay a little more for food if this protected the environment (about the same said they would pay no more to protect the environment; Commission of the European Communities, 1999).

Add to this the strength of the corporate grip on food production, processing and sales. Can we really expect a shift toward homely individualistic production, with PC environmentally, organically sustainable practices to the fore, when corporate control is so heavily weighted? (You might add into the dream world implied in some commentaries on post-productivist practices that transport facilities are expected to be animal friendly, processing procedures squeaky clean, workers paid fairly, in a non-discriminatory work environment, while points of food sale and consumption sparkle with a healthy glow comparable to an operating theatre.)[4] As Nottingham (1998) draws out, the companies that are likely to dictate terms under new food regimes are conglomerate multinational enterprises, with fingers in many pies. Thus, the corporations that are involved in promoting genetically modified organisms tend to be an amalgam of enterprises that incorporate food processing, agro-chemical production, seed sales and veterinary or pharmaceutical products. Recognition of the wide reach of such organizations makes for real caution in expecting major changes in food system regimes. It is in this context that I find it hard to accept commentaries like Pretty's (1998). Here we have recognition of the power of the corporate world. Pretty notes, for example, that 60%-90% of wheat, maize and rice is marketed by just six multinational enterprises. Set against this, there is a tone of Schumacher (1973) about the commentary; an imposition of the intermediate technology ideas in the Third World development literature onto the European food economy, but for me with insufficient acknowledgement of very different economic power contexts. Pretty's (1998) ideas about farmers 'taking the middle back', by running farmers markets or whatever,[5] are appealing, but will they work in the longer term? Lauding the fact that one-third of organic farmers were involved in direct sales to consumers might seem to herald the beginning of a drive toward 'taking the middle back' (Pretty, 1998, p.22), but this idea looks somewhat grey at the gills now Iceland claims to have secured 40% of global organic vegetable production. Farmers' markets might be 'alternative' spaces, but they seem unlikely to become more than ephemeral spaces (Holloway and Kneafsey, 2000). A key point here is that corporations are not static entities, but adapt to new situations; and in ways that generally strengthen their market share and power base (e.g. Wrigley, 1987). Significantly in this regard, Monk (1999) reports that agro-food producers are realizing the ease with which some organic practices can be superimposed on conventional food processing, in ways that eliminate once taken for granted chemical applications. It looks as though corporations will be able to manipulate or adapt to new circumstances in ways that give an appearance of 'newness', but that newness will be tightly constrained within the existing corporate fabric. This point applies irrespective of government regulation. Perhaps, as Banks and Marsden (1997) note for the dairy industry, food production is seeing increasing external pressure on quality and safety standards. But we have seen this occur before. When it does occur, it usually results in the closure of smaller processing units, and the removal of smaller farm producers from the food chain, as the dictates of meeting improved quality and safety criteria usually involve the installation of expensive new equipment (or procedures). Commonly these can only be justified economically if the scale of production is large. If this trend toward larger production units is appears to run counter to the mythology of post-productivism, a dose of reading about the politics of corporate-state relations should help dispel over-idealized imageries. Take a look at Perkins (1997), for example, to see how state and corporate sectors combine in the promotion of particular agricultural regimes. States 'use' corporate agents in many contexts, if only because they seek exports, lower food costs or economic growth that will help improve their nation's (and its government's) standing. Anyone looking for visible signs of musings on this issue need only listen to the UK Prime Minister or his Minister of Agriculture talking about why the UK should have GMO field trials, for the technology we are told is such that the UK should not be left behind if this is to be the future.[6]

In no sense does this mean that change is not occurring in either farming or food processing. As Murdoch and Miele (1999) point out, the predominant trend in the food sector is not toward standardization and globalized production, but toward fragmentation, as in the development of 'natural' products. This takes a variety of different forms, including an emphasis on quality networks (e.g. van der Meulen and Ventura, 1995), which help induce dual market structures. Critically, what has to be recognized is that none of this should be equated with post-productivism (or more broadly with a stepping back from the dominant productivist ethos that permeates farm and food processing practices). For some commentators, the shift toward more complex market arrangements and speciality foods is rather bizarrely grasped as signifying a new post-productivist rationale for the farm sector (as Morris and Evans, 1999, point out for some definitions of post-productivism). It might be that this stems from those who wishfully think that environmentalism is taking a firm grip on the agricultural sector (read Tovey, Chapter Six, and Paniagua, Chapter Seven, for two sharp messages that should disabuse you of too ready an acceptance of this view). The word 'bizarre' is appropriate for such views, for they reveal a major flaw in not linking what is occurring in agriculture to what is happening beyond the sector. Fundamental change has been occurring in the European economy, with production shifts from so-called Fordist production relations to post-Fordist ones (Meegan, 1988; Nilsson and Schamp, 1996). No longer can you have any colour car as long as it is black. Now production is organized such that mass producers output cars in many colours and styles, catering for a wide variety of preferences. Agriculture might have been slow in being drawn into this productivist mentality (albeit the greater diversity of restaurants that now exist in many European nations reveals that the food industry as a whole is embedded within it), but its operatives are not driven by fundamentally different values from economic sectors that are dominated by mass producers, which embody small-scale firms with a specialized product and a limited market. That said, have you heard anyone refer to the car industry as post-productivist? What is it that makes commentators think agriculture is so different? Certainly it is not that there is a new 'quality' insignia on certain production practices, for there are very different discourses on what quality is (Morris and Young, 2000). You can guarantee that the corporations that have dominated the food industry for so long are much better placed to manipulate messages about quality than farmer organizations, who have been outplayed in 'controlling' the food sector for so long (e.g. Vogeler, 1981; Goodman *et al.*, 1987; Bowler, 1992).

Perhaps then it is the farmers themselves who offer something that is distinctive? Agricultural transformation toward new rules of engagement might be due to changes in the disposition of farmers toward what they produce, and how they produce it? Available evidence suggests this is unlikely, even if a minority of farmers clasp more environmentally-friendly or organic practices close to their chests (e.g. Clunies-Ross and Cox, 1994; Schmitt, 1994). Illustrative of this, we find evidence that farmers are unable to see themselves as environmental actors (Tovey, 1994) and resist attempts to integrate agricultural and environmental legislation (Deverre, 1994). Where integration between farm and conservation policy appears to attract farmer interest is when either conservation and commercial interests are not in conflict, as for rare breeds in UK (Evans and Yarwood, 2000), or where farmers are concerned that failure to act will lead to greater 'urban' influence on their production decisions (Tovey, 1997). Even when more environmentally-sound production practices seem to offer better market prospects, farmers fear getting their fingers burnt (Remmers, 1994). Such attitudes feed into the slow take-up of initiatives like the UK's Organic Aid Scheme, which was introduced in 1994 with a much lower uptake than expected (Gilg, 1999, p.85). If Kaltoft's (1999) work is more broadly applicable, then this reluctance would not have arisen from narrowly circumscribed views of organic farming, for the views of organic farmers incorporate a variety of practices and interpretations on what 'nature' is. More likely, it stems from a realistic appraisal of the costs of changing production practices, alongside a belief that change is unnecessary. On the former, from an eight nation study, Huylenbroeck and Whitby (1999) conclude that the transaction costs of EU Regulation 2078/92 were about 20% of total spending (some 40% of local expenditure; also Falconer, 2000), with Winter (2000) noting how farmer participation in the Environmentally Sensitive Areas scheme was lessened by the view that payments were too low, with rejection of Stewardship schemes arising more from the amount of paper work involved with participation. Add to which, farmers do not seem to believe that their actions need to change. Seymour and associates (1997) provide one illustration, in reporting that only 22% of interviewed farmers saw pollution as reprehensible in itself. As Izcara Palacios (1998) reports for Campos de Dalías in south-east Spain, farmers see their actions as non-polluting and regard nitrates as innocuous, so they are reluctant to change farming practices. What spurs farmers to contemplate such change is the fear that inaction (over pollution, for example) could lead to legal trouble (with 62% reporting this as a concern in the Seymour and associates work).

What is needed for change to occur is an outside 'push' (or the 'pull' of extra funding). This has been seen across a broad canvass in recent publications. Thus, van der Meulen and Ventura (1995) found that it was farmers moving into Umbria from other areas who helped revitalize the farm economy, by introducing new techniques and philosophies. Similar findings are reported by Martin (1996) on the role of in-migrants in bringing needed economic diversification to Languedoc and by Remmers (1994) over the introduction of ecological wine-making in Contraviesa in the Spanish Alpujarras. This need for outside prompts, which at times can be seen as unwelcome by farmers, as with the pressures for less farm pollution that come from incoming middle-class householders in the English countryside (Lowe *et al.*, 1997), places a heavy premium on governmental initiatives, if coordinated efforts are sought. But within the EU state agency responses to agricultural change are far from convincing. In part, as Winter (2000) points out, this is because environmental objectives in the 1992 CAP reforms were not explicit. Moreover, as the blank spaces have been filled-in, policies have been shown to have loose, ill-defined objectives (Huylenbroeck and Whitby, 1999). As a result, as in France, original agri-environmental objectives that sought to protect the environment have been transformed into measures to support marginal agricultural areas, so as to maintain landscape and provide new subsidized services and quality regional products (Alphandéry, 1994; Billaud *et al.*, 1997). This does not mean there have been no environmental benefits, but: "It is difficult to escape the conclusion that what has happened in the CAP so far is that some token concessions have been made in the direction of incorporating environmental policy considerations" (Grant, 1997, p.213). Thus, summarizing the findings of a multi-nation research project on the implementation of EU Regulation 2078/92, Buller (2000) concludes that what distinguishes most (national) schemes is that they maintain existing farm practices. Most nations have subscribed to the lower tiers of the Regulation, so potential environmental benefits are at best only capable of a limited environmental impact, even though a key feature of the public's and governmental attention is often (or in the latter case, often stated to be) environmental gain.

In this context, we should not come down too hard on agri-environmental policy, for the mixing of objectives, and compromises over implementation measures, are integral parts of so much policy-making. Paniagua (2000) highlights one element of this, in noting how Spanish early retirement policy for farmers has not had a major effect on farm restructuring, as policy initiatives have mixed social and economic goals, with many farmers renting out their land so those taking it over have restricted capacities to restructure their farm operations (on the imposition of social criteria on broad aspects of farm policy, see Granberg, 1999). That said, as Grant (1995, p.162) points out, for EU agricultural policies "... success of reforms may be undermined by the limited administrative capabilities of member states which, intentionally or unintentionally, lead to reforms not being implemented years after they have been approved by the Council of Ministers". In many regards agriculture remains an 'exceptional' policy arena, in which collective practices that are unacceptable in other spheres linger on.[7] The sector is changing, but its policy frameworks are not being transformed rapidly.

Is there uniformity?

The message for this section is not about differences between commodities, about which clear divergences exist (Charvet, Chapter Two). Neither is it about disparities between small-scale and large-scale producers, for evidence on this score makes it very clear that we are dealing with two different populations when looking at the extremes. In this regard, the idea of 'the farmer' owes more to spin-doctoring than it does to the 'reality' of farm operations (e.g. Newby *et al.*, 1978). Rather attention in this last short section is devoted at variation across localities.

This train of through has been prompted by a number of recent publications. Henk de Haan (1997) provided one such impetus, in his articulation of the local character of globality. Papadopoulos (1997) offered another, in putting forward a case for recognizing that EU regulations are not an anonymous force. Rather, as shown for the Greek case, they are internalized and transformed into a resource that is manipulated to best local advantage (albeit, 'local' might largely mean to best advantage of powerful local interests; see Osti, 1997). This point is taken up at the local and the national level by a number of researchers, examining a variety of policy arenas of economic scenarios. Gray (2000) offers a convincing argument in this regard, in showing how farmers reconfigure their activities in response to favourable price regimes and structural measures of CAP. In this his argument has many similarities with Ray's (1999) work on LEADER, which likewise shows the ability of local activists to transpose themselves into a (seeming) manifestation that attracts bounties from the Brussels coffers. This does not mean that direction does not come from outside forces, for there is little doubt that even distinctive local power structures are subjected to pressures to adapt to broader policy directions; as Martin (1996) reveals in work on Languedoc syndicalism.

At the national level, as Buller (2000) makes clear, nations bring their own agricultural, rural and environmental concerns into decision arenas. As regards EU Regulation 2078/92, for instance, there are 12 specific goals or actions, with member states having significantly different emphases across them. Even basic concepts are interpreted in dissimilar ways. For one, extensification is interpreted as maintaining traditional farm systems in France, (parts of) Germany, Portugal and Spain, but as de-intensification in Denmark and (other parts of) Germany. Noteworthy in this context is the work of Tanaka and associates (1999), who found that the nation-state retains a capacity to restructure the global rape-seed sector to benefit national interest through laws and policing. In doing so, what we see in policy implementation is a combination of cultural values and power relationships. So as not to belabour the point, just two examples will be given on this. The first is the marked impact that the 'Norwegian food culture' has on both the nature of food retailing in the country and on the products that are grown (and imported), with concerns about food safety linked to strategies to raise consumer confidence through local (viz. national) sourcing (Nygård and Storstad, 1997, 1998). More directly as a result of national policy initiatives, Shortall (1999) offers exposition on how the state has a key role in improving women's involvement in farming, as seen from policies as diverse as inheritance laws through to training programmes (Shortall, 1996).

The simple answer to the question posed by this chapter is thereby two-fold. Seen in a temporal context, despite all the changes that have occurred over the last two decades, agriculture is very definitely the same animal as it was 20 years ago. "A potentially interesting debate about a post-productivist 'myth' has yet to establish itself in the literature" (Morris and Evans, 1999, p.353). Agriculture today might have more cuts and bruises. It might even have a few growths and contractions that distort its appearance compared with 20 years ago. But the basic precepts of the sector are unchanged. The efforts to re-write its fundamental being has been capture by forces of inertia (or more accurately forces that wish for more of the same rather than something different). As for the geographical realm, here we see repeated signs that locality and nationality are important dimensions in agricultural change. This does not diminish the importance of commodity groups, size of farm operation or the like, but it does bring home that core understandings about what farming is and should be continue to differ across the European Union. If expansion to the east take place, these differences are likely to become all the more profound. This provides a strong impetus for dynamic, innovative thinking in the formulation and implementation of food policies for the future. Without this, expansion eastwards is likely to occur largely on terms that suit the manufacturing and finance sectors. Agriculture will be the rump policy arena, whose inadequately prepared and presented programmes open the door to practices that damage the image of the sector, the health of the populace at large and the vitality of the rural environment.

Notes

1 Readers should not get carried away by this point, as the literature is not crystal clear on the relative importance of farm labourers leaving agriculture of their own volition or as a result of redundancy. In a UK context, Armstrong (1981) is one of many who leave the strong impression that the uncertainties, low pay and discomforts of farm labouring

encouraged workers to seek other employment. In the nineteenth and early twentieth centuries at least the irregularity of work would have provided ample incentive to look for other jobs (Howkins, 1985; Hussey, 1997). Yet, as we get closer to the present-day, the farm workforce came to be more obviously full-time and permanent (Armstrong, 1981). In this setting, investigations provide a stronger message than many labourers were told to go (e.g. Drudy, 1978).

2   This refers to the annual reviews of recent literature that Andrew Gilg provided in the book series that preceded this one; namely, the two series *Countryside Planning Yearbook* and *The International Yearbook of Rural Planning*, and the series, *Progress in Rural Policy and Planning*. The volumes were published by GeoBooks, Belhaven and Wiley.

3   If one wished to be cynical about the potential self-interest that lies behind claims that a farm crisis exists one could ask about the basis on which a crisis can be said to exist. A sustainable case could be put forward holding that the farm sector has been in permanent crisis, at least in so far as the cost-price squeeze of production relationships has forced huge numbers of farmers out of business. Yet as Thompson (1991) points out in a commentary on the so-called Great Agricultural Depression of the late nineteenth century, in the UK more farmers lost their farm occupation in the 'golden years' of 1851-1871 than during the Depression years of 1871-1901. The fact that these latter years have come to be seen as crisis years probably owes a lot to too much attention being given to cereal prices – especially given that falls in these prices tended to feed through to depress the rents received by large landowners. In the twentieth century we have likewise seen little complaint from governmental or farm organization representatives about the large number of small-scale farmers who have been 'forced' off the land. Could it be that a distinguishing feature of current farm sector change, which prompts many to ascribe a 'crisis' title to contemporary events, is little more than a repeat of nineteenth-century patterns? (One might add to this the political uncertainty, as farmers have lost their dominant local power positions, such that they might even be contrived to be represented as 'others' in a largely non-farm population; Yarwood and Evans, 1998.) Perhaps the distinguishing attribute of post-1992 reforms, and potentialities for change in the future (Charvet, Chapter Two), is that large-scale farmers are seeing their potential for extracting huge subsidies from government coffers diminish? Like the nineteenth-century aristocracy, perhaps the trauma arises because an adjustment in lifestyle will be needed amongst larger landholders, much as it has done for smaller scale producers in vast numbers for more than a century? As Thompson (1991) found for the nineteenth-century depression, while there were serious commodity price falls, these impacted unevenly. How far is

the imagery of a severe economic trauma today associated with the unevenness of which farm groups it impacts on, as in the past?

4 This point is written on a day (19 July 2000) when BBC Radio 4's Today Programme announced that inspections show that half of the restaurants visited in the UK do not meet environmental health standards; whether this be due to the presence of cockroaches in the food preparation area or simply that the kitchen is not kept clean. The point is not that anyone has been daft enough to suggest the list of 'idealizations' provided above will result from post-productivism but that in many commentaries the implication the reader is left with is that more environmentally-friendly farming will induce marked health and other improvements. In reality much more will be needed than changes in farming practices.

5 Amongst those who would like to see less corporate control of the economy (and fresher food), there will no doubt be hope that Pretty is right. According to Pretty (1998), the first farmers market in the UK was only established in Bath 1997, so they are still at an early stage of their potential market presence. Set against this, look at the manner in which supermarket chains are capturing increasing shares of food sales, with independent retail outlets, like butchers, increasingly losing out.

6 This comment could be extended to the Environment Minister as well, although many of the comments here are less about the UK being left behind than being couched in terms of needing to see what effect GMO might have (see "Farmer's GM crop destroyed by family trust", *Guardian*, 8 June 1999, p.7; "Public unease on GM crops 'not irrational' ", *Guardian* 19 October 1999, p.5; "Brown backs US on hormone beef", *Guardian*, 13 June 2000, p.10).

7 The messages here are that prices are raised for consumers, income is redistributed in a highly regressive manner toward large-scale farm producers, and farm policies create a drag on economic growth (as many publications sought to show during the Uruguay Round of GATT negotiations; e.g. Johnson *et al.*, 1985; Stoeckel *et al.*, 1989). All this is occurring in a framework in which policy change in other countries shows that reducing farm subsidies does not lead to devastation, even if it does speed up existing trends in farm restructuring (e.g. Valdés, 1994; Cloke, 1996). Added to which, existing farm policy arrangements are creating environmental damage of unknown long-term consequences (e.g. Pitman, 1992). Linked to this, Vail (1994) reports that Sweden has moved forward with de-regulation for agriculture, with the driving force for this being widespread public concerns about the long-term sustainability of production, cultural-historical landscapes, rural communities, biological diversity and aquatic ecosystems. In this context, Sweden is in the vanguard in developing policies to foster sustainable agriculture and green initiatives. Throughout Europe, agriculture has been declining in economic

and demographic importance (Hoggart *et al.*, 1995), but this Swedish initiative is effectively abandoning propping-up commercial production in the name of environmental improvement, such that only hobby farming is likely to survive in the north of the country. This initiative shows what can be done, but as Grant (1997) argues, getting broad agreement across the Union to implement innovative policies that are environmentally constructive will be extremely difficult. This point is understandable, for while the Swedes have taken this stance for reasons linked to environmental enhancement, others fear the destructive potential of policy change for countryside management (e.g. Potter, 1999).

References

Alphandéry, P (1994) Agricultural practices and environmental perceptions in the Manche Département, *Sociologia Ruralis*, 34, pp.329-339.

Armstrong, W.A. (1981) The workfolk, in G.E. Mingay (ed.) *The Victorian Countryside: Volume Two*, Routledge & Kegan Paul, London, pp.491-505.

Banks, J. and Marsden, T.K. (1997) Regulating the UK dairy industry: the changing nature of competitive space, *Sociologia Ruralis*, 37, pp.382-404.

Bessière, J. (1998) Local development and heritage: traditional food and cuisine as tourist attractions in rural areas, *Sociologia Ruralis*, 38, pp.21-34.

Billaud, J-P., Bruckmeier, K., Patricio, T. and Pinton, F. (1997) Social construction of the rural environment: Europe and discourses in France, Germany and Portugal, in H. de Haan, B. Kasimis and M.R. Redclift (eds.) *Sustainable Rural Development*, Ashgate, Aldershot, pp.9-34.

Blekesaune, A. (1994) Structural changes in Norwegian agriculture: from family farms to one-man farms?, in D. Symes and A.J. Jansen (eds.) *Agricultural Restructuring and Rural Change in Europe*, Wageningen University Press, Wageningen, pp.111-127.

Bowler, I.R. (1992) The industrialization of agriculture, in I.R. Bowler (ed.) *The Geography of Agriculture in Developed Market Economies*, Longman, Harlow, pp.7-31.

Brandes, S.H. (1975) *Migration, Kinship and Community: Tradition and Transition in a Spanish Village*, Academic Press, New York.

Brandt, B. and Haugen, M. (1997) Rural women, feminism and the politics of identity, *Sociologia Ruralis*, 37, pp.325-344.

Bruckmeier, K. and Grund, H. (1994) Perspectives for environmentally sound agriculture in East Germany, in D. Symes and A.J. Jansen (eds.) *Agricultural Restructuring and Rural Change in Europe*, Wageningen University Press, Wageningen, pp.180-194.

Buller, H. (2000) Regulation 2078: patterns of implementation, in H. Buller, G.A. Wilson and A. Höll (eds.) *Agri-Environmental Policy in the European Union*, Ashgate, Aldershot, pp.219-153.

Campagne, P., Carrère, G. and Valceschini, E. (1990) Three agricultural regions of France: three types of pluriactivity, *Journal of Rural Studies*, 6, pp.415-422.

Cloke, P.J. (1996) Looking through European eyes? a re-evaluation of agricultural deregulation in New Zealand, *Sociologia Ruralis*, 36, pp.307-330.

Clunies-Ross, T. and Cox, G. (1994) Challenging the productivist paradigm: organic farming and the politics of agricultural change, in P.D. Lowe, T.K. Marsden and S.J. Whatmore (eds.) *Regulating Agriculture*, David Fulton, London, pp.53-74.

Commission of the European Communities (1999) *What do Europeans Think About the Environment*. Office for Official Publications of the European Communities, Luxembourg.

Damianakos, S. (1997) The ongoing quest for a model of Greek agriculture, *Sociologia Ruralis*, 37, pp.190-208.

Danziger, R. (1988) *Political Powerlessness: Agricultural Workers in Post-War England*, Manchester University Press, Manchester.

Deverre, C. (1994) Rare birds and flocks: agriculture and social legitimization of environmental protection, in D. Symes and A.J. Jansen (eds.) *Agricultural Restructuring and Rural Change in Europe*, Wageningen University Press, Wageningen, pp.220-234.

Djurfeldt, G. and Waldenström, C. (1999) Mobility patterns of Swedish farming households, *Journal of Rural Studies*, 15, pp.331-344.

Drudy, P.J. (1978) Depopulation in a prosperous agricultural region, *Regional Studies*, 12, pp.49-60.

Drummond, I., Campbell, H., Lawrence, G. and Symes, D.G. (2000) Contingent or structural crisis in British agriculture?, *Sociologia Ruralis*, 40, 111-127.

Efstratoglou-Todoulou, S. (1990) Pluriactivity in different socioeconomic contexts: a test of the push-pull hypothesis in Greek farming, *Journal of Rural Studies*, 6, pp.407-413.

Eikeland, S. and Lie, I. (1999) Pluriactivity in rural Norway, *Journal of Rural Studies*, 15, pp.405-415.

Evans, N.J. and Yarwood, R. (2000) The politicization of livestock: rare breeds and countryside conservation, *Sociologia Ruralis*, 40, pp.228-248.

Falconer, K. (2000) Farm-level constraints on agri-environmental scheme participation: a transactional perspective, *Journal of Rural Studies*, 16, pp.379-394.

Fanfani, R. (1994) Agricultural change and agro-food districts in Italy, in D. Symes and A.J. Jansen (eds.) *Agricultural Restructuring and Rural Change in Europe*, Wageningen University Press, Wageningen, pp.87-101.

Fink, M., Grajewski, R., Siebel, R. and Zierold, K. (1994) Rural women in East Germany, in D. Symes and A.J. Jansen (eds.) *Agricultural Restructuring and Rural Change in Europe*, Wageningen University Press, Wageningen, pp.282-295.

García Ramon, M.D. and Cruz, J. (1996) Regional welfare policies and women's agricultural labour in southern Spain, in M.D. García Ramon and J. Monk (eds.) *Women of the European Union*, Routledge, London, pp.247-262.

Gasson, R.M. (1974) Socio-economic status and orientation to work: the case of farmers, *Sociologia Ruralis*, 14, pp.125-141.

George, J. (1999) *A Rural Uprising: The Battle to Save Hunting with Hounds*, J.A. Allen, London.

Gidarakov, I. (1999) Young women's attitude towards agriculture and women's new roles in the Greek countryside, *Journal of Rural Studies*, 15, pp.147-158.

Gilg, A.W. (1999) *Perspectives on British Rural Planning Policy, 1994-97*, Ashgate, Aldershot.

Goodman, D., Sorj, B. and Wilkinson, J. (1987) *From Farming to Biotechnology: A Theory of Agro-Industrial Development*, Blackwell, Oxford.

Gourdomichalis, A. (1991) Women and the reproduction of family farms: change and continuity in the region of Thessaly, Greece, *Journal of Rural Studies*, 7, pp.57-62.

Granberg, L. (1999) The emergence of welfare state rationality in Finnish agricultural policy, *Sociologia Ruralis*, 39, 311-327.

Grant, W. (1995) Is agricultural policy still exceptional?, *Political Quarterly*, 66, pp.156-169.

Grant, W. (1997) *The Common Agricultural Policy*, Macmillan, Basingstoke.

Gray, J. (2000) The Common Agricultural Policy and the re-invention of the rural in the European Community, *Sociologia Ruralis*, 40, pp.30-52.

Greenwood, D.J. (1976) The demise of agriculture in Fuenterrabia, in J.B. Aceves and W.A. Douglass (eds.) *The Changing Faces of Rural Spain*, Schenkman, Cambridge, Massachusetts, pp.29-44.

Haan, H. de (1997) Locality, identity and the reshaping of modernity: an analysis of cultural confrontations in two villages, in H. de Haan and N. Long (eds.) *Images and Realities of Rural Life*, Van Gorcum, Assen, pp.153-177.

Hart-Davis, D. (1997) *When the Country Went to Town: The Countryside Marches and Rally of 1997*, Excellent Press, Ludlow.

Hill, B.E. (1993) The 'myth' of the family farm: defining the family farm and assessing its importance in the European Community, *Journal of Rural Studies*, 9, pp.359-370.

Hill, B.E. (1999) Farm household income: perceptions and statistics, *Journal of Rural Studies,* 15, pp.345-358.

Hoggart, K., Buller, H. and Black, R. (1995) *Rural Europe: Identity and Change*, Arnold, London.

Holloway, L. and Kneafsey, M. (2000) Reading the space of the farmers' market: a case study from the United Kingdom, *Sociologia Ruralis*, 40, pp.285-299.

Howkins, A. (1985) *Poor Labouring Men: Rural Radicalism in Norfolk 1870-1923*, Routledge, London.

Hussey, S. (1997) Low pay, underemployment and multiple occupations: men's work in the inter-war countryside, *Rural History*, 8, pp.217-235.

Huylenbroeck, G. van and Whitby, M.C. (1999) Conclusions and policy recommendations, in G. van Huylenbroeck and M.C. Whitby (eds.) *Countryside Stewardship*, Pergamon, Oxford, pp.177-191.

Ilbery, B.W. and Kneafsey, M. (1998) Product and place: promoting quality products and services in lagging rural regions of the European Union, *European Urban and Regional Studies*, 5, pp.329-341.

Ilbery, B.W. and Kneafsey, M. (2000) Producer constructions of quality in regional speciality food production: a case study from south west England, *Journal of Rural Studies*, 16, pp.217-230.

Ingersent, K.A., Rayner, A.J. and Hine, R.C. (1998) Postscript, in K.A. Ingersent, A.J. Rayner and R.C. Hine (eds.) *The Reform of the Common Agricultural Policy*, Macmillan, Basingstoke, pp.189-199.

Izcara Palacios, S.P. (1998) Farmers and the implementation of the EU Nitrates Directive in Spain, *Sociologia Ruralis*, 38, pp.146-162.

Jervell, A.M. (1999) Changing patterns of family farming and pluriactivity, *Sociologia Ruralis*, 39, pp.100-115.

Johnson, D.G., Hemmi, K. and Lardinois, P. (1985) *Agricultural Policy and Trade: Adjusting Domestic Programs in an International Framework*, New York University Press, Trilateral Commission Triangle Paper 29, New York.

Kaltoft, P. (1999) Values about nature in organic farming practice and knowledge, *Sociologia Ruralis*, 39, pp.39-53.

Lowe, P.D., Clark, J., Seymour, S. and Ward, N. (1997) *Moralizing the Environment*, UCL Press, London.

Marsden, T.K. (1999) Rural futures: the consumption countryside and its regulation, *Sociologia Ruralis*, 39, pp.501-520.

Martin, J.P. (1996) Wine growers' syndicalism in the Languedoc: continuity and change, *Sociologia Ruralis*, 36, pp.331-339.

Meegan, R. (1988) A crisis of mass production?, in J. Allen and D.B. Massey (eds.) *The Economy in Question*, Sage, London, pp.136-183.

Moissidis, A. and Duquenne, M-N. (1997) Peri-urban rural areas in Greece: the case of Attica, *Sociologia Ruralis*, 37, pp.228-239.

Monk, A. (1999) The organic manifesto: organic agriculture in the world food system, in D. Burch, J. Goss and G. Lawrence (eds.) *Restructuring Global and Regional Agricultures*, Ashgate, Aldershot, pp.75-86.

Moran, W. (1993) Rural space as intellectual property, *Political Geography*, 12, pp.263-277.

Morris, C. and Evans, N.J. (1999) Research on the geography of agricultural change: redundant or revitalized?, *Area*, 31, pp.349-358.

Morris, C. and Young, C. (2000) 'Seed to shelf', 'teat to table', 'barley to beer' and 'womb to tomb': discourses of food quality and quality assurance schemes in the UK, *Journal of Rural Studies*, 16, pp.103-115.

Murdoch, J. and Miele, M. (1999) 'Back to nature': changing 'worlds of production' in the food sector, *Sociologia Ruralis*, 39, pp.465-481.

Navarro, C.J. (1999) Women and social mobility in rural Spain, *Sociologia Ruralis*, 39, pp.222-235.

Naylor, E.L. (1994) Unionism, peasant protest and the reform of French agriculture, *Journal of Rural Studies*, 10, pp.263-273.

Newby, H.E. (1972) The low earnings of agricultural workers, *Journal of Agricultural Economics*, 23, pp.15-24.

Newby, H.E. (1977) *The Deferential Worker: A Study of Farm Workers in East Anglia*, Allen Lane, London.

Newby, H.E., Bell, C., Rose, D. and Saunders, P. (1978) *Property, Paternalism and Power*, Hutchinson, London.

Nilsson, J-E. and Schamp, E.W. (1996) Restructuring of the European production system: processes and consequences, *European Planning Studies*, 3, pp.121-132.

Nottingham, S. (1998) *Eat Your Genes: How Genetically Modified Food is Entering Our Diet*, Zed Books, London.

Nygård, B. and Storstad, O. (1997) The struggle surrounding the distribution of food in Norway, in H. de Haan, B. Kasimis and M.R. Redclift (eds.) *Sustainable Rural Development*, Ashgate, Aldershot, pp.73-89.

Nygård, B. and Storstad, O. (1998) De-globalization of food markets? consumer perceptions of safe food - the case of Norway, *Sociologia Ruralis*, 38, pp.35-53.

Oldrup, H. (1999) Women working off the farm: reconstructing gender identity in Danish agriculture, *Sociologia Ruralis*, 39, pp.343-358.

Osti, G. (1997) Sustainable development in the Italian mountains, in H. de Haan, B. Kasimis and M.R. Redclift (eds.) *Sustainable Rural Development*, Ashgate, Aldershot, pp.179-196.

Paniagua, A. (2000) Analysis of the evolution of farmers' early retirement policy in Spain: the case of Castille and León, *Land Use Policy*, 17, pp.113-120.

Papadopoulos, D.A. (1999) Side effects of bureaucratic formalism: some administrative aspects of CAP implementation in Greece, *Sociologia Ruralis*, 37, pp.287-301.

Perkins, J.H. (1997) *Geopolitics and the Green Revolution: Wheat, Genes and the Cold War*, Oxford University Press, Oxford.

Pitman, J.I. (1992) Changes in crop productivity and water quality in the United Kingdom, in K. Hoggart (ed.) *Agricultural Change, Environment and Economy*, Mansell, London, pp.89-121.

Potter, C. (1999) Agricultural liberalization and the double dividend, in M.R. Redclift, J.N. Lekakis and G.P. Zamias (eds.) *Agriculture & World Trade Liberalization*, CAB International, Wallingford, pp.88-103.

Pretty, J. (1998) *The Living Land: Agriculture, Food and Community Regeneration in Rural Europe*, Earthscan, London.

Ray, C. (1997) Towards a theory of the dialectic of local rural development within the European Union, *Sociologia Ruralis*, 37, pp.356-362.

Remmers, G. (1994) Ecological wine-making in a depressed mountainous region in southern Spain, in J. van der Ploeg and A. Long (eds.) *Born From Within*, Van Gorcum, Assen, pp.101-127.

Repassy, H. (1991) Changing gender roles in Hungarian agriculture, *Journal of Rural Studies*, 7, pp.23-29.

Schmitt, M. (1994) Women farmers and the influence of ecofeminism on the greening of German agriculture, in S.J. Whatmore, T.K. Marsden and P.D. Lowe (eds.) *Gender and Rurality*, David Fulton, London, pp.102-116.

Schumacher, E.F. (1973) *Small is Beautiful: Economics as if People Really Mattered*, Harper Torchbooks, New York.

Seymour, S., Lowe, P.D., Ward, N. and Clark, J. (1997) Environmental 'others' and 'elites': rural pollution and changing power relations in the countryside, in P. Milbourne (ed.) *Revealing Rural 'Others'*, Pinter, London, pp.57-74.

Shortall, S. (1996) Training to be farmers or wives? agricultural training for women in Northern Ireland, *Sociologia Ruralis*, 36, 269-285.

Shortall, S. (1999) *Women and Farming: Property and Power*, Macmillan, Basingstoke.

Stoeckel, A.B., Vincent, D. and Cuthbertson, S. (1989, eds.) *Macroeconomic Consequences of Farm Support Policies*, Duke University Press, Durham, North Carolina.

Strijker, D. (2000) Agriculture: still a key to rural identity?, in T. Haartsn, P. Groote and P.P.P. Huigen (eds.) *Claiming Rural Identities*, Van Gorcum, Assen, pp.47-53.

Tanaka, K., Juska, A. and Busch, L. (1999) Globalization of agricultural production and research: the case of the rape-seed sector, *Sociologia Ruralis*, 39, pp.54-77.

Thompson, F.M.L. (1991) An anatomy of English agriculture 1870-1914, in B.A. Holderness and M. Turner (eds.) *Land, Labour and Agriculture 1700-1920*, Hambleton Press, London, pp.211-240.

Tovey, H. (1994) Rural management, public discourses and the farmer as environmental actor, in D. Symes and A.J. Jansen (eds.) *Agricultural Restructuring and Rural Change in Europe*, Wageningen University Press, Wageningen, pp.209-219.

Tovey, H. (1997) 'We can all use calculators now': productionism, sustainability and the professional formation of farming in Co. Meath, Ireland, in H. de Haan, B. Kasimis and M.R. Redclift (eds.) *Sustainable Rural Development*, Ashgate, Aldershot, pp.113-127.

Tracy, M. (1989) *Government and Agriculture in Western Europe 1880-1988*, third edition, Harvester Wheatsheaf, Hemel Hempstead.

Vail, D. (1994) Sweden's 1990 food policy reforms, in P. McMichael (ed.) *The Global Restructuring of Agro-Food Systems*, Cornell University Press, Ithaca, pp.53-75.

Valdés, A. (1994) Agricultural reforms in Chile and New Zealand, *Journal of Agricultural Economics*, 45, pp.189-201.

van der Meulen, H. and Ventura, F. (1995) Methods of identifying and reinforcing endogenous rural development experiences in Umbria, in J. van der Ploeg and G. van Dijk (eds.) *Beyond Modernization*, Van Gorcum, Assen, pp.147-178.

Vega, M., Bontoux, L. and Kern, M. (1999) European agriculture and future world food demand, *IPTS Report*, 39, pp.26-32.

Villa, M. (1999) Born to be farmers? changing expectations in Norwegian farmers' life courses, *Sociologia Ruralis*, 39, pp.328-342.

Vogeler, I. (1981) *The Myth of the Family Farm: Agribusiness Dominance of US Agriculture*, Westview, Boulder, Colorado.

Walford, N. (1999) Geographical transition from productivism to post-productivism, in N. Walford, J. Everitt and D. Napton (eds.) *Reshaping the Countryside*, CAB International, Wallingford, pp.25-38.

Winter, M. (2000) Strong policy or weak policy? the environmental impact of the 1992 reforms to the CAP arable regime in Great Britain, *Journal of Rural Studies*, 16, pp.47-59.

Wrigley, N. (1987) The concentration of capital in UK grocery retailing, *Environment and Planning*, A19, pp.1283-1288.

Yarwood, R. and Evans, N.J. (1998) The changing geographies of domestic livestock animals, *Society and Animals*, 6, pp.137-166.

90 0470953 5